# The Hidden Power of Lotus 1-2-3: Using Macros

# The Hidden Power
# of Lotus 1-2-3:
# Using Macros

*Richard W. Ridington, Jr.*
*Mark M. Williams*

**Brady Communications Company, Inc.**
A Prentice-Hall Publishing Company
Bowie, MD 20715

The Hidden Power of Lotus 1-2-3: Using Macros

**Library of Congress Cataloging in Publication Data**

Ridington, Richard W. (Richard Warren), 1954–
    The hidden power of LOTUS 1-2-3.

    Includes index.
    1. Lotus 1-2-3 (Computer program) 2. Business—Data processing. I. Williams, Mark M., 1948–    . II. Title. III. Title: Hidden power of L.O.T.U.S. one-two-three.
HF5548.4.L67R52    1984        001.64'25        84–27423

ISBN 0-89303-517-3

Prentice-Hall of Australia, Pty., Ltd., *Sydney*
Prentice-Hall Canada, Inc., Scarborough, *Ontario*
Prentice-Hall Hispanoamericana, S.A., *Mexico*
Prentice-Hall of India Private Limited, *New Delhi*
Prentice-Hall International, Inc., *London*
Prentice-Hall of Japan, Inc., *Tokyo*
Prentice-Hall of Southeast Asia Pte. Ltd., *Singapore*
Editora Prentice-Hall Do Brasil LTDA., *Rio de Janeiro*
Whitehall Books, Limited, Petone, *New Zealand*

Printed in the United States of America

85 86 87 88 89 90 91 92 93 94 95          3 4 5 6 7 8 9 10

Publishing Director: David Culverwell
Acquisitions Editor: Sue Love
Production Editor/Text Designer: Michael Rogers
Art Director/Cover Design: Don Sellers
Assistant Art Director: Bernard Vervin
Manufacturing Director: John Komsa

Copy Editor: Jolanta Obrebska
Indexer: Deborah L. Corson
Typesetting: Alexander Typesetting, Indianapolis, IN
Printing: R.R. Donnelley & Sons Company, Inc., Harrisonburg, VA
Typefaces: Aster (text), Helvetica (display), OCR-B (computer material)

# CONTENTS

# Preface

1-2-3 is a joy to use. Powerful, productive, convenient—the characteristics of the program exceed anything that preceded it. As popular as it has become, few people know the true power of 1-2-3 available through macros. From the simplest things like controlling worksheet posting and printing through sophisticated applications like stock and commodities analysis, insurance claims analysis, and small business accounting, macros open the door to results most users of 1-2-3 don't even suspect are possible. I have met and trained people from a wide variety of professions who have become expert macro users through their enthusiasm for the flexibility and power it gave them. Writing macros has been a hobby as well as an occupation, and I hope you'll come to feel the same way after using this book.

I would like to recognize the contributions of the many people who provided assistance or feedback during the writing of the book, including those at the Brady Communications Company and Lotus Development Corporation, and Cynthia W. Harriman.

Richard W. Ridington, Jr.
Middletown, Connecticut

I became a coauthor of this book for three reasons. First, I was very impressed with the capabilities of Lotus 1-2-3. It was the first program that I felt was powerful enough, yet easy enough (and fun enough!) to really be useful for managers and staff. Second, I found that the macro language that gave 1-2-3 the tremendous ability to automate functions, expand its capabilities, and develop systems was skimmed over in its otherwise excellent manual. I wished to share the understanding I gained in my work with macros. Third, I found that Mr. Ridington and myself were able to overlap our talents, to produce one comprehensive text instead of our writing two books on special applications.

I appreciate programs that make things simple . . . I want to spend my time getting the job done! Lotus has done this admirably with 1-2-3. 1-2-3 simplified the use of commands, made the program "visually" based so that it is easy to see what the commands will do, and added the macro abilities so that commands could be automated. I even use 1-2-3 as a word processor. In fact, much of this book was written with 1-2-3!

While I was doing research for this book I used quite a few different computers. 1-2-3 was identical on each computer, and most of them could share 1-2-3 data files. The differences in how fast 1-2-3 worked on them is shown in Section 3.8. My favorite machine was the Wang Professional with a hard disk. I don't like to memorize commands, so its menu-driven operating system was a joy to use. The Wang ran so fast that I had to rewrite some of my systems when I saw how slow they became on the IBM PC.

I have enjoyed watching the new, powerful software come out. The tools that are now available can be a great help, without requiring us to become computer programers. It was fun writing this book to show how to put 1-2-3 to work. I hope it proves useful to you!

Mark M. Williams, CPA
Kirkland, Washington

# About the Authors

RICHARD WARREN RIDINGTON, JR. provides support for productivity computing through consulting, training, speaking, and writing. He has provided training services to firms such as the Hartford Insurance Group and Home Box Office and has written for Business Computer Systems Magazine, the Wang Professional News, and the Connecticut Business Times. He has been a guest speaker at the University of New Hampshire Graduate Summer Computer Program and has given presentations and clinics for the Boston Computer Society and the Connecticut Computer Society.

"Like many other people, I was interested in computers around the time the Apple II came out, so I took a short course at a computer store (the course turned out to be on the programming language BASIC). BASIC didn't strike me as a very productive tool, and I decided to wait and see what else might develop. When 1-2-3 arrived, everything just took off: here was the kind of tool I'd been hoping for several years earlier.

"Computing brings together a lot of the things I enjoy and value: the logic inherent using software, consulting with others to solve problems, and motivating others to exercise greater creativity and productivity."

Mr. Ridington became involved with personal computers while working as a Production Control Manager when he attended a course given by computer author and teacher Russ Walter. Mr. Ridington's background includes functional job analysis, competency-based training development, career counseling, and rehabilitation counseling. In his leisure time, he enjoys swimming, racquetball, studying history, and autumn in New England.

MARK WILLIAMS has recently returned with his family to the Seattle area after living in Anchorage and Boston.

He received his CPA in Alaska while working with clients to improve their accounting systems. In Boston he managed the accounting group of a Trust operation.

Then he founded his own company, Useful Computing, Inc. Useful Computing specializes in helping people gain the full use of productivity tools such as Lotus 1-2-3. It has developed training classes, workbooks, and trainer's guides to accompany this book. If you are interested in taking their courses, obtaining the workbooks or guides, or would simply like to have a question answered, please call or write:

21909 N.E. 156th
Woodinville, WA 98072
(206) 788-5334

Mr. Williams is the president of the Northwest Computer Society and is working to coordinate many special interest user groups in the area. He was the director of the Integrated Software Clinics in the Boston Computer Society.

Mr. Williams has written articles for several computer magazines. He is currently writing books on using the data base capabilities of 1-2-3 and the macro capabilities of Symphony (also to be published by Brady Communications Company, Inc.).

# Foreword

**Adam B. Green**

Arlington, Massachusetts

When Mitch Kapor first called in August 1982 to invite me to look at a "spreadsheet program" he was working on, I wasn't too enthusiastic. After all, with VisiCalc, Multiplan, and Supercalc on the market, who needed another spreadsheet? I decided to take a look anyway because I respected Mitch's other works: Tiny Troll, VisiPlot, and VisiTrend.

Over the last few years, I've looked at more software products than I care to remember, and I've learned to trust my "gut reaction" to new products. I'm also rather critical, and eager to voice any negative impressions I might have about a program. Many software developers are aware of these traits, and they often ask me, and others like me, to look at new products several months before their release. I get a tremendous kick from making suggestions for changes; but, I know better than to ever claim responsibility for any final features of a program.

I arrived at Lotus Development Corporations's offices to find a rather laid-back company of about a dozen employees, most of whom seemed to live in their doorways, holding cups of coffee. This was a good sign. When I find a company filled with three-piece-suited salesmen, I know I can expect better advertisements than product. Lotus seemed to be the kind of environment where creative juices flowed freely.

Mitch brought me into his office and gave me a thrilling demonstration of 1-2-3, which was called Trio at the time. His enthusiasm was almost as fascinating as the product. My "gut" told me instantly that this was going to be a hit.

I quickly accepted Mitch's offer to join a small group of "beta-testers" being formed. Another member of this beta-test group was to be Doug Cobb, who later authored *Using 1-2-3*. Doug happened to have his office in the same building as Lotus.

Beta-testers are knowledgeable individuals who use a product before it is released and give the developers a preview of the final end-user's reactions. They often take part in a "pruning" process, in which the final features of a program are selected from the many possibilities under development. This goes on for several months until the "freeze" date, after which nothing can be added.

Along with the pre-release copy of 1-2-3, we were given a preliminary copy of the documentation. This documentation included a two or three page description of something called "typing alternative commands," later to become known as macro commands.

Over the next few months I fell in love with 1-2-3. Yes, it is possible to love software. I also came to feel that the macro capability would make 1-2-3 stand out from all of its competition. Consultants and programmers would be able to customize the program for any application. I had worked with dBASE II extensively and knew that its programming language was responsible for its success.

When the time came for the final beta-test meeting before the freeze date, most of us were adamant about one thing: Macros must be included in the final version. Surprisingly, many of Lotus' people were against the inclusion of macros. They were worried about the potential technical support requirements. The cries of the beta-testers and the desire to reach the application development market eventually prevailed, and macros were not cut from 1-2-3.

Lotus' corporate ambivalence towards macros manifested itself again in the final version of the manual. In my opinion, macros were deliberately "anti-documented." The documentation was written to discourage the timid from exploring macros. In this way, the experienced programmers could take advantage of them, but nonprogrammers would never get far enough to need technical support.

When 1-2-3 was released, I wasn't surprised to find that many users were fascinated with macros. Developers quickly began producing 1-2-3 application templates. Even nonprogrammers understood that putting time into learning macros would result in greatly increased efficiency.

To help people harness the power of 1-2-3, I added a seminar on 1-2-3 to my regular program of dBASE II seminars. Of course, a major part of my seminar was spent on macros. I wasn't alone in training 1-2-3 users. A flood of books, videotapes, and other training aids appeared on the market. Amazingly, none of these products ever concentrated exclusively on macros.

Almost two years after 1-2-3's release, the book that we have all been needing has finally been written. When Mark Williams gave me a copy of this book to preview, I was so pleased that I offered to write this Foreword. Again my "gut" told me that this was a product the public needed.

I'm sure you'll find this book as useful and well written as I have. Follow along with the clear and complete examples provided, and the wonderful world of macros will soon be yours.

# Who This Book Is For, What You Need To Use It

This book is for people who already know how to use 1-2-3 and now want to know how to use it more effectively through macros. It presents a complete course on the use of macros, with sections dealing with introductory, intermediate, and advanced skills. It also provides many macros you can use "as is" to save time and enhance the performance of your current worksheets.

Three things will affect your use of this book:

1. Your knowledge of 1-2-3
2. The release of 1-2-3 you are using
3. The make of computer you are using to run 1-2-3

The effects of each are explained here.

## Your knowledge of 1-2-3

As a starting point, we have assumed you are already comfortable using 1-2-3 and have developed your own worksheets. Accordingly, we won't side track you with explanations of basic operations you can find in an introductory 1-2-3 book. However, we assume no prior knowledge of macros. The book presents detailed descriptions of how to use macros to automate and customize 1-2-3 operations, along with complete descriptions of all the commands specific to macros, such as "/XM" and "/XG".

Regardless of your background, 1-2-3 is such a diverse program it's likely you'll encounter at least a few commands unrelated to macros that will be unfamiliar to you while reading this book. Because this book focuses exclusively on macros, we recommend you obtain a good 1-2-3 reference book where you can look up any command, dictionary style. This will give you quick answers to questions about any non-macro commands. All macro related questions will be dealt with here.

## The release of 1-2-3 you are using

This book is designed for use with Lotus 1-2-3, Release 1A or greater (that includes Release 1A with the "*" below it). You can easily check the release number of your 1-2-3 program by loading it into your computer. After selecting

"1-2-3" from the Lotus Access System menu, a screen showing Lotus' copyright notice will display. The release number of your 1-2-3 program is shown just below that notice. You can use the book with Release 1 of 1-2-3, but you won't be able to take advantage of release 1A's additional features (including macro subroutines, custom prompts, and "single-step" macro mode) explained in the book.

## The make of computer you are using to run 1-2-3

The instructions for writing macros correspond to the IBM Personal Computer keyboard. If you are using an IBM compatible personal computer by Compaq, Corona, or Columbia, your keyboard layout is identical to IBM's, and you will be able to follow the instructions without any adjustments.

If you are using a keyboard differing from IBM's layout, such as the ones supplied with the Wang Professional Computer or Texas Instruments Professional Computer, there will be some differences between what we tell you to type and what you see on your keyboard. The CHARACTERS you should type won't vary from the ones presented in the text, but the KEYS you must press to type those characters occasionally will.

For example, on the IBM PC keyboard the backslash character is located in the lower left corner next to the space bar. On the Wang Professional keyboard there is no backslash character at all. However, the Lotus 1-2-3 manual for the Wang Professional will tell you the backslash character can be typed by pressing the second key and the slash key. So if you are using a computer with a keyboard layout differing from the IBM PC and should not see a key we tell you to type, consult your 1-2-3 manual for the keystrokes to use instead. The differences will be minor (a computer with one of those "non-IBM PC" keyboards was used to write half of this book).

## Limits of Liability and Disclaimer of Warranty

## Note to Authors

Have you written a book related to personal computers? Do you have an idea for developing such a project? If so, we would like to hear from you. Brady produces a complete range of books for the personal computer market. We invite you to write to David Culverwell, Publishing Director, Brady Communications Company, Inc., Bowie, MD 20715.

## Registered Trademarks

# 1

# The Access System

# What's In This Chapter

This chapter provides you with an overview of the book. It will help you understand the purpose of the book, and focus on those parts that can benefit you most.

# 1.1 The Benefits Of Macros

What can macros do for you? Here's a review of the diverse benefits macros offer:

1.  *Save Time.* A macro can save you time in your use of 1-2-3. For example, should you need to print several copies of a report, or need to print several different print ranges from one worksheet, a macro can easily handle that *unattended.* This frees you from waiting around for the printer to finish so you can reset print ranges.

2.  *Fewer Keystrokes.* The execution of an operation requires fewer keystrokes when using a macro as compared to executing the same operation manually. For example, to manually round the entry 12.2345 to two decimal places you'd have to edit it to read @round(12.2345,2). This requires thirteen keystrokes, if you make no mistakes. A macro will do the same thing with *only two keystrokes,* execute the operation in about *a second,* and *won't make any mistakes.* Imagine the time you'll save if you have a lot of rounding to do. Most frequently used operations can be more efficiently performed by a macro than by hand. But that's a conservative example. Larger macro applications routinely *save their users hundreds of keystrokes.*

3.  *Save Mental Effort.* Macros also help those who tend to forget the commands they want to use. By storing a complex sequence of commands in a macro, you *eliminate the need to remember* these commands. Since macros also provide for pauses where you can type in data or make a key choice, they even allow you to *automate complex procedures* that will not be done exactly the same way each time.

4.  *Customize* 1-2-3. Macros can customize 1-2-3 to meet a variety of specific needs. They can allow you to use the IBM Personal Computer's numeric keypad for data entry (without switching in and out of "NUMLOCK") by moving the cursor for you. They can replace the generic 1-2-3 command menus with ones that show choices you designate. Instead of "Worksheet, Range, Copy" the choices could read "Post, Erase, Save." You can also use macros to write custom prompts to control data entry. These are a few of the features macros offer that will *allow inexperienced persons to use 1-2-3 effectively.*

5.  *Ensure Consistency.* Macros can be used to ensure consistency in the manner critical operations are performed, regardless of who performs them. Many applications must be posted in a certain sequence, and require error checking. Macros can guide the operators to certain cells, prevent them from moving ahead before posting a cell, check their entry to ensure it falls within an acceptable range, and prompt them to make a correction if needed.

While the above points are by no means a complete listing of all the benefits you can expect to obtain from macros, at least one more item deserves mention. We separate this last point because its personal nature makes it unique, though no less important.

6. *Sharpen Your Mind.* Creating a new and useful macro is like a good game. Not only is it *fun* to see a new macro work successfully, but the process of creating it sharpens logical and creative faculties. The evidence for this one is subjective, but widespread enough to merit attention. For your own part, we can only suggest you read on and prove it for yourself.

## 1.2   The Makeup of a Macro

What are these powerful tools? How are they written? Here's an introduction to the methods of macros.

Macros execute 1-2-3 operations automatically by reading a "record" of the keystrokes you would use to perform those operations manually. You create this special record by entering the 1-2-3 keystrokes as a label entry on the worksheet.

Example: since you normally type the first letter of a 1-2-3 command to execute it, the command Worksheet is written as "w" in a macro. The sequence of commands needed to adjust column width, / Worksheet Column-width Set, would look like this in a macro:

```
/wcs
```

Thus, the 1-2-3 commands you know become the "vocabulary" of your simple macros.  As you learn more commands, your ability to create more powerful, versatile macros expands proportionately.

While simple macros use the 1-2-3 commands you already know, more advanced macros can take advantage of a special set of commands that are used only in macros. These special commands offer you the ability to customize 1-2-3, including the ability to create your own command menus and data entry prompts.

## 1.3   How to Take Advantage of Macros

The purpose of this book is to teach you how to take advantage of macros. It teaches by example, so you'll always see the concepts working. Here's a summary of those examples:

1.   Simple Operations:
     • date a worksheet
     • write labels and formulas on the worksheet
     • enter boiler-plate text in mid-sentence

- indent labels
- round numbers and formulas
- set column widths
- justify and merge text

2. Intermediate Operations:
   - print multiple worksheet ranges
   - print multiple copies of a worksheet
   - automate cursor movement while posting a worksheet
   - round an entire row (or column) of entries
   - enter a warning in a cell when its value drops below a limit
   - display a sequence of graphs automatically
   - prompt operators for data entry
   - display custom-written command menus to allow inexperienced operators to make selections in 1-2-3
   - create counters, loops, and other worksheet control macros
   - suppress irrelevant or unneeded material from displaying on the screen
   - control screen display to create messages

3. Advanced Operations—create entire macro systems to:
   - manage address lists
   - record payroll tax registers
   - maintain check registers
   - manage a note control system
   - provide menu-driven word processing
   - create a dedicated data base program

You'll be able to use most of these macros on your own worksheets just as you find them in the book. The exception to this is the advanced macro systems described in item 3, "Advanced Operations." These macros illustrate advanced techniques appropriate for larger, more complex macro operations than those found in the other sections. Due to the sheer size of the actual applications, no attempt has been made to reproduce them wholly in the book. Instead the focus is on explaining their critical elements, where the important lessons lie. So while you'll be able to transfer specific techniques from these chapters, the only practical way to transfer the entire macro systems these chapters discuss is to use the optional diskette.

## *Summary*

Whether you're satisfied with using the macros we give you, wish to modify them somewhat, or want to create entirely new ones, this book offers the tools and step-by-step instructions you'll need to meet your goal.

## 1.4   Using the Diskette

The diskette contains every macro example presented in the book (there are over 300 individual macros) in an easy-to-use format, and also allows you to combine any of these macros directly into your own worksheets. The macros are arranged in the same order as the book itself. Refer to Appendix A.1 for instructions on using the diskette. Use the diskette as you read the book. We suggest that you try each of the examples yourself, and then check the sample in the book to correct any errors.

To use the macros, load Lotus 1-2-3 with the book diskette in drive B. This will automatically load the File Manager. Select the macros you wish to see. The system will retrieve the file, and let you VIEW the macros or USE them. To bring the macros into your own worksheets, use the File Combine commands (see Section 2.8 for an explanation). Each macro within the book diskette has been given the same Range Name as its macro number in the text.

### *Summary*

We urge you to purchase the diskette with the book. While we designed the book so that a reader can type in each of the macros, this task will become laborious as the longer macros in the later sections are covered. The systems discussed in Chapter 4 and the Appendix are both learning tools and useful applications. Having the diskette will allow you to take full advantage of them.

As another bonus, we included a worksheet with all 256 ASCII characters that IBM-type computers are capable of reproducing. As Lotus 1-2-3 can only reproduce the characters on the keyboard, this gives you access to the other graphics, line drawing, Greek, and special characters. By File Combining these into your worksheets and editing them to fit your application, your worksheets will look better and have greater utility.

## 1.5   How to Get the Most From This Book

While preparing to write this book, one of the people we interviewed made an important point: people need to know about macros in order to solve problems, not to satisfy any intrinsic interest in macros. That was Sheila Karp, who was at that time a supervisor of Lotus Development's customer support. Sheila was absolutely right—macros are a problem solving tool, and you'll learn fastest if you begin using them to solve problems as you read.

As we introduce a macro, put it to work on your 1-2-3 worksheets. The macros are all proven utilities—you'll save time, get more work done, and solve problems through using them. But that's only part of the point: you'll gain experience creating and using macros. This experience will help you to master the art of macros, and thereby accomplish things with 1-2-3 most people never suspect are possible. Then the next time you come up against a tricky problem, you'll know how to create a macro to deal with it.

Read the book in any way that pleases you: front to back, back to front, skim through it, or use the tables of contents located at the front of the book and the beginning of each section to select just the things you consider most relevant. Once you've found what you're looking for, using it on your 1-2-3 worksheets is the way to mine that knowledge from the book, and thus convert it into the skills and models you can use.

## *How To Find The Sections That Will Help You Most*

This book provides a complete course on the use of macros. To help you focus on the parts that address your needs most closely, read the description following each number below. If it seems to describe you, consider the suggestions beneath it.

1.  *For those who don't know about macros at all.*

    Before getting into the procedures of creating macros, you need to know what macros can do for you and how they make 1-2-3 significantly more powerful. This is the job of this entire "Introductory Chapter." If you haven't read the pages preceding this, do so now.

2.  *For those who know about macros but want to know how to get them to work (perhaps you couldn't understand the 1-2-3 manual's instructions).*

    You need direct, clear instruction in order to begin using macros for the first time. The "Basics of Macros" will have you writing simple macros in five minutes, then proceeds to provide a rigorously complete and easy-to-follow tutorial covering all the essentials of macros, right through creating your own menus. After completing this section you'll not only understand everything in the macro section of your 1-2-3 manual, you'll know much more!

3.  *For those who have used macros to do simple things, and now want to explore their more advanced uses.*

    Everything from writing a macro for the first time through the use of the X commands is contained in the "Basics Of Macros"—Chapter 2. If any of those areas have given you problems, check the guide at the beginning of that chapter to find the material you want. Once you've mastered that material and are ready to create more powerful applications, look into the "Macro Techniques"—Chapter 3 to find all the methods necessary to develop complete customized 1-2-3 systems of macros. This uses a customized 1-2-3 application (a menu-driven word processor) to illustrate techniques such as loops, counters, moving data around, methods of controlling the screen to hide the work the macros are doing behind a pleasant message—all the undocumented tricks you need to really turn on the power of macros.

4. *For those who have read all the techniques, and now want to see some larger macro systems incorporating these methods.*

Other sections of the book include numerous examples of useful macros, but each section in the "Advanced Macro Systems" chapter, and the first three sections in Appendix A, are devoted exclusively to explaining one sophisticated system of macros that provides a completely customized 1-2-3 application. Included are a word processor, payroll register, a check register, an address list manager, a file management system, and a note control system. As with the other examples in the book, these macros are not only useful as written, but present specific concepts which can be adapted to other applications as well. The address manager shows how any 1-2-3 data base can be completely automated and customized so that it can be used by anyone. The mortgage manager is an example of completely automated file management under macro control.

# 2

# The Basics of Macros

# What's In This Chapter?

This section will teach you how to write simple macros. It is the best place to start if you've never written macros before.

## 2.1   5 Minutes To Your First Macro

This chapter will show you how to write a simple macro in a matter of minutes, and is intended for those of you who are anxious to use a macro without waiting for detailed explanations. A more systematic and comprehensive treatment of this process follows in the next section.

Here's a simple macro to automatically adjust the width of a column from the standard nine spaces to twenty-five. To do that, the macro will execute the command sequence in the order shown below:

| / | **Worksheet** | **Column-Width** | **Set** | **25** | **ENTER** |
|---|---|---|---|---|---|
| (1) | (2) | (3) | (4) | (5) | (6) |

Syntax Note: **ENTER** means press the Enter key, located where the typewriter Return key would be.

Load 1-2-3 into your computer so that you are looking at a blank worksheet. Type /wey (/ Worksheet Erase Yes) to ensure you're working with a fresh worksheet. Your cursor is in cell A1 now, so *type* the following:

```
'/wcs25~
```

Notes:

**'**   Type the *apostrophe* first.  The apostrophe is located on the middle row of the alphanumeric keyboard, to the far right side.  It is on the same key with the double quote ( " ) mark.  Do *not* confuse it with the similar looking accent mark just to its right.

**/**   The *slash* that appears next is on the lower *right* side of the keyboard.

**~**   The symbol after the 25 is called a tilde (rhymes with "Matilda"). On an IBM-style keyboard it is found on the key just to the *left* of the **ENTER** (or Return) key, in the *uppercase* position of that key. When used in a macro, this tells 1-2-3 to press the **ENTER** key.

There should be *no* spaces between any of these characters.

Now press **ENTER** to place the label in cell A1 on the worksheet. Note that the apostrophe *disappears* on the worksheet (when the apostrophe is the first character typed in a cell, it acts as a "control character", aligning the entry with the left margin of the cell). If you neglect to type the apostrophe, the slash that follows it will activate 1-2-3's command menu, rather than typing a label.

Your first step is complete, and you've just written a macro. Now you are going to give cell A1 (where the macro is written) a special range name. Follow along with this command sequence:

| You Press: | Which means: |
|---|---|
| / | Slash displays command menu |
| r | Range |

| | |
|---|---|
| **n** | Name |
| **c** | Create |
| **\a** | In response to prompt to "Enter name:" |
| **ENTER** | Confirms name entry |
| **a1** | In response to prompt to "Enter range:" |
| **ENTER** | Assigns cell A1 the name "\a" |

Note: the range name " \a " you were instructed to enter in the sequence above uses a backslash ( \ ), located on the lower *left* side of an IBM-style keyboard, *not* the slash ( / ) located on the lower right side of the keyboard. The distinction is an important one.

This sequence should return 1-2-3 to the "READY" mode, with no menu display. If not, press **Esc** (the ESCAPE key) until 1-2-3 does return to READY mode, and start the command sequence over again. Slowly follow the steps once more; they work.

You are now ready to "run" your first macro, as follows:

1. Press the **ALT** key (located directly to the left of the space bar), and *hold* it down.
2. Now type the **A** key and *watch the worksheet*.
3. Release the **ALT** key.

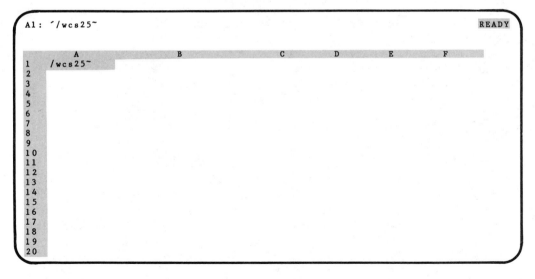

**Screen 2-1. First macro (Macro 2-1).**

Observe carefully. Cell A1 is now 25 spaces wide (It started out 9 spaces wide). Congratulations: your macro did that! That's a basic macro: automating what you could have done manually. Now move to cell B1. Press **ALT** and **A** again (You can execute your macro from *anywhere* on the worksheet, not just in cell A1). Macros can get very fancy and produce all kinds of sophisticated programs, but this is the fundamental process for them all.

In the next section you'll learn all the basics of writing macros. It includes instructions for writing macros that fall into the category of worksheet utilities. They enter labels on the worksheet, enter dates and numbers, and execute longer sequences of commands. As "utilities," these macros are useful on any number of worksheets, and are a good foundation for the more sophisticated systems presented in later chapters.

## 2.2   The Basics of Macros

The last chapter presented a quick and simple example of a macro. In this chapter, you'll learn a comprehensive, systematic method for writing any kind of macro, be it simple or complex. The steps of this method are described below in this macro-writing outline.

| Step | Explanation |
|------|-------------|
| **1.  Defining** | Manually execute the 1-2-3 operation. Type the commands and enter any data you want to automate with the macro. On a piece of scratch paper, write down EACH KEY you press during this operation. |
| **2.  Writing** | Find an out of the way area on the worksheet to place the macro. Using your keystroke notes from step 1, type the macro on the worksheet as a label or, in the case of a multiple line macro, a series of labels in one column. Spaces should never be entered between macro characters unless you pressed the space bar at that point when you executed the operation manually. Leave a blank cell directly beneath the macro. |
| **3.  Naming** | Range Name the first (top) cell in the macro with the **/ Range Name Create** command sequence. Assign the cell a name consisting of the backslash (\) and any single letter of the alphabet. |
| **4.  Protecting** | **/File Save** the worksheet to make a copy of the file. If the macro erases or damages the worksheet, the original worksheet can be File Retrieved from disk intact. |
| **5.  Executing** | Hold down the ALT key and press the letter included in the name. If the name given the macro was \a, then hold down ALT and press **A**. |

A reminder on syntax: when you read **ENTER** in the examples that follow, press the **ENTER** key.

## Step One: Define the Macro

The first kind of simple macro types labels for you. It could be used to enter report headers, or store frequently used entries (like a long company name). As an example, let's try a name. Here's how to do it manually:

James  Johnson  **ENTER**

That operation is easy to keep a record of, because you don't need any 1-2-3 command menus to enter a simple label.

## Step Two: Write it on the Worksheet as a Label

This operation is easy to translate into a macro. Type the name into cell A1 and follow it with the symbol representing the ENTER key, the tilde (˜). The ˜ key takes the place of the ENTER key in every 1-2-3 command that is written into a macro.

James  Johnson˜

Now make sure the cell beneath it (cell A2) is blank. That will terminate the macro.

## Step Three: Name it as a Macro

All macros take a special kind of range name, a backslash followed by a single letter, such as "\a". This is a very specific format:

- a backslash followed by a single letter
- The order cannot be reversed
- the letter may NOT be replaced with a number
- There can only be ONE letter
- The backslash (\) CANNOT be replaced by the slash (/).

Place your cursor on cell A1, which contains the macro, and execute the following steps to give that cell the special range name:

| You type: | Which means: |
|---|---|
| / | Slash displays 1-2-3 command menu |
| r | Range |
| n | Name |
| c | Create |
| \a | In response to prompt "Enter name:" |

| **ENTER** | Press the Enter key, confirming name |
| **ENTER** | Press Enter key, confirming current cell as recipient of that name |

## Step Four: Protect Your Work

If you have a two-drive floppy disk system, place a formatted disk in drive B (where you normally keep your data). If you are using a hard disk, you will store your file on the hard disk. The name for the file in this example is SAMPLE, so if you already have a file named SAMPLE on your disk, substitute a DIFFERENT name for this file or you will overwrite, and destroy, your original SAMPLE file.

| **You type:** | **Which means:** |
|---|---|
| **/** | Slash displays command menu |
| **f** | File |
| **s** | Save |
| **sample** | In response to prompt "Enter save file name:" |
| **ENTER** | Press Enter to save the file on disk |

## Step Five: Execute the Macro

Move the cursor to any blank cell (except the one directly beneath the macro) where you wish to enter the name. Leaving the cursor on the macro cell would overwrite the macro itself. Now follow the intructions below:

| **You type:** | **Which means:** |
|---|---|
| **ALT** | HOLD DOWN the ALT key, do not merely press |
| **a** | The letter used in the name ( \a ) |
| | NOW release the ALT key |
| | (some computers require pressing the keys one at a time) |

Congratulations, you've reached a milestone on your first time out: you've completed the process for writing a simple macro. Let's run through that process again with each of the three types of simple macros:

1. Macros that enter labels.
2. Macros that enter numbers.
3. Macros that execute commands.

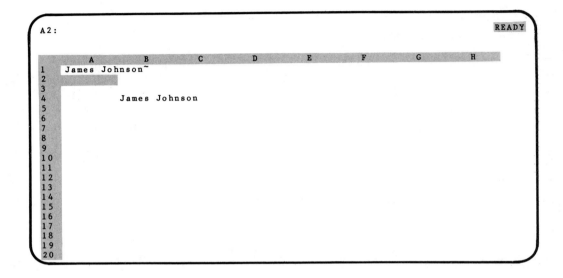

**Screen 2-2. Label macro (Macro 2-2).**

You've just done the "type 1" macro, entering a label on the worksheet. Other possible uses for that include entering: (1) frequently used long labels, (2) headings for reports, (3) month name headers for spreadsheet columns, and (4) entire sentences that are used frequently. Later on we'll see how to insert text into the middle of a sentence.

## Entering Numbers

Let's now look at a macro that enters a number (the second type of macro). To manually enter a number on the worksheet simply type the number and press enter:

**234.23 ENTER**

To make that number entry into a macro, place the cursor on a blank cell and follow these steps: type the left label alignment character ('), the number, and the tilde:

**'234.23~**

Of course, when you enter this on the worksheet, the label alignment character disappears, leaving a left aligned label looking like this:

**234.23~**

If you don't make the entry into a label by preceding it with the label alignment character, (1) you won't be able to enter it on the worksheet with the tilde after it; and (2) the macro won't read it. Macros can't read VALUE entries, only LABELS (so values must be made into labels).

The next step is to give the cell containing the macro a Range Name. Use the name "\b". There's not much chance of this macro damaging a worksheet so there's no need to File Save before executing the macro. Move the cursor to a blank cell and execute the macro by pressing **ALT B**.

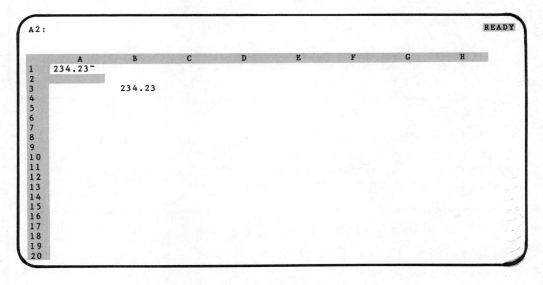

**Screen 2-3. Number macro (Macro 2-3).**

## Entering Commands

We'll change that macro and expand it a bit. Start off by writing a macro to enter a number. This time the number will be a formula, such as @today. This formula calculates the number of days from the beginning of the century until today's date (which is the date you put into the computer when you turn it on). Here are the steps to write the macro: type the left alignment character, then @today, then a tilde. It should look like this when it appears on the worksheet (don't forget that left alignment character):

**@today~**

That will enter a number on the worksheet, but the number lacks the formatting needed to display as a date. Move to the cell just below the macro and enter the following keystrokes there:

| You type: | Which will mean: |
|---|---|
| ' | Left label alignment |
| / | Slash opens command menu |
| **r** | Range |
| **f** | Format |
| **d** | Date |
| **2** | Select second date format (day/mon) |
| ~ | Accept default range (current cell) |

Here's the way the macro looks now:

```
@today~
/rfd2~
```

Observe how a command sequence is entered in a macro—in the precise manner you would use if entering the commands from the keyboard. Try executing these commands manually, omitting the label alignment character, to verify their accuracy.

Now Range Name the top macro cell containing the entry **@today~**, with the macro name "**\c**". Move to a blank cell and press **ALT C** to execute it. Note what happens: the macro enters **@today** in the cell (producing a value), then formats the cell as a date (so the value displays today's date).

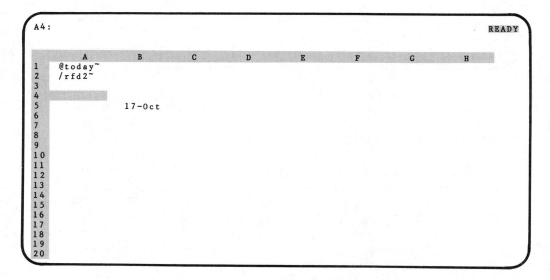

**Screen 2-4. Command macro (Macro 2-4).**

## *Additional Notes About Macros*

Note 1: Macros can be written on more than one line, and will read from the top cell down to the bottom. If you added another statement to the macro, it would be placed in the next cell below. When the macro reads downward and encounters an EMPTY cell, it ends. This is the reason to ensure there is a blank cell at the bottom of any macro.

Note 2: When beginning a line of a macro with an entry that is not normally read as a label, such as the "/" slash that normally activates the command menu, or a value, a label alignment character must be typed first to turn it into a label. This can be any one of the four 1-2-3 label alignment characters (' ^ " \), but the most common one is the left label alignment character (').

The next section gives you an explanation of an important principle governing the way macros work, called "Flow of Control." Understanding the Flow of Control principle is crucial in more advanced work with macros.

# 2.3   Flow of Control

"Flow of Control" is a concept we'll use throughout the rest of the book to describe the way macros work. This chapter will explain it and prepare you for more sophisticated macros to come.

Macros are little sets of instructions—programs. 1-2-3 reads these instructions from left to right, just as we read. Unlike us, however, 1-2-3 will only read a macro from left to right in a SINGLE column. It will not read across the worksheet from, say, cell A1 to cell B1. The flow of control of the macro runs from left to right in a cell, and then down to the next cell below.

Example: If cell A3 depicted on page 20 was given a macro name and executed, the instructions /wcs25~ would be read. However, the contents of cell B3 would be ignored, because the macro only reads from left to right across a single column.

### Diagram 2-1. Flow of Control—A.

```
===========================================================================

Example macro:          A               B               C

                1
                2
                3 /wcs25~         $34.95
                4
                5


----------------------------------------------------------------------------

Flow of control:        ----->          (not read by macro)


===========================================================================
```

In the last section you learned that all macro cells must be labels. Consequently, every macro cell begins with a label alignment character, even though that character is invisible on the worksheet.

When a macro is executed, it reads the cell the way we would. Ignoring the invisible label alignment character, it begins execution with the first visible character. In the example above, the first character to be executed is the slash (/), used to begin a command sequence.

The sequence of execution (or "flow of control") then passes to the next character to the right, until all characters in the cell have been executed. The macro then drops to the next cell below (cell A4 in this example) to read it in the same fashion. If that cell is blank, the macro terminates.

Let's return to the example of the "today" macro to learn more about how the flow of control works.

**Diagram 2-2. Flow of Control—B.**

```
=====================================================================

Example macro:          A                 B                 C

                    1
                    2
                    3 @today~            $34.95
                    4 /rfd2~
                    5


=====================================================================
```

When executed, this macro will first execute the instruction in cell A3 (enter the @TODAY function on the worksheet), then drop to cell A4 and execute the instruction there (display the number in Day/Month format). The macro terminates after this since nothing is entered in cell A5. The technical term for this last step is "terminating macro control."

The flow of control in the preceding example can be mapped as shown in Diagram 2-3.

**Diagram 2-3. Flow of Control—C.**

```
=====================================================================

Cell A3      @    t    o    d    a    y    ~          (read  first)

            ->   ->   ->   ->   ->   ->   ->

Cell A4      /    r    f    d    2    ~               (read  second)

            ->   ->   ->   ->   ->   ->

Cell A5                                               (read  third)

       ->      (macro ends)


=====================================================================
```

But what would happen if some non-macro entry was in that last cell, A5? Let's set up an example where we inadvertently write a column heading "Totals" just below the macro, depicted below.

**Diagram 2-4. Flow of Control—D.**

```
========================================================================
Example macro:          A               B               C

                1
                2
                3 @today
                4 /rfd2~
                5 Totals
                6

========================================================================
```

Here's what happens when that macro is executed, in the sequence each event occurs:

1. The formula @TODAY will be placed in the current cell.
2. The current cell is given the Date—2 format.
3. The label "Totals" is typed, and appears on the Edit line of the control panel. The mode indicator, in the top right corner of your screen, changes to "LABEL" to indicate the type of entry. Since no tilde follows to represent the **ENTER** key, 1-2-3 remains in LABEL mode, and the word "Totals" is not entered on the worksheet. The macro is now terminated.

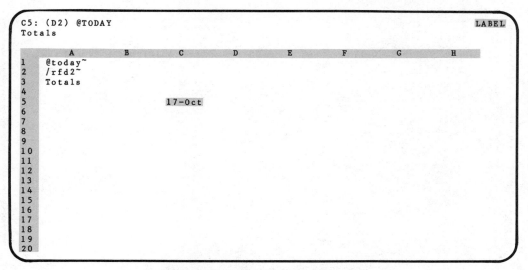

**Screen 2-5. Entry beneath macro (Macro 2-5).**

Note that although the word "Totals" wasn't intended as part of the macro, its careless placement in the cell beneath the last macro instruction forced 1-2-3 to read it as part of the macro. This example offers an excellent demonstration of the "literal nature" of macros. They have no ability to discern what you intend to be read as a macro versus what you don't. If an entry is placed in the next cell down from an active macro, it will ALWAYS be read as part of the macro.

We've already reviewed the need to always leave a blank cell below the macro in order to terminate it. But how do you prevent inadvertent entries from being placed there after you've written the macro?

Move down to the cell two places below the last macro entry cell and enter a continuous line across the cell (or even across all eight cells on the screen). Such a "borderline" will warn against placing any entry in the blank cell above. You can enter the repeating label entry \- in the cell and copy it across as many cells as you wish.

Here's how it looks on the worksheet (see Screen 2-6).

```
A4:  \-                                                        READY
        A          B        C        D        E       F       G        H
  1  @today~
  2  /rfd2~
  3
  4  --------------------------------
  5
  6
  7
  8
  9
 10
 11
 12
 13
 14
 15
 16
 17
 18
 19
 20
```

**Screen 2-6. Macro with blank cell (Macro 2-6).**

Another approach uses a very long label of dashes, without the repeating label character. This is more difficult to write. You must start with the left label alignment character, then hold down the dash key (the minus sign) until you think the entry is long enough to cover the cells. If it isn't, you just edit it until you have it right. Why take the trouble? This method allows you to do something that adds a nice touch to your worksheet.

A macro can type this for you, but in order to type the single line across the worksheet the macro must begin with TWO label alignment characters. Not only must the macro entry be preceded with a label alignment character, but the actual worksheet entry it makes must also be preceded by one. Try it manually first. Type a few dashes (----) on the worksheet and press ENTER. 1-2-3 will beep and go into EDIT mode. What's needed is a label alignment character to force the numeric operator " - " (read as a minus sign) to be viewed as a label.

The macro should be TYPED on a single line, using the following keystrokes.

**Keystrokes:**   **which mean:**

| | |
|---|---|
| ' | Label alignment character |
| ' | Label alignment character |
| -------------- | Minus sign (as long a line as you wish) |
| ~ | Tilde represents **ENTER** |

It will APPEAR like this on the worksheet:

'------------------------~

And will PRODUCE the following when executed:

```
------------------------
```

This type of label makes a nice tool for placing titles and labels inside it. If you make the line 72 dashes long, and execute it from the far left cell on the worksheet, it'll create a line across the entire page, like this:

```
-----------------------------------------------------------
```

If you then move to one of the cells it overwrites, around the middle of the screen, and type this:

`<Space Bar>Title<Space Bar>`**ENTER**

Here's what you get:

```
----------------------- Title -------------------------
```

The word "Title" with spaces on either side blocks the long line and gives a nice appearance to set off a section. We'll use that more later on.

Before leaving this section, it's important to return to one point made earlier. We presented an example showing the "literal nature of macros" as a problem, but to leave it as such would be misleading. It is precisely because macros follow rules so consistently that they are such effective tools. The better you understand their logic the better you will be able to innovate macros to improve the performance of your 1-2-3 applications. We will show you the results of such innovation with macros throughout the book, but the better you grasp those rules, the better you'll be able to innovate for yourself.

# 2.4   Printing Macros

Now that you have some skills in writing macros it's time to put them to work. Here's an example of a macro we use frequently, automatically printing worksheets, that's well within your abilities. When does it make sense to do that?

1.  When you have to print multiple print ranges on a large worksheet, and must wait between printings to adjust print ranges and restart the operation.
2.  When you have to print multiple copies of the same worksheet for filing and distribution. You'll find large worksheets much easier to reprint than to attempt photocopying them piecemeal due to their size.
3.  When you have to print worksheets from more than one file. While it makes sense to have macros doing this work, we won't show you this example until later, when the special commands it requires are introduced.

In addition to the new macros, you'll see a new organization for your macros that'll make them easier to write and read.

```
A2:                                                              READY

         A          B         C        D       E       F       G       H
1   \p           /ppcrr               Clears and resets print range
2                A1.D34~              Range to print
3                agp                  Print and advance page
4                crr                  Clears and resets print range
5                E17.L63~             Range to print
6                gpq                  Print, advance page, and quit
7                                     Blank space to end macro
8
9
10
11
12
13
14
15
16
17
18
19
20
```

**Screen 2-7. Example 1 (Macro 2-7).**

The clear documentation built into this example allows you to easily check the macro's name, and augments each line of the macro with a line of explanation. Here are some of the advantages of this format:

1. The name, macro, and comment information are contained in *separate* worksheet columns.
2. The Range Name of each cell is shown in the left column. Often several cells in a macro will be given Range Names. They can be quickly found and identified with this method.
3. The Macro can be given a Range Name by using the command **Range Name Labels Right**. This uses the macro name to create the Range Name in the cell to the right. With the cursor in the cell displaying the name, the cursor can be moved down the column to encompass any other entries. Thus, many Range Names can be created with one command.
4. The Range Names and cell addresses are all in uppercase. This makes it very easy to separate the WHAT of each macro (the macro commands), from the WHERE (the location on the worksheet that is being affected).
5. The macro is written in modules—only one type of command is written on each line of the macro. This makes it easy to follow what the macro is doing, and to use the macros as building blocks for other macros.
6. The comments serve to quickly tell what each portion of the macro is doing. This task is difficult if the code itself must be read.

Now suppose you had to change those print dimensions frequently. We'll rewrite the macro, moving the tilde that follows the print range to the beginning of the following line. The instructions will be read in exactly the same *sequence* by the macro, but the change in design will leave the print ranges on lines by themselves, so they can be changed easily.

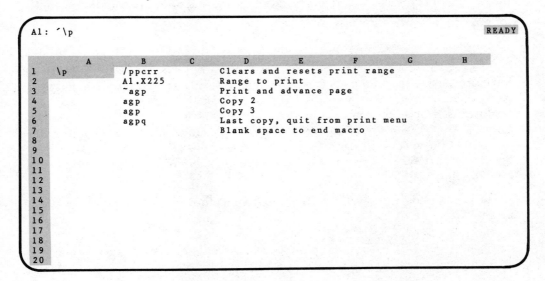

```
A1:  '\p                                                              READY

          A         B         C         D         E         F         G         H
 1  \p          /ppcrr              Clears and resets print range
 2              A1.D34              Range to print (can be revised)
 3              ~agp                Print and advance page
 4              crr                 Clears and resets print range
 5              E17.L63             Range to print (can be revised)
 6              ~gpq                Print, advance page, and quit
 7                                  Blank space to end macro
 8
 9
10
11
12
13
14
15
16
17
18
19
20
```

**Screen 2-8. Example 1 revised (Macro 2-8).**

Even with a fast printer, printing a large worksheet is going to take awhile. Printing the worksheet more than once makes matters worse. This macro takes care of all that for you:

```
A1:  '\p                                                              READY

          A         B         C         D         E         F         G         H
 1  \p          /ppcrr              Clears and resets print range
 2              A1.X225             Range to print
 3              ~agp                Print and advance page
 4              agp                 Copy 2
 5              agp                 Copy 3
 6              agpq                Last copy, quit from print menu
 7                                  Blank space to end macro
 8
 9
10
11
12
13
14
15
16
17
18
19
20
```

**Screen 2-9. Example 2 (Macro 2-9).**

These macros are nice for two reasons: (1) they are relatively simple to write (macros need not be complex to be useful), and (2) they can probably be used on every worksheet you have. In section 2.11 we'll show you how to write a custom menu to control which of the above macros is executed—then you can have anyone print worksheets for you.

### A Tip For Finding Macro Names

Here's a tip for those times when you wish to move quickly to a macro you've written. In the worksheet containing the macro, press the **GOTO** (F5) and **NAME** (F3) function keys to display a menu of range names you've created for this worksheet. If you have more range names than can display at once, press the **END** key to move to the very end of the range names listing. Range names are arranged according to an information code called ASCII, which happens to place the backslash character close to last in its list. Since all macro range names begin with a backslash, they are almost always listed last. Highlight the one you wish, and press **ENTER**. If you place all your macros in the same area on the worksheet you can review them all at once with this method.

## 2.5   The {Bracketed} Macro Commands

Before showing you more macros, it's time to introduce an important addition to your macro vocabulary: the **{bracketed}** commands. These commands allow macros to control 1-2-3's function keys and cursor control keys. What's more, they include a special command allowing macros to pause and accept user input at critical points.

### Overview

The {bracketed} commands extend the control you can exercise with macros to three new areas. The brackets (sometimes called "curly braces") used to enclose each command are located on an IBM-style keyboard on the keys directly ABOVE the double quote and tilde, and reside on the UP-SHIFTED position of those keys. Be careful. If you mistakenly use the brackets that reside on the UNSHIFTED position, [ ], the commands will not work when you execute the macro.

The commands and the three functional areas they cover are shown in Diagram 2-5.

### Diagram 2-5. Bracketed commands.

1.  *To represent the function keys:*

|      |          | F2  | {edit}   |
|------|----------|-----|----------|
| F3   | {name}   | F4  | {abs}    |
| F5   | {goto}   | F6  | {window} |
| F7   | {query}  | F8  | {table}  |
| F9   | {calc}   | F10 | {graph}  |

*Note: every 1-2-3 function key except "HELP" can be written into a macro, thereby invoking the function(s) automatically.*

2.  *To represent the cursor control keys:*

| {home} | {up}   | {pgup}  |
|--------|--------|---------|
| {left} |        | {right} |
| {end}  | {down} | {pgdn}  |

3.  *To represent editing and "special" keys:*

| {esc} | Escape key |
|-------|------------|
| {bs}  | Backspace key |
| {del} | Delete key (use while in EDIT mode only) |
| {?}   | Pause to accept user input |
| ~     | ENTER key (known as tilde), this is uppercase of key to the right of double quote key on IBM keyboards |

The special bracketed command, {?}, needs some explanation. It provides the first step in making your macros interactive with their user. Whenever the macro encounters {?}, it will pause and await keyboard input from the user. Let's look at a simple example of this.

Here was our first macro:

/wcs25~

which was used to execute the command sequence:

/  Worksheet  Column-width  Set  **25**  **ENTER**

We can change it so the column setting can be varied each time it's used, by replacing the number "25" with the {?}:

/wcs{?}~

When this macro executes on a worksheet it pauses with a prompt displayed in the control panel, and CMD POINT in the Mode indicator.

```
B3:                                                      CMD POINT
Enter column width (1..72): 9

        A        B        C        D       E       F       G       H
 1  /wcs{?}~
 2
 3
 4
 5
 6
 7
 8
 9
10
11
12
13
14
15
16
17
18
19
20
```

**Screen 2-10. Pause macro (Macro 2-10).**

This allows you to set the column width yourself. To complete the operation, type in the number of spaces for the column width setting and press **ENTER**. This is an important feature—you can now take advantage of the power of macros for operations where only *some* of the commands will be the same each time you use them. Let's take a look at some examples of macros using a wider range of the bracketed commands.

## *Example #1: @ROUND Macro*

Here's a macro you can now use to fix a common 1-2-3 problem. 1-2-3's Range Format commands alter the display of numbers but not their true value. When you use **Range Format** to set the number of decimal places to something less than the unformatted display, the appearance of the formatted numbers occasionally disagrees with a total calculated from them. Here's an example:

| Display Unformatted: | Same Figures Formatted With Range Format Fixed with 1 Decimal Place |
|---|---|
| 0.25 | 0.3 |
| 0.49 | 0.5 |
| ---------- | --------- |
| 0.74 Total | 0.7 Total (appears incorrect) |

The total on the right isn't wrong; the Range Formatting just makes it appear that way. The total still reflects the unchanged underlying values shown in the left column. While that explanation may be OK for other 1-2-3 users, you don't want to print and distribute a worksheet with this problem. The solution is to apply 1-2-3's @ROUND function to the numbers being added.

| The same entries with the Rounding Formulas applied: | The Rounded entries now display correctly: |
|---|---|
| @ROUND(0.25,1) | 0.3 |
| @ROUND(0.49,1) | 0.5 |
| ----------------- | --------- |
| 0.8  Total | 0.8  Total (now appears correct) |

The problem with this method is the tedium and redundancy involved. You have to apply this long formula to every entry being added. Writing this function adds ten keystrokes to any numeric entry, editing an existing entry requires thirteen keystrokes per entry.

Here's a macro to round an entry with only two keystrokes (and no errors!).

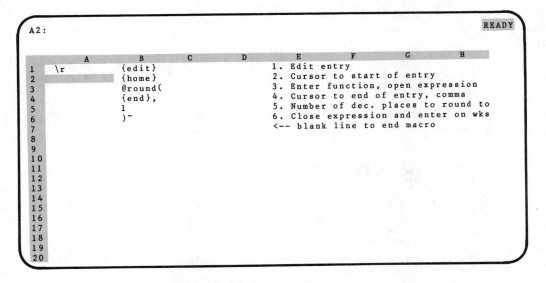

**Screen 2.11. @Round macro (Macro 2-11).**

This macro would normally be written on fewer lines, but we've spread it out to make its explanation easier. To use this macro, place your cursor on the entry to be rounded, then press **ALT R.** Here's how it works:

{edit}                                            1.   Edit entry

With the cursor on the entry to be rounded, the first command, {edit}, places 1-2-3 in EDIT mode to prepare to rewrite the entry.

{home}                                          2.   Cursor to start of entry

In EDIT mode the cursor control keys are redefined so that the {home} command moves the cursor to the far left, the beginning of the entry, where we need to add the @round.

**@round(**                                    3.   Enter function, open expression

The first part of the expression, the function name **@round** and the open parenthesis character, are typed in front of the entry.

**{end},**                                    4.   Cursor to end of entry, comma

The **{end}** command is also redefined in EDIT mode, moving the cursor to the far right of the entry being edited. Note the comma following the **{end}** command. A comma is used in an @round expression to separate the two "arguments" used: the number being rounded and the number of decimal places.

**1**                                         5.   Number of decimal places to round to

The number "1" provides the number of decimals to round the entry to (a setting which can be varied).

**)~**                                        6.   Close expression and enter on worksheet

The parenthesis ends the @round expression, followed by the tilde to enter the revised entry on the worksheet. The last line is blank to end the macro.

## Example #2: @ERR Macro

Another, more frequent problem, is the presence of unwanted ERR displays on the worksheet. The ERR display was created to warn you when a formula cannot be calculated, either because:

1.   it asks a mathematical impossibility, such as dividing a number by zero, or
2.   the deletion of a row or column removes a cell needed to calculate a formula.

Unfortunately, this safety feature sometimes creates unforeseen trouble on the worksheet. If you create some of your formulas in advance of supplying values to the cells they reference, 1-2-3 will generate ERR displays. If these formulas link into other formulas, the ERR display will spread across the worksheet to every other related cell.

Unwanted in your onscreen displays, this is absolutely unacceptable in a printed report. There is a method for dealing with them, but like @round, it is cumbersome to invoke. Here's an example.

The formula +B5/A4 generates the value ERR when A4 hasn't been given a value. In effect, the formula is then trying to divide the value in cell B5 by zero, a mathematical impossibility. Novice 1-2-3 users often solve this problem by entering a zero over the offending formula. That solution creates another problem. Your original formula is now gone and will have to be re-entered later when the data is available. The formula below solves both problems. It converts the offending ERR display to zero, but will automatically change when the value in cell A4 is entered:

`@IF(@ISERR(B5/A4),0,B5/A4)`

Translated into English, this would read:

"If (B5/A4) IS ERR, then display the value zero in the cell.
If (B5/A4) does not equal ERR, but has a meaningful value,
then display the value generated by the formula (B5/A4)."

Effective, but a bit complex to write. Revising the formula as shown above usually requires (1) looking in the manual to figure out how to use @ISERR and (2) editing the formula into a much longer version. What we need is a quick, reliable method for writing this any time we need it. This is shown in Screen 2-12.

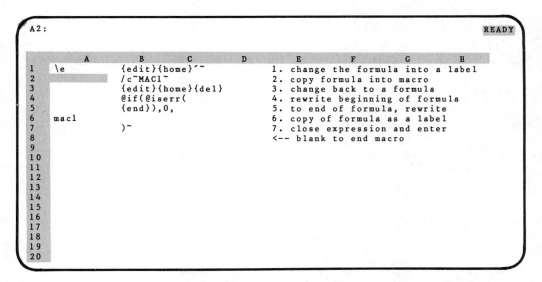

**Screen 2-12. @ISERR macro (Macro 2-12).**

Note: the cursor must be placed on the formula cell before using the macro.

This macro uses some old tricks in new ways, and adds a twist or two of its own. We've numbered the comment lines as a reference for the explanations below. We are editing the formula B5/A4. Our final formula,

@IF(@ISERR(B5/A4),0,B4/A5) contains the original formula in two places so it must be copied twice. The original formula must be turned into a label both to keep the addresses absolute, and to let the macro read it.

   \e       {edit}{home}'~       1.   Change the formula into a label

With the cursor on the formula to be modified, line one puts 1-2-3 in EDIT mode, moves the cursor to the beginning of the formula entry with the HOME key, inserts a left label alignment character, and re-enters the formula on the worksheet as a label. This is necessary because we are going to copy the formula into a line in the macro itself, and the macro requires that it be a label.

          /c~MAC1~        2.   Copy formula into macro

This line copies the formula (now a label) into the cell named MAC1 in the macro (located on line 6). That formula will later be used in the macro.

       {edit}{home}{del}       3.   Change back to a formula

Line 3 puts 1-2-3 back into EDIT mode, moves to the front of the entry and deletes the label alignment character we inserted in Line 1. Notice that no tilde follows: we stay in EDIT mode for the next line as well.

         @if(@iserr(        4.   Rewrite beginning of formula

As line 4 is executed, 1-2-3 is in EDIT mode, with the cursor at the very beginning of the formula entry. The macro writes the first part of the formula there and opens the expression to enclose the formula. Note that when you write this line of the macro, you must start with a label alignment character to force it to be a label. Supposing we are editing the formula B5/A4, the rewritten formula now looks like this:

   @IF(@ISERR(B5/A4

   {end}),0,            5.   Move to end of formula, rewrite

Line 5 starts with the {end} instruction, moving the cursor past the last character in the original formula. It enters a parenthesis to close the first expression, then enters the comma and zero for the "if true" condition, then a comma to separate it from the "IF FALSE" condition. At this point the rewritten formula looks like this:

```
@IF(@ISERR(B5/A4),0,
```

mac1                           6.   Copy of formula as a label

Line 6 is the cell that will have the original formula copied into it, as a label, by line 2 of the macro. After lines 3, 4, and 5 modify the formula, line 6 writes the original formula back into the expression. It will be the value used when the @ISERR function proves false. At this point the rewritten formula looks like this:

```
@IF(@ISERR(B5/A4),0,B5/A4
```

)~                             7.   close expression and enter

Line 7 closes the @IF expression and enters the new formula on the worksheet. The final formula entered into the original cell reads

```
@IF(@ISERR(B5/A4),0,B5/A4)
```

Of course, the last line is left blank to terminate macro control.

This macro would take any formula and substitute it in both places in an @IF function. Use these tricks—copying relative formulas as labels and editing formulas—in your own macros!

## 2.6  Macro Utility Library

There are a number of "utility" macros useful in many worksheet situations. Each is relatively simple, but a real workhorse. A macro utility library is a tool to allow you to transfer useful macros between worksheets without rewriting them. The macros are stored in their own file, and then combined into other worksheets when needed via the **File Combine Copy** command. In this section we'll show you some of the macros we use this way, and describe the procedure you can use to set up your own macro utility library.

To facilitate the testing of macros, 1-2-3 was used to write this book. Using 1-2-3 to write the reports that accompany your worksheets is also the easiest way to integrate data the worksheets contain with those reports. Let's look at some macros that can smooth the task of word processing with 1-2-3. After using them we think you'll agree that with the proper macros, 1-2-3 makes a much more effective word processor than anyone suspects. Here they are (explanations follow):

## The Macros

| | | |
|---|---|---|
| FileSave | \f | /fs{?}~ |
| Xtract | \x | /fxf{?}~{?}~{?}~ |
| Print | \p | /ppcar.{right}{right}{right}{right}{right}<br>{right}{right}{?}~omt0~mb10~s\027\069~qagpq |
| Justify | \j | /rj{right}{right}{right}{right}{right}{right}{right}<br>{down}{?}~ |
| Indent | \i | {?}~ |
| Move | \m | /m.{right}{right}{right}{right}{right}{right}{right} |
| Double | \d | ===================================================~ |
| Single | \s | '-------------------------------------------------~ |
| Type | \t | Using Macros |
| Hide | \h | \              {?}~ |

## The Macros Explained

**File Save (\f)** The macro saves a file for the first time. If the operation replaces an existing file, the macro will terminate with the "Cancel—Replace" menu displayed in the control panel. This allows the user to decide whether or not to overwrite the current file.

**Xtract (\x)** This macro extracts portions of a file to create another file, or replaces the current file with the data included in the Xtract range. The third pause command, **{?}~**, is to allow you to select "Replace" when replacing the current file. When creating a new file, this command will cause the macro to pause after it's finished, requiring you to press ENTER one last time. Without this last pause, the macro may overwrite existing files against your wishes.

**Print (\p)** The first part of the macro clears the prior settings. Use this macro with the cursor in the far left column of a normal eight-column screen. The macro expands the print range across the eight-column page, then pauses for you to extend it downward as many rows as you wish to print.

Following that are our preferred margin settings and a custom setup string for an Epson FX printer. The **\027\069** puts it into emphasized mode (darker printing). Your printer manual will have a listing of the codes it uses.

It will have codes that alter the darkness of the printing, increase the spacing between lines, and change other print characteristics.

**Justify (\j)**      After writing some text, the use of the justify macro arranges the text within the specified area. This macro expands the justify range across the page, down one row, and pauses for you to extend it downward to cover the rest of the paragraph. Why the solitary {down} command in the macro?

If the Justify range indicates only one row, it will justify all the text below the highlighted line. This is useful for the last paragraph of a document. But if there is text below the paragraph, the rows may become misaligned.

If more than one row is highlighted, only the indicated area will be justified. The macro highlights two rows to prevent the accidental misalignment of all the text below. The user can move the cursor up or down to get the desired result.

**Indent (\i)**      This macro will indent sections of text as far as needed, because it can be repeated. Although it can't be seen, the indentation is accomplished by the five blank spaces preceding the {?}~. Should you need more indentation than five spaces, press **ALT I** repeatedly and it will indent repeatedly. This macro also works effectively in EDIT mode to insert spaces in front of a worksheet entry you want indented.

**Move (\m)**      This macro is used to move sections of text. The use of the seven {right}s means this macro is to be used from the far left column of a standard eight column wide 1-2-3 screen. The macro must extend across the entire screen if it is to move text written in the other seven columns. Since writing text in these other columns is a useful way of indenting text (such as this paragraph), the Move range MUST extend across the entire screen.

The macro has no tilde at the end, which ends macro control with the "Enter range to move FROM:" prompt in the control panel. You can then indicate the range to be moved, and where it's to be moved to.

**Double (\d)**      Both the double- and single-line macros provide a quick way to write dividing lines across a single screen, such as you would use in word processing. In this situation, they are

**Single (\s)**      more useful than the more commonly used method of copying a repeating label (\-) across the screen's seven cells, for two reasons:

1. the label is all in one cell and can be moved by moving just that cell.
2. If text is placed in one of the cells the line overwrites, a very clean continuous "line and text" effect is created, as shown in the "Sample text" line here.

-------------------- Sample text --------------------

**Type (\t)**    This macro offers a novel and useful technique. It will insert a phrase whenever it is needed. You can execute this macro in the middle of typing a sentence and it will type the words "Using Macros" instantly, then return control to you.  Since there is *no* tilde following it, the macro doesn't enter the line on the worksheet, only in the control panel Edit line. This leaves 1-2-3 in "LABEL" mode so you can continue typing.

All dedicated word processors offer this capability—you can use it too. Merely insert your word or phrase in place of "Using Macros."

**Hide (\h)**    People frequently ask how to hide labels on the worksheet. Here's a macro to do it. Assuming your column width is set to the default nine spaces, this macro types the repeating label character, inserts nine spaces, and pauses for you to type your entry. The entry will not appear on the worksheet, but will show in the control panel to be read when the cursor is placed on the cell. This is an effective method for placing "invisible" documenting remarks on a worksheet.

## Creating The Library File

The most efficient means of handling frequently used macros is to place them in a "macro library" file. A macro library is a worksheet file containing a group of macros you use frequently. Whenever you need these macros in a worksheet, use 1-2-3's File Combine function to bring the macros directly into the current worksheet from the LIBRARY file.

We'll assume the word processing macros shown earlier are in a worksheet file called LIBRARY. Here's the procedure to use:

1. Retrieve the worksheet file with which you are going to use the macros.
2. Make sure the data disk with the LIBRARY file on it is in the drive.
3. Move the cursor to the location on the worksheet you want to store these macros. It must be a space large enough to hold them without overwriting any other data.
4. Execute the commands as follows:

| You press: | Which means: |
|---|---|
| / | Displays command menu |
| f | File |
| c | Combine |
| c | Copy |
| e | Entire File |
| **LIBRARY** | Name of file to combine |
| **ENTER** | Press ENTER key |

5.  Move your cursor to the label \f to the left of the first macro, and execute the commands as follows:

| You press: | Which means: |
|---|---|
| / | Displays command menu |
| r | Range |
| n | Name |
| l | Labels |
| r | Right |
| **(expand pointer down the column)** | Indicate range of labels to be used as names for macros |
| **ENTER** | Press the enter key to complete operation |

Why is this last step necessary if the macros are already named in the LIBRARY file? File Combine only brings in the data, *not* the Range Names. Presumably Lotus made this restriction to eliminate the potential for conflicts between Range Names in the current file and the file being combined. At any rate, lining the macros up with their names to the left makes it a snap to reassign the names.

Make up your own LIBRARY file of macros you use frequently. If you find LIBRARY is too long a name to type, substitute the name UTIL (for utility). Another variation of this method is to use a short name for the file, such as LIB. Then you can add a suffix to the name to denote what KIND of library file it is— for writing, spreadsheet work, or whatever.

| File name: | Contains macros for: |
|---|---|
| LIB_S | Spreadsheet work |
| LIB_W | Word processing |
| LIB_G | Graphics |
| LIB_D | Data base management |

Note: the underscore joining the two words that make up the file name in the example is a useful way of breaking apart two strings of characters in 1-2-3 file names. Instead of using the name FEBSALE for a file containing February sales data, use the name FEB_SALE. The underscore is the only nonalphabetic or nonnumeric character allowed in a file name. Keep in mind you must still keep your file names to eight characters or less, including the underscore.

A more efficient approach to macro libraries is to use one large library file for all your most frequently used macros. Within that file, give Range Names to the groups of macros you use for particular 1-2-3 operations. Call the range containing all your spreadsheet macros (such as the @ROUND and @ISERR macros) "S", call the range containing the writing macros "W", call the range with your data base macros "D". Now you can use this command sequence to File Combine just the group of macros you want into your worksheet:

| You press: | Which means: |
|---|---|
| / | Displays command menu |
| f | File |
| c | Combine |
| c | Copy |
| n | Named Range |
| W | Name of range to combine |
| **ENTER** | Press the ENTER key |
| **LIBRARY** | Name of file to combine |
| **ENTER** | Press the ENTER key |

The advantage to using the single file approach is the efficiency it offers. This one LIBRARY file can contain all the macros you want to store. You only have to place that one file on any diskette to have immediate access to any of your utility macros. The Range Names allow you to select just those macros you want to bring into your worksheet.

# 2.7   Protecting Your Work

As your applications become more sophisticated and your data more valuable, it becomes more important to protect them properly. Here we'll review three related issues:

- protecting your data from accidental loss
- security
- archival documentation

### Protecting Your Data From Accidental Loss

In order to protect your work from accidental destruction, you must have more than one copy of each file. Many people feel confident that once they've put their worksheet file on disk they have protected it. There are three reasons this is not true:

1. The obvious: if anything happens to that diskette, you will have lost your work.

2. The not so obvious: suppose you've just updated a file and have executed the File-Save-Replace command to resave the file. Should anything happen during that process, such as a power failure or the computer is turned off for any reason (or fails), chances are your file will be completely destroyed. The reason for this is that when the power is off you've lost what's in RAM. The only file you had was in the process of being rewritten when the failure occurred. 1-2-3 can't retrieve a file in this state (the error message on this one says "Part of file missing").

3. The obscure: suppose you've Retrieved a file from the disk and done some work, adding to the file's size in the process. When finished, you execute File-Save-Replace to update the file. The drive light goes on as 1-2-3 writes the changes back to the disk, but then you get an error message: Disk Full. You don't have another disk handy, what do you do? You find one or lose ALL your work! Although you wouldn't suspect it, your original disk file has been destroyed because 1-2-3 began to overwrite what was stored there. When it ran out of space on the disk, the operation was terminated, leaving you with an incomplete file, unreadable and worthless.

Any of these situations could cause you to lose valuable information and a great deal of unique and creative work if you don't have a backup file. Heed this warning. Worksheets can be hard work to generate, but as data in a computer, they can easily be lost. Use common sense and back up your work on another disk.

## Things You Should Know About Security

If you're keeping sensitive information in your worksheets, such as payroll data or company earnings, you must deal with the issue of security. Here are some points to consider:

1. The final security for your data in a floppy disk system is to save your file, exit to DOS, take the floppy with you, and lock it up.

2. There are various password protection schemes available on the market. We haven't evaluated all of them, but we'll tell you that macros are NOT a solution to this problem. A macro only works from inside a file, and can be disabled by pressing **Control-Break**. If a macro is used for password protection from within the file, all you have to do to gain access to the file's contents is to press **Control-Break**. That's no protection.

3. It isn't possible to protect your macro code from a knowledgeable user.

A.   Finding macros on a worksheet is as easy as pressing **GOTO, NAME,** then pressing the **END** key to move to the end of the range names listed. That's where the macro names (all preceded by a backslash) will be listed. Highlight a name, press **ENTER**, and you'll see the macro.

B.   It's possible to obscure a macro from view by hiding it beneath other entries. However it will show in the control panel when the cursor is placed on it using the above method.

A way to prevent this is to place 79 spaces in front and in back of the macro code. When the cursor is moved to the cell the control panel will remain blank, and if **EDIT** is pressed, the code will still be off the screen. This method requires {esc} to be placed in front of each line of code to keep the spaces from becoming part of the macro code.

C.   To make macros very hard to understand, break them into many parts, have cells reference one another in a confusing sequence. Hide portions of the code as explained above, and have the macro create and delete parts of itself as it progresses. A macro written this way is very difficult to interpret. But, the bottom line is this: there is no true protection for your macros once someone has access to the file containing them.

## Documentation For Your Worksheets

As your use of macros expands, the complexity of your worksheets will increase. Whether you are developing worksheets for yourself or others, good documentation is another form of protection for your work. After you have left a project for a time, you will forget the reasons for the unique methods you used, and may have difficulty explaining it to others, or modifying it yourself.

Documentation explains the work so that both you and other people will (1) understand how to use it, (2) be capable of revising it for new uses, and (3) have a paper record of your work.

Here we'll discuss the archival type of documentation you need, so that both worksheets and macros are placed in paper form. We'll cover documentation to explain macros later. Lotus provides one method of documenting that is adequate for interactive 1-2-3 applications, printing the worksheet with the commands: "/ **Print Printer Options Other Cell-Formulas Unformatted**". This produces a report of the contents of each cell, showing formulas instead of values. The report is in the form of a list, one cell address beneath another (not in grid-like worksheet format). Although cumbersome to interpret, this is acceptable for simple applications.

When you begin using macros more extensively you'll need more than that. All the Range Names used in the macros, as well as settings for graphs, queries, and tables used, need documentation. One solution is a program such as DocuCalc (by Micro Decision Systems, Pittsburgh, PA). These are some of the 1-2-3 settings they document:

- Global format, column-width and label prefix settings
- Individual cell formats (Range Format)
- Bottom right cell position (worksheet size)
- Recalculation settings
- Iteration settings
- Protection status
- Print set-up, margins, and range
- Named ranges and their locations
- Ranges used for all Data commands (Sort, Query, etc.)
- Named graphs and the default (current) graph
- Warnings on any "@ERR" values present in the worksheet

This provides the essential information you should maintain on any important worksheet, but especially one with macros. These programs can document an entire worksheet or just part of one, and can print worksheet entries and formulas in grid-like worksheet format (much easier to comprehend than a line by line listing). Extra long formulas can be printed at the end.

DocuCalc is only one of several programs of its type. We used DocuCalc because of its breadth of features; the program is easy to use and comes with a good manual. Reviews indicate that not all spreadsheet documentation programs are as fully featured as this one, so be sure to evaluate the one you select.

## 2.8 File Combine Macros

As we move into more complex macros, the importance of properly documenting your work, as presented in the previous section, will quickly become apparent.

The **File Combine** commands bring all or part of one file INTO another. This presents possibilities many people haven't fully explored with 1-2-3. It's possible to design a series of worksheets that electronically connect reports from different departments in much the same way those reports are now linked manually.

In many businesses, Finance does pricing for the coming year, and Marketing uses that data to put together sales and income projections. Those same sales projections go into a production planning model, and are translated into purchased and manufactured parts requirements. The purchased parts requirements can then be combined into a purchasing planning model with vendor lead times. 1-2-3 makes the planning for each individual group much easier. With **File Combining**, it is easy to transfer data developed in one department so it can be used by another without rekeying.

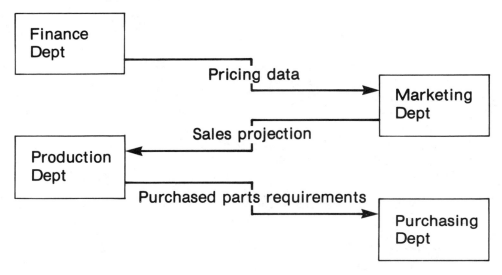

**Diagram 2-6. Exchanging data.**

That, then, is the potential for **File Combine**. There are problems, however, because of its complexity and destructive potential. The complexity results from the range of choices Lotus provided with this operation. You must select the file to combine data from, choose to combine the entire file or just a named range (and specify the range), choose to add, subtract, or copy data into the current file, and determine the position of the incoming data.

The potential for destruction exists because the position of the incoming data is determined by the position of the cursor when the command sequence is executed. If the cursor is in the wrong position, the data "lands" in the wrong position, and may overwrite the rest of the worksheet.

A macro is an excellent way to eliminate these problems. It'll simplify the operation from numerous keystrokes down to two. More importantly, it will standardize the operation by controlling the position of the incoming data, preventing accidental overwriting of data. Let's look at a worksheet we'll use to perform a file consolidation.

```
F4: (,0) @SUM(B4..E4)                                              READY

          A              B        C        D        E        F
 1  SALES ANALYSIS FOR:          APRIL
 2                              - WEEKS -
 3  SALESPERSON            -1-      -2-      -3-      -4-     TOTAL
 4  Barton                618      907      387      870     2,781
 5  Corey                 110      386      608      937     2,041
 6  Garner                752      425      772      746     2,695
 7  Karsten               193      537       87      576     1,392
 8  Martin                207      394      845      672     2,118
 9  Swezey                198      269      397       84       948
10  Taggart               167      379      874       79     1,499
11                      --------------------------------------------
12  TOTAL               2,245    3,297    3,969    3,964    13,475
13
14
15
16
17
18
19
20
```

**Screen 2-13. Sales analysis.**

In the worksheet above, each week's sales are listed by salesperson to form an entire month of sales information. The far right column summarizes the month's sales for each salesperson, and will be used to represent this month's sales in the quarterly report.

1-2-3's **File Combine** function can be used to consolidate this column out of each monthly worksheet file into a quarterly worksheet. The files containing the monthly data are named for the month's data that they contain, such as, April, May, and June. This **File Combine** operation consolidates only part of the monthly files, so a named range must be used to identify the part of each file to be combined. In each file, that range has been named TRANSFER, and in the worksheet shown above, that is the range F4..F10. The worksheet shown on page 46 represents the quarterly sales analysis, as yet unposted.

```
E4: (,0) @SUM(B4..D4)                                              READY

              A              B       C       D       E       F
 1   SALES ANALYSIS FOR:        SECOND QUARTER
 2                              - MONTHS -
 3   SALESPERSON          -1-     -2-     -3-   TOTAL
 4   Barton                                        0
 5   Corey                                         0
 6   Garner                                        0
 7   Karsten                                       0
 8   Martin                                        0
 9   Swezey                                        0
10   Taggart                                       0
11                      ------------------------------------
12   TOTAL                0       0       0       0
13
14
15
16
17
18
19
20
```

**Screen 2-14. Quarterly sales analysis.**

The macro that will combine each of the three month's data into the quarterly sales analysis will be a part of the quarterly sales analysis worksheet, since it is combining data *into* that worksheet.

### Macro 2-13. File combine—A.

| Name | Macro | Comments |
|------|-------|----------|
| \c | {goto}B4~ | Move cursor to first range |
| | /fcanTRANSFER~ | Combine range "transfer" from APRIL sales |
| | APRIL~{?}~ | and pause |
| | {goto}C4~ | Cursor to second range |
| | /fcanTRANSFER~ | Combine range "transfer" |
| | MAY~{?}~ | from MAY sales and pause |
| | {goto}D4~ | Cursor to third range |
| | /fcanTRANSFER~ | Combine range "transfer" |
| | JUNE~ | from JUNE sales |
| | {goto}A1~ | Move to top of data |
| | | End macro |

Let's translate that into English.

### Table 2-1. Macro translation.

| Macro from above: | Means this: |
|-------------------|-------------|
| {goto} | Press the **GOTO** function key |
| B4 | Position cursor at top of first month column |
| ~ | Press ENTER to execute **GOTO** |

## Table 2-1. Macro translation (continued).

| *Macro from above:* | *Means this:* |
|---|---|
| / | Slash displays command menu |
| f | **File** |
| c | **Combine** |
| a | **Add** data from another file |
| n | **Named range** |
| TRANSFER | Name of range to combine |
| ~ | Press enter to confirm range |
| APRIL | File containing the "TRANSFER" range |
| ~ | Press enter to execute combine operation |
| {?} | Pause for operator to change disks, if needed |
| ~ | Press enter when ready to continue |
|  | (From here, the macro repeats itself to |
|  | combine each of the different monthly files.) |

## Enhancing The Macro...

The File Combine macro uses three different files with no guarantee that they will all be on the same disk. In addition to the pause already included in the macro to permit an operator to switch disks, it would be helpful to include a prompt stating which file is needed at each stage of the macro.

A sample of that prompt is shown below as it would be written on a worksheet.

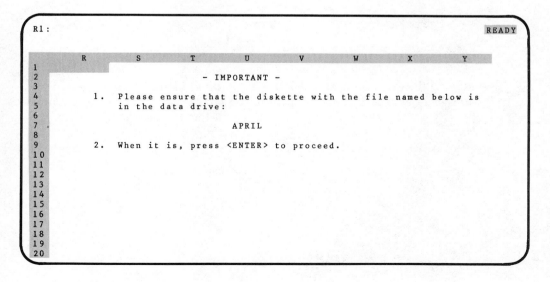

The macro can take care of putting the right month in the message and displaying it when needed. Here's how to do it:

1. Place the above message somewhere on the worksheet.
2. Name the top left hand cell of the area MESSAGE (cell R1 in this example).
3. Name the cell where the label APRIL appears MONTH (cell U7 in this example).
4. Edit the macro so it reads as shown in Macro 2-14.

## Macro 2-14. File combine—B.

| Name | Macro | Comments |
|---|---|---|
| \c | /cONE~MONTH~ | Put month name in prompt screen |
| | {goto}MESSAGE~{?}~ | Tell user to put right disk in |
| | {goto}B4~ | Position cursor for combine |
| | /fcanTRANSFER~ | Combine range "transfer" |
| one | APRIL |    from this sales file |
| | ~/cTWO~MONTH~ | Put month name in prompt screen |
| | {goto}MESSAGE~{?}~ | Tell user to put right disk in |
| | {goto}C4~ | Position cursor for combine |
| | /fcanTRANSFER~ | Combine range "transfer" |
| two | MAY |    from this sales file |
| | ~/cTHREE~MONTH~ | Put month name in prompt screen |
| | {goto}MESSAGE~{?}~ | Tell user to put right disk in |
| | {goto}D4~ | Position cursor for combine |
| | /fcanTRANSFER~ | Combine range "transfer" |
| three | JUNE |    from this sales file |
| | ~ | |
| | {goto}A1 | Move to top of data |
| | | End macro |

5. Place the cursor on the cell containing the entry \c in the Names column; execute the command sequence / **Range Name Labels Right**; extend the pointer down the column to include the labels one, two, and three and press **ENTER**. This step uses the labels in the Name column as Range Names for the cells to their right. For example, the cell containing the entry APRIL has been Range Named ONE.

```
F1:                                                                   READY

              A             B         C         D        E         F
 1  SALES ANALYSIS FOR:             SECOND QUARTER
 2                                    - MONTHS -
 3  SALESPERSON                -1-       -2-       -3-      TOTAL
 4  Barton                    2,781     1,844     2,368    6,993
 5  Corey                     2,041     2,374     1,983    6,398
 6  Garner                    2,695     1,935     1,749    6,379
 7  Karsten                   1,392     1,147     2,321    4,860
 8  Martin                    2,118     2,854     1,736    6,708
 9  Swezey                      948     2,103     1,875    4,926
10  Taggart                   1,499     1,723     2,017    5,239
11                           ------------------------------------
12  TOTAL                    13,475    13,980    14,049   41,504
13
14
15
16
17
18
19
20
```

**Screen 2-16. Consolidated sales analysis.**

## Comments

The macro repeats the same cycle once for each of the three files, so we'll just run through it now with the first file, APRIL:

Line 1:

**\c**        **/cONE~MONTH~**        Put month name in prompt screen

Line one of the macro copies the contents of the range ONE to the range MONTH. The range named ONE is several lines down in the macro, and contains the label APRIL. It will be copied into a range called MONTH, which is a blank cell in the middle of the message screen. This label completes the message, telling the user which file to place in the data drive.

**{goto}MESSAGE~{?}~**    Tell user to put right disk in

Line two moves the cursor to the range named MESSAGE, which displays the prompt to the operator, and then pauses. The pause allows the operator to change disks, if necessary.

**{goto}B4~**        Position cursor for combine

Line three repositions the cursor prior to beginning the File Combine operation. This cell is the beginning of the row where the totals from the monthly file will be entered on the worksheet.

**/fcanTRANSFER~**        Combine range "transfer"

Line four executes the commands **File Combine Add Named-Range**. The named range it will copy data from is called TRANSFER.

    one          APRIL                from this sales file

Line five is the named range ONE (indicated by the label **one** in the NAME column of the macro). This line serves two purposes. In the very first line of the macro, line five was copied into the MESSAGE screen. As the macro reads it now, the line provides the name of the file to combine data from. The name of the month has been isolated on this line to allow you to easily modify it. You can keep this macro in a library file and use it again with next quarter's files by changing the lines with APRIL, MAY, and JUNE to JULY, AUGUST, and SEPT.

A more complicated approach to prompting the user involves using 1-2-3's **Worksheet Window Horizontal** commands to display a window containing a message. This offers a little classier look, as the screen never leaves the original worksheet. The design of this macro is a bit trickier, however, and we'll leave it for Chapter 3.

In the next section, you'll learn to use a new set of commands available only in macros, commands which offer a vast increase in the potential power of your macros to serve your needs.

# 2.9  The Macro X Commands

Up to this point we've looked at the simplest function of macros: automating commands you could have keyed in manually. This chapter introduces a vast increase in the power of your macros, including the abilities to:

- display easy-to-understand menus, allowing operators to choose which macro they want to execute.
- display custom prompts that not only ask the operator for specific information, but will enter that information in the proper cell on the worksheet automatically.
- make macros "smart" by having them evaluate worksheet conditions and then execute one of several commands.
- string together numerous small macros to allow you to develop longer, more useful macros.

All of the above features are implemented through the macro X commands and are covered in the following "Dictionary of the X Commands". Following that, this chapter will introduce you to "Macro Autoexecute Features" that allow 1-2-3 to automatically load worksheets and/or automatically execute macros without any operator intervention.

# *The X Commands: A Quick Dictionary*

Whether you are looking for a few simple enhancements or wish to completely customize 1-2-3 using all your own menus and prompts, the **/x** commands are the key. The name "X commands" derives from the way they are written. All the the X commands start with **/x**. Since these commands do not appear in any 1-2-3 command menu and can only be used in a macro, you might think of them as "Xtra" commands. As you will see in the examples in this section, the X commands can be appended to any of the macro operations you've already learned.

Here's an overview of the X commands:

| Command | Mnemonic | Function |
|---------|----------|----------|
| **/xm** | **(Menu)** | Displays a custom menu allowing the user to choose from several different macros. |
| **/xi** | **(If)** | "If-then" statement to test worksheet conditions and execute certain operations as a result. |
| **/xl** | **(Label)** | Displays a custom prompt, accepts a character string (label) in response, and places the label in a specified location on the worksheet. |
| **/xn** | **(Number)** | Displays a custom prompt, only accepts a number in response (rejects labels), and places the number in a specified location on the worksheet. |
| **/xg** | **(Goto)** | After reading this command, the macro will begin reading keystrokes in a specified cell on the worksheet, rather than at the next cell below. |
| **/xc** | **(Call)** | Redirects macro flow of control to read keystrokes in a specified location, called a subroutine, but only until an **/xr** command is read. |
| **/xr** | **(Return)** | Returns flow of control to the macro that used the **/xc**, to the command following the **/xc**, continuing to read keystrokes where it left off. |
| **/xq** | **(Quit)** | Ends macro control the same way a blank cell does, without requiring you to leave a blank cell. |

In the following dictionary of the X commands each entry is arranged in the following order:

1. The Name of the command.
2. A listing of the purpose of the command, the command itself, the format for the command, and an example of that format in use.
3. An explanation of how to write the command, where it can be used effectively, and an example application.

## /XM: Custom Menus

| Purpose | Command | Format | Example |
|---------|---------|--------|---------|
| Menus | /xm | /xm[location]~ | /xmB94~ |

The /xm command is used to display a menu that looks and works like a 1-2-3 menu, except it is one you have written yourself, and the choices it executes are your macros. Instead of having to remember the names of all the macros, an operator need only remember one name now: the name of the macro to display the custom menu. All other macros can be executed directly from menu choices.

Here's how it works. First, select a place to write your menu on the worksheet, preferably right next to your macro.

Now write each menu choice in its own cell. The choices must be written in cells side by side. You may include a maximum of eight choices and no more than 79 characters in the entire menu (those limits are described in more detail later in this section). Here's a simple menu:

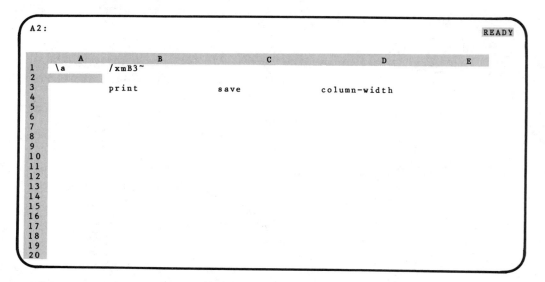

**Screen 2-17. Menu construction—A (Macro 2-15).**

In English, the /xm command shown above says, "Display a custom menu using the range of cells whose top left corner is cell B3." This special range of cells, known as a "menu range", begins with the cell named in the /xm command (cell B3 in this case). The menu range extends from cell B3 across all NON-BLANK, contiguous cells to its right. In the example above, the menu range includes cells B3, C3, and D3. The menu range ends after D3, because E3 is blank.

Observe that:

1. This menu has three choices: "print" is written in cell B3, "save" is written in cell C3, and "column-width" is in D3. Up to five more choices could have been included.
2. Each choice is a label in a separate cell. Each label can include more than one word, as in "column width", as long as it is in one cell.
3. When displayed, the choices will appear in the same order as they appear in the menu range, with "print" being the default (far left) choice.
4. The macro command used to display the custom menu is written like this: /xmB3~. It consists of /xm, a cell address, and a tilde.
5. It is advisable to leave a blank cell between the /xm command (in cell B1) and the menu range (beginning in cell B3). The reason involves a rather technical point for this stage of instruction, so we'll only explain it briefly here. If an operator presses **ESCAPE** while a custom menu displays, the macro will try to continue reading down the column. The blank cell below the /xm command will act to cancel the macro. Without the blank cell, the result will likely be that part of the macro will write itself on the worksheet (wherever the cursor is) possibly overwriting other data. To protect yourself, leave a blank space after the /xm command.

## Menu Explanation Lines

As with normal 1-2-3 menus, macro generated menus have the ability to display an explanatory line when a choice is highlighted. To include an explanation line for a menu choice, write it in the cell directly beneath each choice. In order to show you each of our explanation lines in the example below, we've widened the columns they're written in to prevent any overwriting of one explanation line on another. We emphasize we have only widened the columns for the purpose of instruction. You need not widen the columns in your macros. 1-2-3 will display the explanation lines separately when you execute the menu, even if they overwrite the cells to their right in the macro.

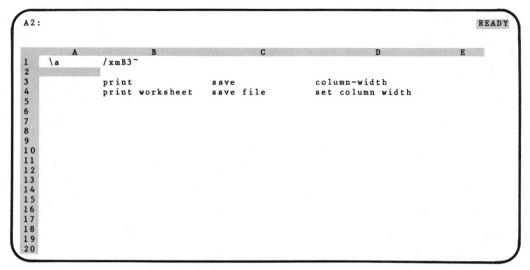

**Screen 2-18. Menu construction—B (Macro 2-16).**

## Cautions and Limits For Writing Custom Menus

If an entry were placed in cell E3, it would also become part of the menu range, because a menu range automatically expands to include all contiguous, non-blank cells to the right of the first menu choice. It's essential you leave a blank cell to the right of your menu range or you will inadvertently add menu choices. For example, if you later enter something in cell E3, such as the number 1098, that number will be displayed as a menu choice the next time the /xm command executes. If you already have eight choices in your menu, an inadvertent extra entry will cause an Error when the menu command executes.

The size limits for a menu range are these:

1.  No more than eight choices total. That means no more than seven cells directly to the right of the first menu choice can have anything entered in them.

2.  There are 79 characters available in the entire top line of the menu. 1-2-3 reserves two characters per menu choice to create spaces between them in the display. The sum of the characters in all choices, plus two extra spaces for each choice, must not exceed 79, or you will get an Error message. Using one word for each menu choice, you will not usually have to be concerned with this limit.

3.  There's no limit on the number of characters 1-2-3 will allow in each explanation line. However, the screen will only display 79 characters, so the practical limit for EACH explanation line is 79 characters. Since each explanation line is written in the cell directly beneath the menu choice it

explains, they will usually overwrite each other in the macro. That will NOT cause any problems. They will still display separately when the menu executes.

4. If all menu choices have different first letters, the menu will work the same as all other 1-2-3 menus. The user can either select by highlighting and pressing **ENTER**, or by pressing the first letter of one choice. If two choices have the same first letter such as "Post" and "Print", and the operator presses "P", 1-2-3 will execute whichever choice is farthest to the left in the menu.

Now you know how to write the menu itself and make it display in the control panel. The next step is to have it execute choices, which are your macros.

When the user of the macro selects a menu option, the macro skips down two cells beneath that choice, and begins reading its instructions there. If an operator selects the "print" choice in the sample macro, the flow of control will skip to cell B5 to continue reading instructions. That's the cell where you will write the first line of the macro to be executed in response to that choice. Likewise, if "save" is chosen, the macro will skip to cell C5; and if "column width" is chosen, it will skip to cell D5.

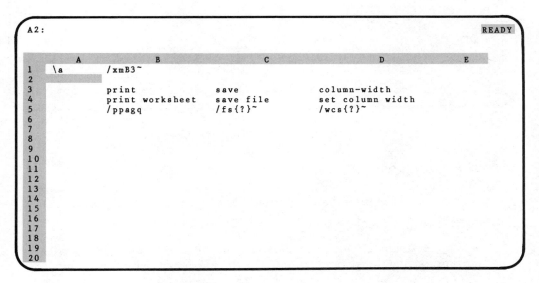

**Screen 2-19. Menu construction—C (Macro 2-17).**

Note: Explanation lines below each macro choice are optional, and do not affect how the rest of the macro should be written. Were no explanation line included in cell B4, the macro for the "print" choice should still be written in cell B5.

## /XQ: Terminate (Quit) The Macro

| For | Command | Format | Example |
|-----|---------|--------|---------|
| Ends macro | /xq | /xq | /xq |

Whenever the macro reads the **/xq** command, it will terminate, regardless of what follows. This command is written just as you see it, no arguments or tilde are needed. The illustration below shows the command added to the end of each macro on row 5. The command forces each macro to terminate, even if entries are inadvertently made on row 6.

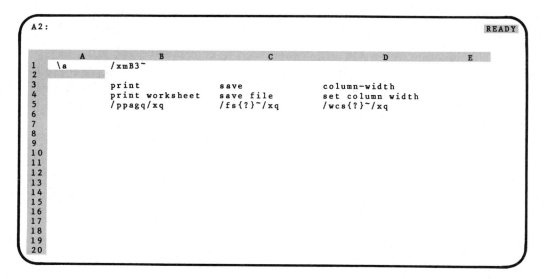

Screen 2-20. Menu construction—D (Macro 2-18).

## /XG: Macro GOTO

| For | Command | Format | Example |
|-----|---------|--------|---------|
| Macro "goto" | /xg | /xg[location]~ | /xgB7~ |

The **/xg** command changes the macro's flow of control from reading cells in the current location to reading them in the [location] named in the command. One common use for this command is to redirect the flow of control beneath custom menus. As you learned in the section on custom menus, the macro instructions for each menu choice must be written two cells beneath that menu choice. Ordinarily, this would force you to write all macros side by side, making it very difficult to read those macros where they overwrite one another.

If you substitute **/xg** commands for the macro instructions in a menu (as shown below), you can redirect the flow of each macro to locations farther down the worksheet where there's more space. This alleviates the need to write all the macros side by side beneath the menu and allows you to write the macros in an organized manner, one beneath the other. Not only will you be able to read the macros more easily, but you'll have enough space to include explanatory comments.

```
A2:                                                                      READY

          A              B                    C                    D              E
1    \a        /xmB3~              display menu below
2
3              print               save                column width
4              print worksheet     save file           set current column width
5              /xgB7~              /xgB14~             /xgB16~
6
7              /ppcrr              Clears and resets print range
8              A21.D34             Range to print (can be revised)
9              ~agp                Print and advance page
10             crr                 Clears and resets print range
11             F17.J173            Range to print (can be revised)
12             ~agpq/xmB3~         Print, advance page, return to menu
13
14             /fs{?}~/xmB3~       Save file, return to menu
15
16             /wcs{?}~/xq         Adjust column width and quit
17
18
19
20
```

**Screen 2-21. Menu construction—E (Macro 2-19).**

## Don't Confuse /xg with {goto}

There's a big difference between the **/xg** command and the **{goto}** command. **{goto}** moves the cursor to a specified cell. **{goto}A37~** moves the cursor to cell A37. **/xg** does NOT affect the cursor, it directs the macro to continue reading keystrokes at the cell address it specifies. **/xgA37~** redirects the macro from reading keystrokes in the current cell, to read keystrokes found in cell A37. Refer back to the discussion of "flow of control" if you have trouble with this concept.

## /XC: Call A Subroutine

| For | Command | Format | Example |
|-----|---------|--------|---------|
| Call subroutine | /xc | /xc[location]~ | /xcB98~ |

An explanation of the term "subroutine" is in order. A subroutine is a macro that acts as an interchangeable part of several other macros. For example, suppose you wanted to show a screen with a message on it every time you displayed a custom menu. The commands for displaying that message could be written into every macro preceding an **/xm** (menu) command, but that would be repetitious. It would be more efficient to write the commands to display the message once, and just "call" those commands before displaying any custom menu. That's known as "calling a subroutine". The **/xr** command is a companion to **/xc**.

## /XR: Return From A Subroutine

| For | Command | Format | Example |
|-----|---------|--------|---------|
| Return from subroutine | /xr | /xr | /xr |

When **/xr** is read in a macro, control is returned to the main routine beginning with the instruction following the **/xc** command. You should understand that 1-2-3 will remember which main routine called the subroutine, and return there.

The command takes no arguments, and no tilde (˜). In this sense it is similar to **/xq**.

```
A2:                                                                   READY

            A              B                   C                D              E
 1   \a           /xcB8~              call message subroutine
 2                /xmB4~              display menu below
 3                                    -----------------------------
 4                print               save              column width
 5                print worksheet     save file         set current column width
 6                /xgB12~             /xgB19~           /xgB21~
 7
 8                {goto}Q31~          Top left corner of message screen
 9                {goto}R41~          Place cursor on message for hilite
10                /xr                 Return to main routine
11
12                /ppcrr              Clears and resets print range
13                A25.D34             Range to print (can be revised)
14                ~agp                Print and advance page
15                crr                 Clears and resets print range
16                F17.J173            Range to print (can be revised)
17                ~agpq/xmB3~         Print, advance page, return to menu
18                                    -----------------------------
19                /fs{?}~/xmB3~       Save file, return to menu
20                                    -----------------------------
```

**Screen 2-22. Menu construction—F (Macro 2-20).**

In the example macro shown above, the first line of the macro (in cell B1) calls the subroutine beginning in cell B8, by reading the command **/xcB8˜**. The macro drops directly to cell B8 and begins reading keystrokes there as a macro subroutine.

The first line of the subroutine moves the cursor to cell Q31, the top left corner of the screen shown below. In this case, moving the cursor to Q31 is the means of displaying the message shown on the screen. The second line of the subroutine moves the cursor to cell R41, creating an inverse video highlight for the message displayed there. Since the width of column "R" has been expanded, the cursor will expand as well, highlighting the entire message. The last line of the subroutine contains the command /xr. /xr causes the macro to return to the very next command following /xcB8~, picking up where it left off before the subroutine.

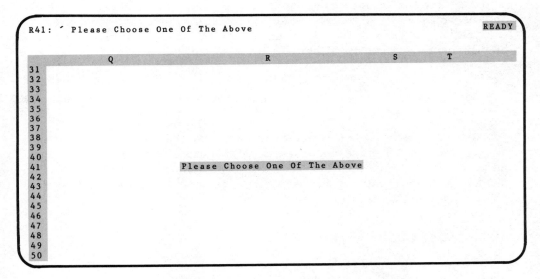

**Screen 2-23. Menu construction—G.**

The sample subroutine can be called by any macro just by including the command /xcB8~. Since 1-2-3 keeps track of which macro calls a subroutine, the /xr command at the end of the subroutine will return control to whatever macro does the calling.

## /XL and /XN: Custom Prompts For Entering Labels And Numbers

| For | Command | Format | /xl[prompt max 39 char.s]~[location]~ |
|---|---|---|---|
| Prompt to accept character entry | /xl | Example | /xlPlease Enter Your Name: ~A34~ |

/xl displays a prompt of a maximum of 39 characters (including spaces) in the control panel and pauses for the operator to type in a response. After the operator presses ENTER, 1-2-3 enters the characters on the worksheet at the [location] specified in the command. Numbers entered in response to the prompt are converted to a label. If the user simply presses ENTER without typing anything a blank space will be recorded at the location specified in the command.

The example shown above includes a prompt followed by a colon and a space. The colon and space improve appearance when the prompt displays, but remember: these must be counted as prompt characters.

Following the prompt is a tilde, a cell address, and another tilde. If the cell address is omitted from the command, 1-2-3 will enter data at the current location of the cursor. If 40 characters are entered in the command, the computer will produce a "beep". This may be useful to draw attention to the prompt in the command line. The extra character will not be displayed.

| For | Command | Format | /xn[prompt max 39 char.s]˜[location]˜ |
|-----|---------|--------|----------------------------------------|
| Prompt to accept numeric entry | /xn | **Example** | /xnPlease Enter The Amount: ˜A38˜ |

/xn is very similar to /xl, with the exception that /xn accepts only numbers in response to the prompt—character entries will cause an error message to be displayed—and the user is REQUIRED to make an entry (Pressing **ENTER** without making an entry generates an error message). The prompt will be displayed again so the user can try again.

## Example of Custom Prompting

An example of the /xl and /xn commands is shown below. First is the macro itself. Below that is the data entry screen used with the macro.

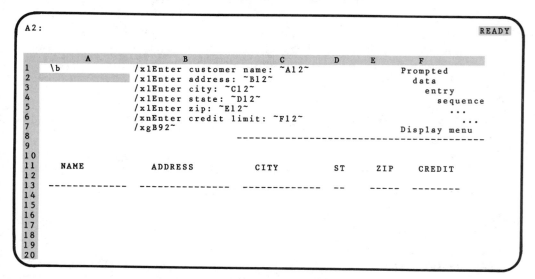

**Screen 2-24. Custom prompts (Macro 2-21).**

The worksheet where the prompts place the data looks like this:

```
========================================================================

        R               S               T           U     V       W
1
2    NAME            ADDRESS         CITY            ST    ZIP    CREDIT
3
4    -------------   ---------------  -------------   --    -----  --------
5


========================================================================
```

Look at the data entry commands in the macro. Five **/xl** commands accept data that should be entered as labels, including the zip code. If the zip code were entered as a number, then a zip code entered as "06450" would display as "6450".

Where we need a number (or value entry) is the credit limit. This will be a dollar amount and will have arithmetic performed on it. The command used to prompt for the credit limit is **/xn**.

## /XI: To Test Values In The Worksheet

| For | Command | Format | /**xi**[logical formula]˜[statement if true] |
|---|---|---|---|
| Conditional branching | /xi | **Example** | /xiT37=10˜/xq |
| | | | {goto}T37˜{?}˜ |

While **/xm** and the **{?}** commands allow the operator to make decisions in the midst of a macro, **/xi** is 1-2-3's way of having a macro make its own decisions. The job of **/xi** is twofold: (1) to evaluate a logical formula as true or false, and (2) to execute additional macro commands if the formula is true. Here's a more detailed explanation.

A logical formula is any formula which can be evaluated as being true or false, such as $+A5+A7=100$. If the values in cells A5 and A7 can be added to total 100, the formula is true. A logical formula always contains at least one of 1-2-3's logical operators: $=, <, >, <=, >=, <>$. A formula by itself such as @SUM(A5..A7) will not work with **/xi**. It doesn't contain a logical operator, so it can't be tested to see if it's true or false. @SUM(A5..A7)$=100$ will work.

If the logical formula is found to be true, the flow of control proceeds normally, reading the very next command on the same line as the **/xi** command. But if the formula is found to be false, the flow of control of the macro skips the remainder of the line and jumps directly to the next line below.

In the example above, if T37 does equal 10, the macro will stop. If not, the cursor will be sent to T37. Before we explore the power of this command, here's a little more detail on how to write it.

The characters /xi are followed by a formula and a tilde. Following that, on the same line, are any commands you want executed ONLY if the formula is true. If the formula is true, and the commands that follow do not change the flow of control, both the additional commands and those in the next line will be read. If the formula is found to be false, this command will be skipped and the macro will move directly to the next line for its next instructions. Keep in mind that the formula contained in the /xi statement must conform to the same rules governing the writing of any other formula. The only thing unusual about this formula is that it's followed by a tilde.

The macro below evaluates cell U90 on Worksheet A. The command in cell B91 says (in effect), "If the value in cell U90 is greater than or equal to .65 (65%), then execute the command in cell B94. If not, then execute the command on the next line." Since cell U90 on worksheet A is less than 65%, the formula is found to be false and the flow of control moves directly to the cell below. The command on the next line saves the worksheet to a disk file.

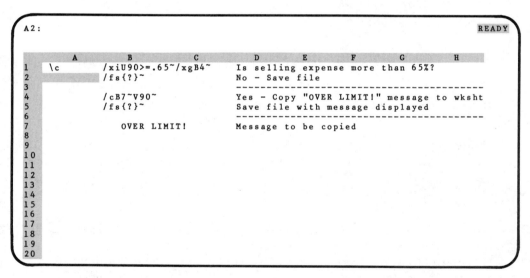

**Screen 2-25. If-Then macro (Macro 2-22).**

```
S87:                                                                    READY

                    S           T           U           V
87                              Amount      Percent
88         --------------------------------------------------------------------
89         Net Sales            30000       100%
90         Cost Of Goods Sold   18000        60%
91         Gross Profit         12000        40%
92
93
94
95
96
97
98
99
100
101
102
103
104
105
106
```

**Screen 2-26. Worksheet A.**

On Worksheet B, we find that cell U90 does exceed 65%. When the macro is run, the formula following the /xi command is found to be true and the macro reads the rest of the line. The command following the /xi is /xgB94~, causing the macro to read the statement in cell B94 as the next command. B94 copies a warning message into the cell next to the excessively high "Cost Of Goods Sold" line item.

```
S87:                                                                    READY

                    S           T           U           V
87                              Amount      Percent
88         --------------------------------------------------------------------
89         Net Sales            30000       100%
90         Cost Of Goods Sold   20400        68%        OVER LIMIT!
91         Gross Profit          9600        32%
92
93
94
95
96
97
98
99
100
101
102
103
104
105
106
```

**Screen 2-27. Worksheet B.**

This simple use of the **/xi** command shows one important way it can be useful. **/xi** can do what the @IF formula can't do, namely, put text messages on the worksheet when a cell value falls outside a specified range!

## Macro Autoexecute Features

Two additional features can add significantly to the power of your macros: the ability to automatically execute a macro upon retrieval of a file, and the ability to automatically retrieve a file upon starting 1-2-3.

**\0**            (Backslash zero) Use this as the name for any macro you want to execute automatically upon retrieval of the worksheet. This is the only time a macro name does not use a letter.

Use care to name the macro backslash zero (the number), not backslash O (the letter).

**AUTO123**    Use this as the name for any file you want retrieved automatically when you load 1-2-3.

### Automatic Macro Execution

In any worksheet, you can now designate one macro you want to automatically execute when the worksheet is retrieved from disk with 1-2-3's "File Retrieve" command. One of the more frequent uses for this feature is to have a macro menu automatically execute when the file is retrieved, thus immediately providing the operator with the available choices.

Once 1-2-3 has returned to the READY mode, the macro cannot be reinvoked by pressing **ALT 0**. However, if you want to be able to invoke the macro from within the worksheet, make a copy of the macro. Give the second copy a standard macro name such as **\m** (for Menu). Then you can use **ALT M** to invoke it from within the worksheet.

Another option is to put a **\m** macro in the cell directly above the **\0** macro. When **ALT M** is pressed, the commands for **\m** will be read, and then the commands for **\0**. The trick here is to have the **\m** macro be a "null" command, or one that does nothing. Use **{esc}**, which has no effect when used by itself.

**\m    {esc}**        Null command
**\0    /xmMENU˜**    Display menu

### Automatic File Retrieval

Beginning with release 1A of 1-2-3, a new feature was added to allow you to designate a file to be retrieved automatically. Every time 1-2-3 starts up, it searches the default disk drive for a file named AUTO123.WKS. If the file is found, it is automatically retrieved. If the file doesn't exist, a blank worksheet displays.

Only one worksheet file on any data disk may be given this name. You name a file AUTO123 when you File Save, in the same manner you would name any other worksheet file. Aside from the autoexecute feature, the AUTO123 file acts no differently than any other worksheet file.

### Synergy

The two macro autoexecute features can be used together to make an exceptionally powerful combination; a worksheet can automatically load itself and execute a macro without any operator intervention. That macro can include custom menus and data entry prompts to guide the operator, and possibly retrieve other worksheet files containing similar autoexecute macros. This enables an operator with little or no knowledge of 1-2-3 to easily post and print reports from numerous worksheets!

## 2.10  Using Range Names In Macros

Now that you know all about menus, goto's, and subroutines, you will begin to develop more sophisticated macros. You will need more sophisticated techniques to manage them.

To be able to plan, write, and debug longer macros effectively you must break them into manageable parts. Each of these parts is known as a routine. A routine accomplishes a specific result, such as printing a report, or displaying a message. Each routine can be given a Range Name. Range Names can be used to describe the routines and to execute the macro code. They can also be used in the macro code. In the example below, an **/xg** statement is used to direct the macro flow of control to cell T234, containing a routine to print the worksheet:

```
/xgT234~
```

If cell T234 were given the range name "print", you could write that same statement a little less cryptically:

```
/xgPRINT~
```

An **/xg** command requires that a cell location be specified, but a Range Name is just as effective a means of specifying a cell location as is a cell address.

Here's an example of this method at work. The illustration below shows a macro calling a menu in cell B3. The menu in turn uses **/xg** commands to call several other macro routines.

```
A2:                                                              READY

          A        B           C        D        E        F        G        H
1    \a      /xmB3~                Display menu below
2                              ---------------------------------------------
3            print                 save              column width
4            print a report       save the file     set current column width
5            /xgB7~                /xgB14~           /xgB16~
6                              ---------------------------------------------
7            /ppcrr                Clears and resets print range
8            F1.L33                Range to print (can be revised)
9            ~agp                  Print and advance page
10           crr                   Clears and resets print range
11           F37.J173              Range to print (can be revised)
12           ~agpq/xmB3~           Print, advance page, return to menu
13                             ---------------------------------------------
14           /fs{?}~/xmB3~         Save file, return to menu
15                             ---------------------------------------------
16           /wcs{?}~/xq           Adjust column width and quit
17
18
19
20
```

**Screen 2-28. Menu with cell address (Macro 2-23).**

Cell A1 contains the name of the first routine, **\a**. Since it's the very first routine of the macro, it must use the special macro Range Name, a backslash followed by a letter. But once the macro has been started using **ALT A**, it can call (execute) any other macro routine with an **/xg** command and a normal Range Name.

Just as you might normally write **/xgB16~** to transfer the macro's flow of control to cell B16, you can give cell B16 a Range Name, and use the Range Name as the cell address in the macro statement. If we give cell B16 the name WIDE, then the **/xg** statement is written **/xgWIDE~**.

Below is a new version of the above macro, using Range Names instead of cell addresses.

```
A2:                                                                   READY

          A        B           C        D        E         F          G          H
 1    \a       /xmMENU1~           Display menu below
 2                                ------------------------------------
 3    menul    print               save              column width
 4             print a report      save the file     set current column width
 5             /xgPRINT~           /xgSAVE~           /xgWIDE~
 6                                ------------------------------------
 7    print    /ppcrr              Clears and resets print range
 8             Fl.L33              Range to print (can be revised)
 9             ~agp                Print and advance page
10             crr                 Clears and resets print range
11             FORM                Range to print (can be revised)
12             ~agpq/xmMENU1~      Print, advance page, return to menu
13                                ------------------------------------
14    save     /fs{?}~/xmMENU1~    Save file, return to menu
15                                ------------------------------------
16    wide     /wcs{?}~/xq         Adjust column width and quit
17
18
19
20
```

**Screen 2-29. Menu with Range Name (Macro 2-24).**

Some of the following comments have been made in other sections of the book. We thought it would be helpful to bring them together in this section.

1.  The "name" column shows each of the range names used in the macro. Each label in the "name" column shows the name given to the macro cell directly to its right. But there are other reasons those labels are there:
    A.  If you place your cursor on cell A1, execute the commands / Range Name Labels Right, extend the pointer down the column through cell A16, and press **ENTER**, you will create all the Range Names for your routines automatically. This sequence of commands is a variation of Range Name Create:
        1.  Instead of asking you to supply the range name, Range Name Labels Right uses existing label entries as the names for the cells directly to their right.
        2.  When the command prompts you to supply a range, it wants the worksheet range containing the LABEL entries, NOT the cells to be named.
        3.  If one of the Range Names already exists on the worksheet, it will be deleted, leaving the new range.
        4.  The command sequence above named 5 cells. This had the same effect as using the Range Name Create Command 5 times.
    B.  The presence of the names on the worksheet also serves as a label identifying the names assigned to each routine.
2.  Note that all the range names and cell addresses used in the macros have been capitalized. We recommend you do this for two reasons: (1) To make them stand out for easier reading, visually separating the WHAT of the commands from the WHERE of worksheet locations. (2) To allow

you to scan the macros quickly to ensure every Range Name you've written in the macro has indeed been created on the worksheet.

If the Range Name hasn't been created and the macro reads it, the macro will terminate with an error. Our programming friends call this a "crash". We just call it undesirable. If you're going to use Range Names (and they are well worth using), make sure you've named them all properly before executing the macro.

3. The presence of these Range Names in the macro also makes the macro much easier to change. For example, if you Move something that has been Range Named, the name itself moves with the data. You do not need to change the macro because the Range Name will now point to the new location.

    But if you have written a cell address into the macro and then change the location of the informaton or routine, you'll have to find all the places you wrote that cell address into your macro and change it.

4. It's easier to comprehend the meaning of a macro that says **/xgPRINT~** than one that says **/xgS345~**. You instantly know that **/xgPRINT~** sends the macro to the printing routine. So use Range Names that communicate the purpose of each macro routine.

The remainder of the book will include Range Names in macros as a standard feature. Please note that whenever you create a macro or get one from another file by using the File Combining command, you must assign each of the Range Names. This must be done before executing the macro. Even if you assign the first cell of the macro an executable name such as **\a**, if you neglect to assign the rest of the Range Names used by the macro, it will terminate in an error. When an unassigned Range Name is read in a macro, 1-2-3 issues the error message "Illegal cell or range address".

## Cautions

For all their conveniences, there are some things you should be aware of in dealing with Range Names, whether or not they are used in macros.

1. Range Names are easily transferred. If cell B5 is given the Range Name A, and you use the Move command to transfer the contents of B5 to cell C6, Range Name A is also moved to cell C6.

2. Range names are easily associated. If cell B5 is given the Range Name A, and later also assigned the Range Name B, those names are associated because they refer to the same cell. If you then issue a command to Move range A to another location, the Range Name "B" will also be transferred to the new location.

3. Another aspect of item two to be aware of: it's possible to use the **Range Name Create** command to redefine an existing range. Just issue the com-

mand **Range Name Create**, supply the range name ("A" in this case), and 1-2-3 will indicate the present range for that name. If you then press Backspace, the range will be cancelled and you can indicate a new range. However, if as in the example above, range names "A" and "B" share the same range, then "B" will also be redefined. To keep "B" from being redefined when you redefine "A", simply issue the command **Range Name Delete "A"**, then reassign "A" by **Range Name Creating** it.

4.   One benefit of the **Range Name Labels** command is that, unlike **Range Name Create**, it will not transfer range names as described above. It deletes any previous reference to the Range Name and creates it in the new location.

5.   The top left and bottom right corner of a range are its anchors to the worksheet. If anything is Moved onto either of these corner cells, that name will be automatically deleted. The same thing happens if a **Worksheet Delete Row** or **Column** command removes an anchored corner of the range. If you then press the function keys **GOTO** and **NAME**, you will still see the name listed in the menu, although it has been effectively deleted, and cannot be used. The latter is a bug in 1-2-3.

6.   A useful rule to follow is that whenever a macro creates a Range Name, it must also delete it. This will help keep different names from becoming associated. When this happens, names can be moved to unexpected places. The worksheet can be damaged if a macro works with a Range Name that has been changed. A looping macro should be sure to build this feature into its loop. If the macro is manipulating a Range Name on the worksheet, it must always delete it before creating it in a new location.

Range Names will be a valuable tool to help you in writing macros from here on. Even in simple macros, we always use the methods outlined above because they make macros so much easier to write and understand.

In the next section we'll show you how to use the X commands and some of the lessons from this section to develop more sophisticated macro applications. We will also show you a powerful new way to use Range Names in macros.

# 2.11   Macros Using the X Commands and Auto-Execute Functions

In this section we'll take two of the macros introduced earlier and show you how to enhance them through the addition of X commands. Then we'll show you how to use the auto-execute functions to set up a worksheet printing queue. First we'll look at the @ROUND macro. This macro was last presented in the following form:

## Macro 2-25. @ROUND Macro—A.

| *Name* | *Macro* | *Comments* |
|--------|---------|------------|
| \r | {edit} | Edit entry |
|    | {home} | Cursor to start of entry |
|    | @round( | Enter function, to end of entry |
|    | {end}, | Cursor to end of entry |
|    | 2 | No. of decimal places to round to |
|    | )~ | Close expression and enter on wkst |
|    |   | ←blank to end macro |

## Consolidating Your Macros

Before we modify this macro, let's take a moment to review the form you use in writing a macro. While we wrote the above macro on six lines, we did this so we could explain it clearly. As your macros become more complex (and longer), you'll want to consolidate the lines to use worksheet space more efficiently. Below is an example of the macro rewritten in less space:

## Macro 2-26. @ROUND Macro—B.

| *Name* | *Macro* | *Comments* |
|--------|---------|------------|
| \r | {edit}{home}@round({end}, | Edit entry to round |
|    | 2 | No. decimals |
|    | )~ | Close expression |
|    |   | End macro |

What's the guideline on this? There are three considerations:

**MEMORY:** Longer macros can take up a lot of worksheet space by extending downward many lines. If this is using too much memory, consolidate what you've got on each line. Also, use /XG statements to move the flow of control of a long macro back to the top of the next column and proceed from there.

**CLARITY:** Put no more on one line than you can reasonably figure out later on. Stuffing too much macro code on one line makes for problems later when you try to retrace your steps to modify the macro.

**LOGIC:** One logical sequence of commands on one line is appropriate; move to the next line for the next sequence of commands. Example: the command sequence to set margins and print: **/ppomt0~mb6~qagpq** can reasonably go on one line of a macro. This modularizes the macro so you can easily change it, by inserting lines of new code, or copying lines into other macros.

Note: some have said that a macro's speed is increased by placing more of it in a single cell, as opposed to writing the same macro down a column of cells.

Our tests failed to show that changes in the number of instructions per line had a significant effect on the speed of a macro. However, a related point did register a significant effect on speed. Two macro routines linked with an **/xg** command run more slowly than the same routines written as one continuous macro, without the **/xg**.

Note: The following three examples use looping techniques. These techniques receive a full treatment in Section 3.3.

## Enhancing The @ROUND Macro

There are three ways you can now enhance the basic @Round macro:

1.  Allow the user to repeat the macro as many times as desired without reactivating the macro.
2.  Use a custom prompt to allow the user to set the number of decimal places to round to.
3.  Have the macro round an entire row or column of numbers automatically.

### Example #1: Allow the operator to repeat the macro

**Macro 2-27. Multiple @ROUND.**

| Name | Macro | Comment |
|------|-------|---------|
| \r | {edit}{home}@round({end}, | Round entry |
|     | 2 | Decimal places |
|     | )~{?}~ | Close entry, pause |
|     | /xg\r~ | Repeat macro |

This macro edits the first entry as usual, but then it pauses. The mode indicator displays CMD READY, and you can use the cursor control keys to move to the next cell to be rounded. When the cursor is repositioned, simply press **ENTER** and the macro will proceed.

You're already familiar with the first two lines of the macro. The addition of the {?}~ to the third line is what makes the macro pause; allowing you to use the cursor control keys to move to the next entry to be rounded. You can even use the **GOTO** function key: the macro will automatically round the cell you GOTO. After you move to the cell, pressing **ENTER** moves the macro flow of control past the {?}~ statement.

The next command in the macro is **/xg\r~**. This is the "macro goto" that redirects the flow of control to the location specified after the **/xg** (remember, this has no effect on the cursor). In this case, the location the macro is sent to continue reading keystrokes is **\r**, the range name for the first cell in the macro, causing the macro to repeat itself. This macro will repeat itself until you end it by pressing **Control Break** (hold down the Control key and press the Break key), which will terminate any macro.

Using the /xl command prior to beginning the rounding process, the next version of the macro allows the user to easily set the number of decimals to round to.

## Example #2: Prompting the user for information

**Macro 2-28. Multiple @ROUND with prompt.**

| Name | Macro | Comment |
|------|-------|---------|
| \r | /xlEnter no. of decimals: ~PUT~ | User prompt |
| loop1 | {edit}{home}@round({end}, | Round entry |
| put | | Decimal places |
| | )~{?}~ | Close entry, pause |
| | /xgLOOP1~ | Repeat macro |

In this macro, the very first line generates a prompt in the control panel asking the operator to specify the number of decimals the entry should be rounded to. Note that the /xl command has been used, not /xn. Since a macro requires each entry to be a label, the /xl command converts the operator's numeric input into a label when it enters it on the worksheet in the location called PUT—the cell to the right of the label put. If /xn were used, the entry would be a value, which a macro cannot read (try it and see).

In this case, we don't want the macro to repeat the prompt after each number is rounded, so the first line containing that prompt must be excluded from the loop. The Range Name LOOP1 identifies the second line of the macro. The /xg command in the macro's last line redirects the flow of control to LOOP1, omitting the prompt for each subsequent rounding operation.

## *Rounding A List Of Numbers*

The above macros are good for rounding numbers scattered over the worksheet. Usually numbers are listed across a row or down a column. Here is how to make the macro considerably more powerful, and handle a whole list at once.

The example we'll use here operates on a column of numbers. The cursor must be positioned at the top of the column of numbers when the macro is executed. It requires that there be a blank cell directly beneath the list. It can easily be modified to handle numbers in a row as well.

## Example #3: Rounding a list of numbers

### Macro 2-29. @ROUND a list.

| Name | Macro | Comments |
|------|-------|----------|
| \r | /xlPlease enter no. of decimals: ~PUT~ | 1. User prompt |
| | {end}{down}{down} | 2. Goto cell below last entry |
| | @na~ | 3. Enter test value |
| | {end}{up} | 4. Return to top of list |
| loop1 | /rncPOINTER~~ | 5. Create test range name |
| | /xi@isna(POINTER)~/xgEND~ | 6. Test range name for value |
| | {edit}{home}@round({end}, | 7. Round entry if false |
| put | | 8. Decimal places |
| | )~ | 9. Close entry |
| | /rndPOINTER~ | 10. Delete range name |
| | {down} | 11. Move to next entry |
| | /xgLOOP1~ | 12. Repeat operation |
| | ------------------------------ END ROUTINE ------------------------------ | |
| end | /re~ | 13. Delete @NA at bottom |
| | {up}{end}{up} | 14. Goto top of list |
| | /xq | 15. End macro |

This example introduces a new level of performance and sophistication in your macros. We've numbered the comment lines so we can explain the macro step by step.

Summary: this macro is designed to round an entire column of entries. It marks the end of the column with a special entry, @NA. Before rounding the items in the list, it performs a test to see if the next item is @NA. If it is NOT @NA, the macro rounds it. When it encounters the @NA entry, the macro terminates.

The first step to take with this macro is to use the Range Name Labels Right commands to create all the Range Names it uses. The only other preparation you must make is to place the cursor at the very top entry of the list of numbers to be rounded before executing the macro.

```
\r          /xlPlease enter no. of decimals: ~PUT~
                 1.   User prompt
```

Line one prompts the operator to enter the number of decimal places to use in rounding entries. When the operator makes an entry, the **/xl** command will enter the number into the cell named **put**. **put** is on line 8 of the macro.

```
            {end}{down}{down}
                 2.   Goto cell below last entry
```

Line 2 moves the cursor from the very top entry of the list to the bottom entry, with the **{end}{down}** commands, and then moves one cell below that with the additional **{down}** command.

     `@na~`       3. Enter test value

With the cursor positioned in the cell below the last entry in the list of numbers, Line 3 enters a value there: @NA. This is the function 1-2-3 uses to stand for "not available". In this case, we're using this entry to mark the end of the column of entries (we're assuming @NA won't be used anywhere else in the list of entries). The `/xi` command in line 6 will test for this value.

     `{end}{up}`     4. Return to top of list

Line 4 uses `{end}{up}` to return the cursor to the top of the list to begin rounding entries.

 Loop1   `/rncPOINTER~~`  5. Create test Range Name

Line 5 creates the Range Name "POINTER" and assigns it to the current cell. At this point in the macro, POINTER will be assigned to the top number in the list. Also note that, as the label in the left hand column indicates, this line of the macro has the Range Name Loop1 assigned to it. Line 12 sends the flow of control back to this line.

    `/xi@isna(POINTER)~/xgEND~`
          6. Test range name for value

  Since the current cell is named POINTER, the macro only has to check to see if POINTER is @NA to know whether the end of the list has been reached. `@isna(POINTER)` is a logical formula that can be translated as: POINTER is @NA. The macro uses the `/xi` command to see if the formula is true (if the current cell contains @NA). If the formula is found to be true, the command `/xgEND~` will be executed, sending the flow of control to the next macro. If the formula is false, the macro will ignore the remaining commands on the same line and skip directly to line 7 to continue rounding entries.

    `{edit}{home}@round({end},`
          7. Round entry if false

The cell is now edited. The first part of the rounding formula is entered, and then moves the pointer to the end of the line. If the value to be rounded is "12.3456", Line 7 will rewrite the entry as far as: `@round(12.3456,`

  `put`        8. Decimal places

Line 8 has the Range Name `put`. The location `put` was used by line 1, specifying where the `/xl` command is to enter the number of decimal places given by the operator. If an entry of "2" is made, line 8 will look like this:

  `put`   `2`     8. Decimal places

As the macro reads this line, "2" will be written into the @round formula, which now looks like this: `@round(12.3456,2`

    )~               9.   Close entry

Line 9 closes the @round expression to complete the formula, and enters it on the worksheet: @round(12.3456,2)

    /rndPOINTER~     10.   Delete Range Name

Line 10 deletes the Range Name POINTER. POINTER was named by line 5. This allows the name to be used in another location.

    {down}          11.   Move to next entry

Line 11 moves the cursor down one row to the next entry in the list.

    /xgLOOP1~       12.   Repeat operation

Line 11 is an **/xg** command, redirecting the flow of the macro back to line 5. Line 5 creates the range name POINTER again, and assigns it to the current cell. Since the current cell has been changed to the next entry down in the list, the range name POINTER is now assigned to the second entry. At this point the macro will repeat the lines following line 5, continuing to test and round cells until the **/xi** command detects the value @NA. When this happens, the macro will execute the command **/xgEND~** and start executing line 13.

    end       /re~       13.   Delete @NA at bottom

Line 13 has the range name END, and will erase the current cell. It will be executed when the cursor reaches the entry @NA at the bottom of the list. Since the macro put the value there for its own testing purposes, it should also erase it from the worksheet when it's finished.

    {up}{end}{up}    14.   Goto top of list

Line 14 moves the cursor {up} one cell to the bottom of the list. Then {end}{up} moves the cursor the rest of the way to the top of the list.

    /xq          15.   End macro

Line 15 terminates macro control.

## Observations

This macro introduces a powerful new tool. The Range Name POINTER became a "traveling Range Name". It was created in the top cell in the list, and used in the first loop of the macro. It was then deleted and created again in the next cell down, to be used by the next loop of the macro. This allowed the macro to use POINTER to sequentially process each entry in the list.

Every time the **/xi** command read the formula **/xi@isna(POINTER)~**, POINTER referred to a different cell in the list. That made a very efficient macro: one command processed an entire list. Because the location of

POINTER varies with each execution of the routine, we say the Range Name acts as a "variable" in this operation. As this example demonstrates, variable Range Names significantly expand the work a macro can perform.

Your selection of these names can make a difference. 1-2-3 will accommodate Range Names up to fifteen characters in length. Since Range Names are read one character at a time by a macro, many long names may slow a macro down somewhat. We suggest you use Range Names that are descriptive of their function, with a length from 4-8 characters.

You should be aware of one more subtle assumption affecting the prior macro example. Line 5 creates the Range Name POINTER with the **Range Name Create** command. We assume that POINTER does not already name another location on the worksheet. If it does, the macro will try to round the wrong cells, because the **Range Name Create** command in line 5 won't change the existing range setting. Under these circumstances, when the macro uses the Range Name in the **/xi** command, it will also evaluate the wrong cell.

If you are ever unsure whether a Range Name will already exist or not, you should include a small routine to make sure the new name will be assigned to the proper cell. It's very simple:

```
/rncPOINTER~~
/rndPOINTER~
/rncPOINTER~~
```

This sequence protects you. Whether the Range Name POINTER exists or not, this routine will ensure that it will be assigned to the right cell. Consider the following three circumstances:

1. If the Range Name does NOT exist, the first line will create the name and assign it to the current cell. The second line will delete the name and the third line will create it again.

2. But if the Range Name POINTER does exist when the macro executes, the macro will work differently. Line 1 will create the name and assign it to the existing location. Line 2 will delete it, and line 3 will assign it to the new location.

3. You may be wondering why line 1 is included at all, since all the work appears to be done by lines 2 and 3. Suppose the range name does NOT exist: then a **Range Name Delete** command will cause an error. The **Range Name Create** command on line 1 is there for insurance. In the event there is no existing range name, it creates one to avoid an error when **Range Name Delete** is executed.

One final point about the structure of this macro: note the separation of the routine END from the other macro routines. Its physical separation clarifies the separation of its purpose from that of the rest of the macro. This is one more tool to help you keep your macros well organized and easy to comprehend.

## *Understanding @ISERR and @ISNA*

In the previous example, we used the @ISNA function as part of an **/xi** command. If you're unfamiliar with this special command and its counterpart @ISERR, the following explanation will clarify their use. These two functions work differently than other @ functions. @ISNA tests for the presence of the value @NA, @ISERR does the same for the value @ERR.

Here's the common mistake: if you want a macro to test for the presence of the value @NA in a cell named TEST, it might appear you should write

```
/xi(TEST)=@na~/xgMAC7~
/xq
```

But you shouldn't. The macro shown above will ALWAYS find the statement true, even when it isn't. This is because the function @NA can only be tested by another function, @ISNA(location). The solution is to rewrite the macro using the @ISNA function in the following format:

```
/xi@isna(TEST)~/xgMAC7~
/xq
```

The macro will accurately test for the presence of @NA and branch depending on the result. The same situation holds true for the function @ERR. The following example substitutes @ISERR for @ISNA:

```
/xi@iserr(TEST)~/xgMAC7~
/xq
```

@ISERR can also be used to suppress the display of ERR on the worksheet. If a formula is generating an unwanted ERR display, it can be placed within a nested @IF/@ISERR function:

Original formula: **+B5/B7**
Revised formula: **@IF(@ISERR(B5/B7),0,B5/B7)**

If the value of the formula is ERR, the cell will display a zero. When the formula has a meaningful result, that result will automatically be displayed instead. A macro that converts the original formula into the revised formula shown above automatically was shown in Section 2.5. Here's another version that does the same thing:

**Macro 2-30. @ISERR.**

| Name | Macro | Comment |
|------|-------|---------|
| \e | {edit}{home}'~ | Change formula into label |
| | /c~MAC1~/c~MAC2~ | Copy formula into macro |
| | @if(@iserr( | Change back to formula |
| mac1 | | Rewrite beginning of formula |
| | ),0, | Rewrite end of formula |
| mac2 | | Insert copy of formula |
| | )~/xq | Close formula and enter |

This version is not better than the earlier one, it's only different. You should be aware there are frequently more ways than one to solve a problem with macros. If one way doesn't exactly suit your needs, use some creativity—often a different one is available that will.

In addition to giving you some useful macros, our point in showing you so many different macros is to demonstrate how flexible a tool they are. Once you grasp the generic principles underlying the specific macros shown here, you can take advantage of this flexibility to adapt solutions of your own.

## Setting Up A Printing Queue With Auto-Exec Macros

Perhaps you've had to print reports from numerous worksheets, each in a separate file, and wondered how you were going to avoid sitting around the computer all morning waiting for your reports to print. The solution is relatively simple with macros. Instead of all morning you'll spend about five minutes setting up the macros to do the work.

In this example, we'll use "auto-exec" macros. Auto-exec is a contraction of the words "automatically execute". Any macro can be made to automatically execute upon retrieval of the worksheet by simply giving it the name \0 (that's backslash ZERO).

To set up a sequence of automatically printing worksheets, do this:

1.  Retrieve your LIBRARY file and add the macro shown here.

**Macro 2-31. Automatic printing of worksheets.**

| Name | Macro | Comment |
|------|-------|---------|
| \0 | /ppcar | Clear prior print settings |
| | | New range |
| | ~of!- # -~ | Page number in footer |
| | h!!@~q | Date in header |
| | agpq | Print and eject page |
| | /rnd\0~ | Delete autoexec name |
| | {home}/fs~r | Resave file without autoexec named |
| | /fr | Retrieve next file |
| | | File name |
| | ~ | Enter |

2. Create a Range Name encompassing the ENTIRE macro; including name, macro and comment columns. Use the name P for printing.

3. Resave the LIBRARY file to disk. Now transfer the LIBRARY file to the disk holding the worksheets to be printed, if it isn't already there.

4. File Retrieve the first worksheet to be printed. Place your cursor on an empty portion of the worksheet and bring the macro into the worksheet file with the following commands:

| You press: | Which means: |
|---|---|
| / | Slash opens command menu |
| f | File |
| c | Combine |
| c | Copy |
| n | Named range |
| p | Name of range to combine |
| ENTER | Confirm |
| library | Name of file containing range |
| ENTER | Confirm |

5. Place the cursor in the "Name" column on the label \0. To easily name the macro, execute the commands:

| You press: | Which means: |
|---|---|
| / | Slash opens command menu |
| r | Range |
| n | Name |
| l | Labels |
| r | Right |
| ENTER | Confirm range as current cell |

Note: you CANNOT get around this step by naming the macro while it's still in the LIBRARY file. Range Names are NOT transferred through a file combine operation. You must rename macros once they have been File Combined, and using the command above is the simplest way to do it.

6. Fill in the range you want printed in the first blank line in the macro (variations that will print multiple copies of a worksheet, or will print multiple ranges on a worksheet, are included in Section 2.4). The Clear All command on the first line will cancel prior print settings, so make sure this macro contains all the new settings (headers, footers, margins, etc.) you need for your reports.

7. Fill in the name of the next worksheet file to be retrieved and printed in the second blank line of the macro. In order for this macro to work, you must enter the file name precisely right . . . any misspelling will abort the

operation. Use the command / **File List Worksheet** to review the files and get the file name spelling.

8. Resave the file to disk with the new macro in it.

9. Repeat this procedure with each file to be placed in the printing queue, with the exception of the very last file. In that file, change the macro so it looks like this instead.

---

**Macro 2-32. Automatic printing—last file.**

| Name | Macro | Comment |
|------|-------|---------|
| \0 | /ppcar | Clear prior print settings |
|      |        | New range |
|      | ~of! - # -~ | Page number in footer |
|      | h!!a~q | Date in header |
|      | agpq | Print and eject page |
|      | /rnd\0~ | Delete autoexec name |
|      | /fs~r | Resave file without autoexec named |
|      | /wey | Display blank worksheet and quit |

---

10. Turn on the printer. Make sure you have a good supply of paper—at least enough to print all the worksheets in the queue. Set the paper to "top of form", and Retrieve the first file in the queue. Check in once in a while to make sure there've been no paper jams in the printer. The last line of the macro is "Worksheet Erase Yes", which will clear the worksheet and terminate the macro. You might also use "Quit Yes", which will leave 1-2-3 and return to DOS.

The macro deletes its own executable Range Name in each file after printing (and resaves the file without the Range Name), so you can File Retrieve those files now without restarting the automatic printing. However, the macros themselves remain in each file. After posting them again, rename the macros before you File Save each file, and you're ready to run your next set of reports.

## A More Efficient Library Set-up

Now that you know the X commands, you can modify the layout of the Macro Utility Library introduced in Section 2.6. Place /xq commands at the end of each entry and eliminate the empty spaces between to make them as compact as possible. The only macro that shouldn't end with /xq is the Indent macro. This is so it can be invoked numerous times within a single entry (allowing you to indent as far as you want). Place the indent macro in the last row of the file so the row beneath will be blank. Each macro should be written on one line only, even though that exceeds what can be displayed on the 80 column screen. This keeps the number of rows to a minimum.

This makes for a very efficient use of space on the worksheet into which the macros are combined. Since these are short routines you are familiar with, you don't need any documentation. The idea is to take up as little memory and space as possible.

Here's the way the **LIBRARY** file of word processing macros looks on the screen (see Screen 2-30).

```
B7:  ´                                                            READY

        A       B        C        D        E        F        G        H
 1   \m   /m.{right}{right}{right}{right}{right}{right}{right}{?}~{?}~/xq
 2   \p   /ppcar.{right}{right}{right}{right}{right}{right}{right}{?}~agpq/xq
 3   \j   /rj{right}{right}{right}{right}{right}{right}{right}{down}{?}~/xq
 4   \d   ===========================================================~/xq
 5   \s   -----------------------------------------------------------~/xq
 6   \x   /fxf{?}~{?}~/xq
 7   \i   
 8
 9
10
11
12
13
14
15
16
17
18
19
20
```

**Screen 2-30. LIBRARY worksheet (Macro 2-33).**

Now that your macros are getting bigger and more complex, it becomes harder to find the errors that keep them from working properly. The next section will help you to deal with those errors.

# 2.12  Dealing With Errors

Errors are an unavoidable result of writing macros, they "come with the territory". So don't worry about making them—just know how to find and correct them. Errors in programs or macros are called "bugs". The process of removing them is called "debugging". The first group of guidelines is for simpler macros, the section following that deals with more complex macros.

## *Debugging Simple Macros*

1.  If the problem is that your macro will not execute, check the following things:

A.  Have you used the right type of name? Press the **GOTO** function key, then the **NAME** function key to display a menu of assigned Range Names. If the macro names are not displayed, press the **END** key to show them. Move the menu pointer to highlight the name of the macro. The range name designating a macro must consist of a backslash followed by a single letter, so check:

- Did you use the BACKSLASH (\), not the slash (/), in the name?
- Is the backslash followed by a SINGLE letter of the alphabet (with no space between them)? The only exception to this rule is where you've used an autoexec macro (which will execute automatically when the worksheet is retrieved). Make sure you've named that \0–that's backslash ZERO (the number) NOT O (the letter).
- If you have named an autoexec macro backslash zero and you can't execute it from within the worksheet there's nothing wrong. These macros execute only upon retrieval of the file from disk. However, you can make a copy of the macro and assign this second macro a conventional name such as \m (for Menu) and use that to execute it from within the worksheet.
- Another option is to put a \m macro in the cell directly above the \0 macro. With a "null" command (one that does nothing). This is discussed in Section 2.9.

B.  Does the macro Range Name refer to the proper macro cell? While still looking at the macro Range Name (using the **GOTO** and **NAME** keys described above), position the menu pointer to select the macro name and press **ENTER**. The cell pointer will go to the cell which has the Range Name: that MUST be the top cell in your macro.

2.  If the macro executes but runs into trouble somewhere along the way, then you need one of these kinds of help:

A.  Execute It Manually: The simplest, most direct method for detecting errors in a macro is described in the original guidelines for writing a macro: execute the macro manually before writing it. This also works AFTER it's written: print a copy of your macro and key in the commands manually, EXACTLY as written, and observe the result of each keystroke. The errors will be apparent as soon as you key them in.

B.  Automated Help: Version 1A of 1-2-3 introduced another method to help you debug your macros. Hold down the **ALT** key and press the **HELP** (F1) function key. The word STEP will appear in reverse video in the lower right of your screen. If you now execute a macro, you will have to press a key—any key—to execute each keystroke in the macro (i.e. "step" through it). This will help you pinpoint where the macro is erring.

When you are through, press **ALT** and the **HELP** function key again. The STEP indicator will disappear.

Here's a checklist of some of the most common errors in macros:

- If 1-2-3 beeps and displays the following error message in the bottom left corner of the screen, "Illegal cell or range address", 1-2-3 can't recognize a cell address or Range Name in the macro. Several things are potential causes:

  A. You have forgotten to supply a range where 1-2-3 expects one. For example, if you place the Copy command in a macro (/c), you must follow it with a range to copy from and a range to copy to. If you merely start writing another command, 1-2-3 will try to use the next command as a range to copy from, and will break down.

  B. You have misspelled a Range Name, and 1-2-3 doesn't recognize it as the Range Name you intended.

  C. You have used a Range Name in your macro, but forgotten to Range Name Create it.

- If 1-2-3 beeps and displays the following error message in the bottom left corner of the screen, "Unrecognized key name {...}": you have used improper syntax for one of the {bracketed} commands, and 1-2-3 doesn't recognize the command. You may have merely misspelled the command.

- Check for the proper placement of tildes ( ˜ ) in the macro. This is one of the most often forgotten steps in a macro.

- Ensure that the slash ( / ) precedes the beginning of every command sequence to put 1-2-3 into "menu mode". All the X commands must also be preceded by a slash. A related problem is the use of a backslash in place of a slash: \xq will cause an error, /xq is correct.

- Another related problem: DON'T use the slash inappropriately. Text and numeric entries in a macro shouldn't begin with a slash because these entries are made directly on the worksheet without using a command menu.

- No spaces should appear between commands in a macro. Think about it. You don't enter spaces between commands when you manually execute them, so you shouldn't in a macro either.

- When an elusive error occurs, it's a natural tendency to think something is wrong with 1-2-3. However, 1-2-3 is relatively bug free—most errors are in the macros. Remember that macros are absolutely literal in their execution of what you have written. Follow the sequence of the command menus precisely.

  If the sequence of commands to change a column width is **/Worksheet Column-width Set 15 ENTER**, then your macro must read **/wcs15˜**. If the c and s are reversed like this: **/wsc15˜** the macro won't work properly. The best way to ensure the commands are right is to execute them manually before you attempt to write them into a macro.

- Ensure that your macros follow "menu etiquette". For example, some command sequences will return 1-2-3 to READY mode by using a tilde at the end, such as the one used to adjust column width: **/Worksheet Column-width Set 15 ENTER /wcs15˜**. In other instances, 1-2-3 requires a Quit command before returning to READY mode.

   An example of this is found in the printing commands: Print Printer Go Quit (**/ppgq**). In this example, if the Quit command were omitted and another command sequence followed, 1-2-3 would respond by "beeping" to indicate an error. Why? 1-2-3 would still be in the Print menu and unable to recognize or execute anything but Print commands.

- Check to ensure you've provided a means to end the macro properly. There should either be an empty cell directly beneath the macro's last cell, or an **/xq** command. If you haven't provided a means to terminate the macro, any label entries in that last cell will be read as part of the macro.

- If you've run the macro and discovered portions of the macro itself written on the worksheet (other than where you wrote them), you've probably forgotten either a tilde to represent the **ENTER** key or a slash to start a new command series. Both of these mistakes can result in the macro writing parts of itself on the worksheet inappropriately.

- The X commands cannot be keyed in and tested manually, so you'll have to observe them running as part of a macro. If you determine an X command is the problem, check the function of the X command you've used. Is it the proper command for the task you want performed? Next check the syntax of the command. Each command has a specific format that must be written correctly.

Those are the methods of dealing with problems you may have with a macro. If you're still having trouble, and you haven't executed the macro manually, do that now. This may take more time than some of the other methods, but it will unerringly pinpoint problems.

## A Simple Debugging Exercise

Here's an exercise that'll sharpen your skills at debugging. Use the techniques described above to find and correct the errors in the macro listed below. These are typical errors, and finding them will help you find similar errors in your own work. When you are done, consult the listing of errors and the corrected model that follows, and compare them with your own findings.

**Macro 2-34. A macro with errors.**

| Name | Macro | Comment |
|------|-------|---------|
| /p | /pohPAGE # | 1. Print options header |
|  | mt15~mb12~ | 2. Margin settings |
|  | brA1.A2~ | 3. Print border row setting |
|  | carA1.Z100~ | 4. Clear prior settings, range |
|  | agpq | 5. Align; print; advance page |

Once you've made your corrections, compare them with this list of errors:

1.  Macro name: the label in the Name column is /p. The character in front of the "p" should be a BACKSLASH, not a slash. It should be \p.

2.  Line 1: the command sequence omits the second "p" needed to send output to the printer instead of a print file; it should read /ppoh...

3.  Line 1: after entering the text for a report Header, you must press ENTER; so the macro must include a tilde after that text: /ppohPAGE #~.

4.  Line 2: the margin settings for top margin and bottom margin exceed the allowable limits (maximum is 10 spaces on top and bottom); the maximum settings this line can use are: mt10~mb10~.

5.  Line 3: the print border settings are the last item to be selected from the Print Options menu; all commands following that are from the main Print menu. A Quit command must be included after the Borders commands to move from the Print Options menu to the main Print menu, or the commands will be misread. This line should end with the Quit command: brA1.A2~q.

6.  Line 4: this line starts with the Clear All command, which clears all prior print settings. The Clear All command should have been issued prior to (not after) all the print settings in lines 1-3, because it will cancel them if it occurs afterward. This setting should be in line 1: /ppcaohPAGE #~.

7.  Also in line 4: the print range duplicates part of the borders range specified in line 3. This will result in double print-outs of the rows contained in the border range. These rows should be omitted from the print range: rA3..Z100~.

8.  Line 5 is fine, but look just below it. That single line will be read as part of the macro because it's in the cell just below the bottom macro cell. There should be a blank space between that line and the last macro cell.

## Macro 2-35. Corrected version of the macro.

| Name | Macro | Comment |
|------|-------|---------|
| \p | `/ppcaohPAGE #~` | 1. Clear settings, print options header |
|  | `mt10~mb10~` | 2. Margin settings |
|  | `brA1.A2~q` | 3. Print border row setting |
|  | `rA3.Z100~` | 4. Print range |
|  | `agpq` | 5. Align; print; advance page |
|  |  | 6. Blank line to end macro |

9. One final possible error: was the macro name assigned to the proper cell? If you press the GOTO function and type the macro's name (\p), does the cell pointer go to the first line of the macro?

# Debugging Complex Macros

As your macros grow more complex, errors in them become more difficult to pinpoint. In this section we'll present some enhancements to the instructions for simple macros to enable you to handle this extra complexity. They include:

1. The renewed importance of saving files
2. Debugging through "playing percentages"
3. Modular testing
4. Logical problems

### 1. Save the Worksheet

Before they are tested, the more complex, more powerful macros you are now writing have just as much potential for negative results as positive ones. Don't underestimate the ability of a macro to wreak havoc on a worksheet: just one wrong {goto} command and the operation may overwrite existing data. We'll reiterate a point we made earlier. Before you first run a macro, make sure that you have File Saved the worksheet. If the macro malfunctions, note the problem. Then File Retrieve the original worksheet and correct the errors. Before you test the corrected macro again, File Save again.

If you want to keep both the original and revised copies of the worksheet separate, save the second version under a different name. Standard names for these files are TEST1, TEST2, etc. When you're finished testing, get rid of the files you no longer need. If you need to transfer portions of macros or data between different test files, don't forget about 1-2-3's File Combine function. It's a lot faster to use than re-entering data.

## 2. Play percentages

Larger macros almost always contain at least a few mistakes when they are first written. These include simple typos, wrong cells being addressed, steps left out in a 1-2-3 command, wrong or misplaced range names being used, and faulty logic in the design of the macro.

With so many possible culprits, be a good detective and narrow down your suspects. Look over the worksheet and observe what happened when the macro executed. What routine was the macro executing when it bombed? Execute that routine manually. Keep an eye out for mistakes you make frequently. Macros are so exacting in their execution that it could be something as simple as using "}" when "{" should have been used. If you're a poor typist, look for common typos such as transposing letters (that'll stop a macro quickly).

## 3. Test the macro in modules

If you are following the guidelines for structuring your macro, you're breaking it into functional segments, known as routines and subroutines, that accomplish specific tasks. Rather than writing an entire macro before testing it, you should debug each routine as you go. This can save you a lot of work later on. Not only will problems be simpler to pinpoint working with a small routine, but changes in an early routine can have significant effects on routines written later. Testing and making corrections as you go will save you a lot of rewriting later.

Here's an example of testing a macro in modules. In the macro shown on page 88, the Print routine can easily be tested after it's written. After you've written a routine, assign it a temporary range name that can be executed directly. To test the print routine shown below, place your cursor on cell B7, give it the Range Name \t (for test), and execute it.

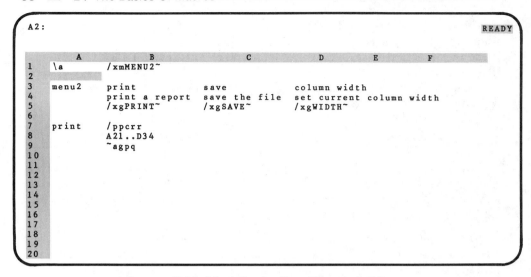

```
A2:                                                                  READY

          A              B                C                D        E        F
 1   \a          /xmMENU2~
 2
 3   menu2       print            save             column width
 4               print a report  save the file    set current column width
 5               /xgPRINT~        /xgSAVE~         /xgWIDTH~
 6
 7   print       /ppcrr
 8               A21..D34
 9               ~agpq
10
11
12
13
14
15
16
17
18
19
20
```

**Screen 2-31. Modular testing (Macro 2-36).**

After you've finished testing, make sure you / **Range Name Delete** the temporary range name \t right away. The reason for this comes from one of the trickiest problems you will encounter with macros: associating range names.

Here's how the problem unfolds. You are using the temporary Range Name \t to test the routine above. It works fine, and you assign the routine the Range Name PRINT, and move on to work on your next routine. After completing the new routine, you assign it the range name \t to run a test. It works fine and you assign it the name FILE. Later, when you run the macros, the menu choice for PRINT runs into trouble. It doesn't execute the print routine at all. Instead, it is running the FILE routine! What's wrong?

After you finished writing the print routine, you assigned it the Range Name PRINT, which would be used by other macros to call that routine. At that time, that routine still had the temporary range name \t assigned to it, left over from when you ran the test. After you finished the next routine you used the **Range Name Create** command to reassign the range name \t to the new routine. And that's where the trouble starts.

Unknowingly, you have also transferred the Range Name PRINT, along with the range name \t, to the new location. Since PRINT and \t refer to the same range, they are associated. Changing one changes the other as well. If you continued testing in this manner, eventually you'd have almost every range name in the macro associated with one another.

How do you avoid this problem and still have the benefit of testing with temporary range names? You must use **Range Name Delete** to eliminate the temporary range name before reassigning it to a new location.

You can create a little macro to deal with this problem as shown here.

**Macro 2-37. Debugging tool.**

| Name | Macro | Comment |
|------|-------|---------|
| \t | /rncTEST~~ | Create Range Name |
|    | /rndTEST~ | Delete Range Name |
|    | /rncTEST~{?}~ | Assign name to current location |
|    | /xgTEST~ | Run macro |

The second line of the macro deletes the Range Name TEST. If this were the first time you'd used the macro, TEST might not exist, causing an error condition when you try to delete it. That's why the first line of the macro creates the Range Name TEST. After its deletion, line 3 creates TEST again and pauses for you to indicate the location of the cell the name is to be assigned to. The last line redirects the flow of control to execute the macro to be tested. The macro leaves TEST in existence, but will delete it before using it again next time.

## 4. Check the logic

Logical problems in macros deal with the improper use of the X commands, and are among the toughest to resolve. In a logical problem, the macro runs without any errors, it just doesn't accomplish what you wanted.

This kind of problem has nothing to do with the technique of execution; it has to do with the thinking behind the macro. Therefore, the way to identify the problem is to review that thinking (or logic). The easiest way of doing that is to translate the macro into something known as "pseudo code".

Pseudo code consists of short, English descriptions of a macro. The descriptions should avoid any 1-2-3 jargon, and concentrate on describing the intent of a step, and its relationship to both prior and subsequent steps. This should enable you to pinpoint the fault in your logic. The comments accompanying each line of these macros are a form of pseudo code.

Of couse, if you write your pseudo code before you start with your macro code, most of the logic of the task will be worked out, and your macros will be much easier to build and debug. One way to do this is to write the comments first, indicating each step the macro will take. Then, write the macro itself. Add, delete, and move lines as necessary. This will help you organize your macro, and it will work better for you.

# 3

# Techniques For Macros

# What's In This Chapter?

This chapter will show you how to make the transition from writing macros for your own use to writing macros for others to use. It will show how to use a variety of techniques and tricks to vastly increase the power of your macros and make them much easier to use.

# 3.1 Screen Management

1-2-3 is a screen-oriented program. The cursor (more properly called the cell pointer) highlights the active worksheet cell in inverse video and displays the cell's contents in the control panel. As you move the cursor around the worksheet, the screen follows automatically.

While these features help make operator interaction with 1-2-3 very visual and easy to grasp, they can create problems in a macro application, where it isn't always appropriate to have the screen follow the cursor around the worksheet. For example, a macro may perform an automated posting operation requiring it to move to many separate areas of the worksheet. However, the operator has no desire or need to watch the screen move around. And there are times when the cell pointer stands out like a sore thumb on a screen displaying a message. It serves no purpose, but how do you get rid of it?

These are just a few of the problems screen management techniques can handle effectively. Here's a more complete list:

1. Instructing an operator with messages and prompts, allowing even inexperienced operators to use 1-2-3 effectively.
2. Highlighting entries and creating screen borders to add emphasis to screen displays, while hiding the display of the cell pointer.
3. Suppressing distracting material from displaying on the screen.
4. Clearing the top line of the control panel of cell content displays during menus and prompts.
5. Providing a screen to help insert dates.

## Displaying Messages

The proper prompts and messages are an important part of advanced macros. Without them an operator can easily become confused (even if the operator and the writer are the same person). With good prompts and messages, macros not only take on a more polished look, but it becomes possible for people with no experience in using 1-2-3 to use them.

Suppose you want to display a brief message when the worksheet loads or to prompt an operator to make a menu selection.

Select a blank part of the worksheet to write a message such as the one shown in Screen 3-1.

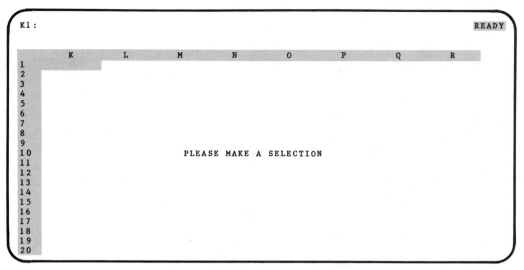

K1 :                                                                 READY

| | K | L | M | N | O | P | Q | R |

PLEASE MAKE A SELECTION

**Screen 3-1. Message screen.**

This message prompts an operator to make a selection from a custom menu. In preparation for the macro, assign cell K1 the Range Name MESSAGE. The macro to display the message looks like this:

---

### Macro 3-1. Message macro—A.

| Name | Macro | Comments |
|------|-------|----------|
| \m | {goto}MESSAGE˜ | Call screen into view |
| | /xmMENU˜ | Display menu |

---

How about giving some help? As much as possible, strive to make your menu choices descriptive and explanation lines clear. Beyond that you can replicate the menu choices onscreen accompanied by a longer explanation of each. Such a screen can be displayed automatically, or be available through a menu choice.

Screen 3-2 is a sample menu screen that provides this sort of extra explanation onscreen.

```
K1:                                                              CMD MENU
Pause  List-files  Select-diskette  Exit
You may now change diskettes in the drive.
           K        L        M        N        O        P        Q        R
 1
 2
 3
 4
 5     Pause                   Allows you to change diskettes in the right
 6                             hand drive prior to reviewing them.
 7
 8     List-files              Displays a list of worksheet files stored on
 9                             the current diskette, and shows available
10                             space remaining.
11
12     Select-diskette         Selects the current diskette for processing,
13                             and presents a menu of files stored there
14                             for retrieval.
15
16     Exit                    Returns to DOS to use other programs.
17
18
19
20
```

**Screen 3-2. Menu with help screen.**

The macro to implement this is the same as the one used in the prior example; the only difference lies in the extra information provided on the screen.

Note two things about this example:

- Each of the menu choices is replicated on the screen, and an explanation of each is given next to it.
- When two words are included as one menu choice, as in List-files, it's helpful to hyphenate them to avoid confusion when the menu displays. Without the hyphen, each word may appear to be a separate selection. Lotus uses this in the **Data Sort Data-range, Primary-key, Secondary-key** selections. Another alternative to using hyphens is to add spaces after each choice to spread them out.

A help screen can be displayed automatically (as shown in the example macro above), or treated as a menu option, to be called only when needed. Here's an example of a menu with one option being HELP:

## Macro 3-2. Message macro—B.

| Name | Macro | Comments | | |
|------|-------|----------|---|---|
| \m | {goto}MESSAGE˜ | Call screen into view | | |
| | /xmMENU˜ | Display menu | | |
| menu | post | save | help | |
| | post worksheet | save a file | obtain helpful information | |
| | /xgPOST˜ | /xgSAVE˜ | /xgHELP˜ | |

## Macro 3-2. Message macro—B (continued).

| Name | Macro | Comments |
|------|-------|----------|
| help | {goto}MESSAGE2~ | Display help screen |
|      | {?}~ | Pause for operator to read explanation |
|      | /xg\m~ | Return to menu screen |

The Range Name **MESSAGE2** used in the Help routine is located at the top right of a screen containing explanations of the menu shown. But in some applications even a full screen of text won't be sufficient. You'll want to offer the same type of menu driven help available in 1-2-3 itself. Using the **/xc** command, that's quite easy to do.

```
A2:                                                                    READY

         A          B              C                D              E
 1   \m         {goto}MESSAGE~  Call screen into view
 2              /xmMENU~        Display menu
 3              -------------------------------------------------------------
 4   menu       post            save            help
 5              post worksheet  save a file     obtain helpful information
 6              /xgPOST~        /xgSAVE~        /xcHELP1~
 7                                              /xg\m~
 8              -------------------------------------------------------------
 9   help1      {goto}MESSAGE1~ Display help screen 1
10              /xmHELPMEN~     Display help menu
11              -------------------------------------------------------------
12   helpmen    return          graph           print          save
13              return to menu  help with graphs help for printing help for savin
14              /xr             /xgHELP2~        /xgHELP3~      /xgHELP4~
15              -------------------------------------------------------------
16   help2      {goto}MESSAGE2~ Display help screen 2
17              /xmHELPMEN~     Display help menu
18              -------------------------------------------------------------
19   help3      {goto}MESSAGE3~ Display help screen 3
20              /xmHELPMEN~     Display help menu
```

**Screen 3-3. Help screen macros (Macro 3-3).**

Here's a step-by-step explanation:

1. The command in cell B2 displays the menu beginning in cell B4. An option on the menu is "help". This selection executes the command **/xcHELP1~**, which calls the subroutine found in cell B9.

2. The **HELP1** routine begins with a command to display a message screen. **MESSAGE1** is a celi at the top right of a screen containing explanations pertaining to the choices on the prior menu. The next command displays another menu, offering help on a wide range of operations used in this macro. It also contains a command called "return", to return to the original menu.

3. Each of the routines executed by menu choices displays a different screen of help messages, and redisplays the help menu. When "return" is selected, it executes the command `/xr`. This changes the flow of control to the command following `/xcHELP1~`, which orginally called the help subroutine. The next command, `/xg\m~`, redirects the macro once more, returning it to the main macro. This moves the screen back to the original message, and displays the main menu.

4. The important point about using the `/xc` command in cell D6 is the portability it provides for the entire help process. Any menu in this macro can now call the same help routines by including the command `/xcHELP1~`. After the operator has explored help screens to his satisfaction, the `/xr` command in cell B16 will return control to whichever menu issued the `/xc` command.

## Message Prompts

You don't always have to set up an entirely separate screen to display a message. If you'd like to maintain the current screen display as well as display a message, there are several options:

1. Place a message at the top of the screen.
2. Use a menu as a prompt.
3. Use a Worksheet Window.

A prompt may be particularly helpful when used with the **Range Input** command. Range Input allows you to define a range within which the operator may only make entries in unprotected cells. While Range Input is in operation, the cursor can ONLY be moved to the unprotected cells, and the arrow keys are used to move between unprotected cells. To terminate Range Input, the operator must press ENTER without making an entry first.

Despite these differences from the standard operating mode, there's no change in the READY indicator in the top right corner of the screen to indicate the special status of this operation. The operator is completely uninformed as to what's happening. This is a good place to use an onscreen prompt to avoid confusion. A simple one for Range Input operations is shown here:

```
============================================================================

Use the arrow keys to move between entries.  Press <ENTER> when done.


============================================================================
```

Prompting with Range Input is handled a bit differently than other operations, so we'll cover it first. Prior to executing this command, you must have Range Unprotected all data entry cells (they will be the only cells the operator will be able to move the cursor into). In the example below, the following cells have been unprotected: T20, V20, T22, V22, T24, V24, and T26. The message is in cells R15, R16, and R17. When the **Range Input** command is executed, it will prompt you for a range. Enter the range R15..V26. 1-2-3 will automatically position row 15 on the top line of the screen (displaying the message), and the cursor will move to the first unprotected cell, ready to begin data entry.

Since 1-2-3 will always position the top row of the Input range at the top of the screen during Range Input, always place your message on that line. Leave the message cells protected because you don't want the cursor to move to them.

The macro to handle this is extremely simple (the work is all in the preparation of the screen and in Range Unprotecting the proper cells):

| macro | comment |
|---|---|
| /riR15..V26~ | Range Input with range |

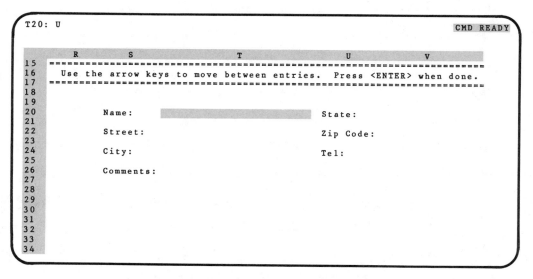

**Screen 3-4. Range Input Screen.**

Using a message for operations which don't use the Range Input command requires an extra step. Since Range Input does the work of adjusting the screen display to place the message at the top of the screen, we'll have to invent some routines to do that for us.

## Macro 3-4. Message macro—C.

| Name | Macro | Comment |
|---|---|---|
| | {home} | Reset screen |
| | {goto}R15~ | Position message at top of screen |

In the above routine, cell R15 contains a message (refer to the prior screen illustration). The purpose of this macro is to move the screen display so that the message is placed in the very top line of the screen, over the area that's to be posted. If this routine contained ONLY the command {goto}R15~, it would place the message at the top of the screen if cell R15 was not currently on the screen.

But what would happen if the cursor was on the same screen as cell R15 when the command {goto}R15~ is executed? The cursor will move, but the screen won't. If the message isn't on the top line of the screen, this command alone won't move it there. So, where there's any possibility the cursor will be on the same screen as cell R15 when you use this routine, you need to "reset" the screen with the {home}command first.

If the cursor is on the same screen as R15, the {home} command will move it to cell A1. Then when the command {goto}R15~ executes, the message will be placed at the top of the screen. The {home} command executes so quickly the operator won't even see it. The effect on the screen will be the same as when you use Range Input; the screen will suddenly shift so that the message is on the top line.

## Using Menus As Prompts

1-2-3's /xm command can also be used to create prompt messages in the control panel. Unlike the more conventional /xl and /xn prompts, these prompts do not accept operator input. The advantages are:

1.  The messages are in the control panel, leaving the entire worksheet operation on the screen.
2.  The macro automatically pauses, allowing the operator to take a moment to attend to printers or disks.
3.  They prevent the operators from writing anything on the worksheet, which could happen if you used the {?}~ command to pause the macro.

Let's look at an example of when this would be appropriate to use.

With some microcomputers, if you attempt to print with the printer off line or turned off, 1-2-3 will "hang up" (go into "WAIT" mode for an extended length of time). If you have printing routines in your macro, you may want to include a prompt to remind the operator to turn on the printer.

In the example below, the label "print" in cell S15 is a standard menu choice. When an operator selects "print", instead of directly executing a printing routine, the macro executes the /xm command found in cell S19. This command displays a custom menu with only one choice: "Make sure the printer is ON and ONLINE". The explanation line (in cell S22) says "Press ENTER when ready to proceed ...". The menu functions as a two-line prompt. Pressing ENTER executes the macro written in cell S23, which is the printing routine.

```
R28:                                                            CMD MENU
Make sure printer is ON and ONLINE
Press <ENTER> when ready to proceed...
           R         S             T             U           V
13   \m         /xmMENU1~                        Display main menu below
14
15   menul      print          enter          quit
16              print report   enter data     return to ready mode
17              /xgPRINT~       /xgENTRY~       /xq
18
19   print      /xmPRINT1~                      Display menu-prompt below
20
21   printl     Make sure printer is ON and ONLINE
22              Press <ENTER> when ready to proceed...
23              /ppagpq                         Print routine
24              /xg\M~                          Return to main menu
25
26
27
28
29
30              Budget Report
31
32              Department:
```

**Screen 3-5. Menu screen with prompt (Macro 3-5).**

Another place this kind of prompting is useful is prior to a macro-controlled Data Query operation. Data Query is case sensitive, so if an operator types the entry "Smith", a query typed in as "smith" won't locate the entry. One solution to this is to force all entries and queries to be made in capital letters. Before any Data Query operations, prompt the operator to press the CAPS LOCK key with a custom prompt.

In the example that follows, we'll show you how to enhance the prompt so that:

1. The operator only needs to press the space bar to continue macro operations.
2. The prompt line can extend across the entire control panel to provide a balanced appearance.

The example shows a custom prompt displayed through the /xmMENU~ command prior to a data base operation. The big difference between this example and the prior one is that the single menu entry has had 21 spaces inserted in front of it, and 20 spaces after it. In the macro, these spaces cause the line to appear as if it's written in the cell to the right; it is not.

Menus highlight the choice where the menu pointer rests. Since this is the only choice in the menu, the menu will display the entire line in inverse video, including the spaces before and after the text. The effect is of one continuous inverse video prompt across the entire top line of the control panel. It will stop just before the edge of the CMD MENU mode indicator in the top right corner of the screen.

To make your prompts display this way, just keep in mind there are 71 characters from the left border of the control panel to the edge of the CMD MENU indicator. Count the number of characters in your prompt, subtract it from 71, and divide the difference with spaces in front of and behind the prompt.

Once the operator has pressed CAPS LOCK, he can proceed with the macro by just touching the space bar, as the menu's "explanation line" points out. This is a nice convenience feature for a menu that serves as a prompt. How is it implemented? Think about it for a moment. You make a menu selection quickly by typing the first character of the selection. In this menu there's only one choice, and it begins with a space.

```
R2:                                                           CMD MENU
                    Please Press The CAPS LOCK Key
                - press the space bar when ready to proceed -
          R         S              T         U          V         W
 1    \a        /xmMENU~
 2
 3    menu                            Please Press The CAPS LOCK Key
 4                            - press the space bar when ready to proceed -
 5                /xmMENU1~
 6
 7    menu1       enter        find            sort       quit
 8                enter data   make inquiries  rearrange  READY mode
 9
10
11
12
13
14
15
16
17
18
19
20
```

**Screen 3-6. Menu screen with two prompts (Macro 3-6).**

## Displaying Messages With Windows

1-2-3's Worksheet Window command is another useful tool for displaying messages to an operator. It's best to use windows when:

1.  You want the message to stay onscreen during an operation, but . . .
2.  The worksheet area is so long that the message will scroll off the screen as the cursor moves down.

To make this work, the macro should move the cursor to the message, create a horizontal window, unsynchronize the windows, and then move the cursor to the area of the worksheet to be worked on. After the work is complete, the window is cleared and the cursor moved to the next work area. The following example uses a subroutine named MESSAGE to create the message on the screen for the insertion of data:

### Macro 3-6. Message macro—D.

| *Name* | *Macro* | *Comments* |
|--------|---------|------------|
| \a | /xcMESSAGE~ | 1. Call message subroutine |
| | /riDATA~ | 2. Show message during input |
| | /wwc{home}/xq | 3. Clear window, go home, quit |

——————————— DISPLAY MESSAGE ———————————

| | | |
|--------|---------|------------|
| message | {goto}MESSAGE1~{down} | 4. Move to message |
| | /wwh/wwu | 5. Create and unsynch windows |
| | {window}/xr | 6. Change windows, return |

Line 1 of the macro calls the subroutine to display the message beginning on line 4. Line 4 moves the screen to where the message is written on the worksheet, a range named MESSAGE1. Since cursor movement to a new screen always leaves the cursor on the top line of the screen, and 1-2-3 cannot create a horizontal window in that position, you must move the cursor down one row. Line 5 creates a horizontal window, and then unsynchronizes the windows. During data entry, the unsynchronize command allows the operator to move around the worksheet without scrolling the top window (and thus hiding the message displayed there).

This macro assumes that the message is written in one row. If the message is more than one line, you must add one more {down} command on line 4 for each additional line of the message. Otherwise the window won't include the extra lines of the message.

## Hiding Macro Operations Behind A Message

While the previous messages are designed to be displayed with the worksheet, some macro operations would be improved if they were completely hidden by a message. For instance, you may have a routine that does a lot of automated copying or posting on different parts of the worksheet. There's no

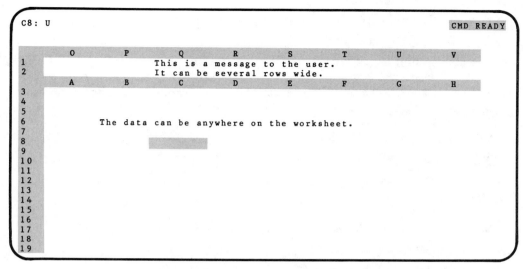

**Screen 3-7. Message with window.**

reason for the operator to watch the operation execute: it requires no input, and the display moves too quickly to be read anyway. Even though you may not want to display it, 1-2-3 forces the screen to follow the cursor wherever it goes, so you'll need some special techniques to prevent 1-2-3 from displaying everything. Here are two methods:

1. Use Range Names in operations such as Copy and Move to eliminate cursor movement.
2. Use an extension of the "message window" techniques to hide any activity you don't want the operator to see.

## Using Range Names To Eliminate Cursor Movement

Operations requiring worksheet range specifications (such as formula building, Copy, Move, and Print) can usually be given that information in one of two ways: either by typing in a location (with a cell address or Range Name), or by pointing to it.

Generally speaking, pointing to ranges is more effective for manual operations, because it's easier to point than it is to type cell coordinates. But the reverse is generally true of macros; they will generally run faster and smoother if you use the typing method.

A good example of that is found in the printing macros you've seen in this book. It's easier and faster to write a print range into a macro than to figure out a routine that points to it. When operations like Copy and Move come up, designate Range Names as both the "Copy from:" range and the "Copy to:" range. This will eliminate any cursor movement at all. It's often easier to Move a value from one range to another range than it is to {goto} the range with the cursor and enter the value directly.

Here are two macros that illustrate this difference. First, the inefficient method:

**Macro 3-8. Using the cursor to enter formulas.**

| Name | Macro | Comment |
|------|-------|---------|
| \a | {goto}A13~ | move to end of list |
|  | @sum($A$1..$A$12)~ | enter formula |
|  | {home}/xq | move HOME, quit |

This macro moves to cell A13, enters the formula @SUM($A$1..$A$12), and then moves the cursor to cell A1.

This next macro accomplishes the same result, without moving the cursor. The real difference in the second macro is the way the formula is written. In the first macro, the formula is a label so the macro can become a real formula when the macro enters it on the worksheet. In the second macro, the cell range named formula has a real formula entered in it. The macro Copies the formula to the designated location.

**Macro 3-9. Using Copy command to enter formulas.**

| \a | /cFORMULA~A13~ | copy formula to list |
|----|---------------|----------------------|
|  | /xq | quit |
| formula | 0      <---------- | @SUM($A$1..$A$12) |

## How To Hide Macro Activity

For the previous operation, you divided the screen horizontally. For this operation, you'll use 1-2-3's ability to split the screen vertically. But before it can be used, you'll have to format a message screen.

The message screen will have only two columns. The left column should be set to 71 spaces wide, the right column one space wide. Write your message in the middle row of the left column. Range Name the top left cell on the screen

TL (cell Y1 in the example). Range Name the bottom right cell on the screen BR (cell Z20 in the example). The message screen might look like the one shown in Screen 3-8.

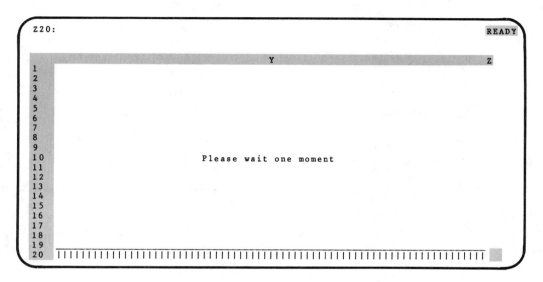

**Screen 3-8. Hide Screen.**

You'll notice we've placed some characters in the bottom two rows of the message screen. When the message routine executes, there will be inverse video borders around the left, top, and right borders of the screen. Without any inverse video border along the bottom, the characters we inserted help balance the screen's appearance. Cell Y20 contains the repeating label entry \¦ . Cell Y19 contains the repeating label \_ . These cells have both been Range Unprotected to make them display in bright intensity.

Here is the macro that uses the screen shown above to hide operations.

### Macro 3-10. "Hide" macro.

| Name | Macro | Comments |
|------|-------|----------|
| | | *Main Routine* |
| \a | /xcHIDE~ | 1. Call HIDE subroutine |
| | ... macro commands ... | 2. Show message, execute commands |
| | /xcUNHIDE~ | 3. Call UNHIDE routine |
| | {home}/xq | 4. Move to home, quit |

## Macro 3-10. "Hide" macro (continued).

| Name | Macro | Comments |
|------|-------|----------|
| | | *Hide Screen* |
| hide | {goto}TL˜ | 5. Move cursor to top left corner |
| | {goto}BR˜ | 6. Move cursor to bottom rt corner |
| | /wwv/wwu | 7. Create and unsynch windows |
| | {window}/xr | 8. Change windows, return to macro |
| | | *Unhide Screen* |
| UNHIDE | /wwc/wws | 9. Clear screen, synch windows |
| | /xr | 10. Return to main routine |

While processing the macro, the screen will look like the one in Screen 3-9.

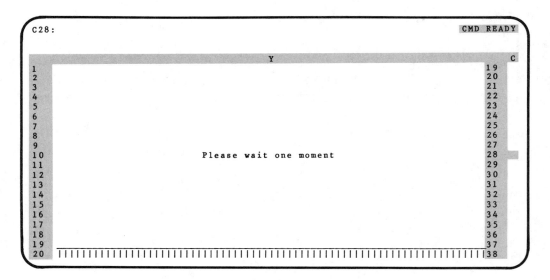

**Screen 3-9. Frozen Screen.**

Line 1 of the macro calls the Hide routine in preparation for macro activity you don't want the operator to see.

The Hide routine begins on line 5 by moving the cursor to the Top Left corner of the message screen. This command positions the screen to display the entire message.

Line 6 moves the cursor to the Bottom Right cell on the screen, Z20. This positions the cursor to split the window in the proper column.

Line 7 has two jobs: split the screen vertically and unsynchronize the resulting two windows. The left window will dominate the screen; the right window that you set to be one space wide will be barely visible. As soon as the windows are created in line 7, 1-2-3 will automatically move the cursor into the left window.

Line 8 moves the cursor back to cell Z20 in the right window. The cursor will barely be visible in the bottom of the one space wide window. At this point the cursor can be moved anywhere on the worksheet. Since the windows are unsynchronized, no movement will register on the large left window containing the message. All movement will register in the right window, but because it's so small, it will be almost unnoticeable to the operator. The /xr command now returns control to the main routine for posting operations to be carried out while the message is frozen onscreen in the large window.

Line 2 of the main routine is representative of whatever commands you might use to do posting, copying, or moving of data without showing it to the operator.

Line 3 calls the subroutine to clear the window.

Line 9 begins the subroutine to clear the window: it executes the Worksheet Window Clear command and resets the windows to be synchronized. It's not imperative to reset synchronization of windows, but that's the default value and you might want to leave it that way. If you don't reset it, the next time you create windows, they'll be unsynchronized from the start. Line 10 returns control to the main routine at line 4.

Line 4 returns the screen home and quits.

Note the design of this macro uses two separate subroutines. The contents of those subroutines could have been written into the main routine. Placing the window creation and clearing operations in subroutines allows any macro routine to call these routines just by including the commands /xcHIDE˜ and /xcUNHIDE˜ in the appropriate places.

## Full Screen Messages

A similar routine can also be used to display a full screen message with a nice inverse video frame surrounding the screen. There are three changes between this macro and the previous one. (1) There is no need to unsynchronize the windows. (2) You will not switch windows to remove the cursor from the screen. (3) The characters in the bottom rows of the screen are not needed.

```
V20:                                                              CMD MENU
 Enter   Find    Sort    Quit
 Enter data
                                      V                                  Z
 1                                                                      1
 2                                                                      2
 3                                                                      3
 4                 ***************************************              4
 5                 *                                     *              5
 6                 *      R. L. HENDRIES CORPORATION     *              6
 7                 *      PERSONNEL HISTORY DATABASE      *              7
 8                 *                                     *              8
 9                 ***************************************              9
10                                                                    10
11                                                                    11
12                                                                    12
13                 -------------------------------------             13
14                     To Return To The Main Menu                    14
15                       Press ALT M At Any Time                     15
16                 -------------------------------------             16
17                                                                    17
18                                                                    18
19                                                                    19
20                                                                    20
```

**Screen 3-10. Bordered message.**

If the top left cell on this screen was Range Named TL and the bottom right cell BR, this subroutine will display a bordered message:

**Macro 3-11. Bordered message macro.**

| *Name* | *Macro* | *Comments* |
|--------|---------|------------|
| message1 | {goto}TL~ | Call screen into view |
|          | {goto}BR~ | Position cursor for window creation |
|          | /wwv | Create window |
|          | /xr | Return to main routine |

The first three lines are the same as the previous macro. They position the screen and create vertical windows. After the windows have been created, the screen displays a perfect inverse video border around all four sides. 1-2-3's normal border frames the left and top sides of the screen. The vertical window creates another border along the left side. When the windows are created, the cursor moves from the bottom cell in the right window into the bottom cell in the left window. The bottom cell in that left window is 71 spaces wide, and the cursor expands to fill it in inverse video, forming the bottom border framing the screen.

## Enhancing Message Displays

If you are using onscreen messages, there's one other technique you can use to make them more effective. This technique solves two problems. While 1-2-3 screens lack much pizzazz in the way of special formats to enhance their appearance, it is possible to expand the cell pointer to display a message in inverse video. However, this results in the entire message being displayed in the top line of the control panel. When a custom menu or **/xl** prompt is displayed at the same time, the operator may become confused by all the entries there. The technique presented below solves both these problems nicely.

On a blank worksheet, here are the keystrokes needed to set up the message display:

| You press | Which means |
|---|---|
| **HOME** | Move to cell B1 |
| **RIGHT** | |
| **/wcs54** | Widen to 54 spaces |
| **ENTER** | |
| **GOTO a10** | Move to cell A10 |
| **ENTER** | |
| **(press the space bar 22 times)** | Enter blank spaces and. . . |
| **Please Choose One Of The Above** | . . . text in cell A10 |
| **ENTER** | |
| **RIGHT** | Move to B10 |

With your cursor in cell B10, you will see your prompt: "Please choose one of the above" displayed in inverse video. This prompt is used with a menu display, the "above" refers to the menu in the control panel. But look in the control panel now. You'll see it's clear—there's no entry displayed on the top line. That's because the label is actually entered in the cell to the left (A10).

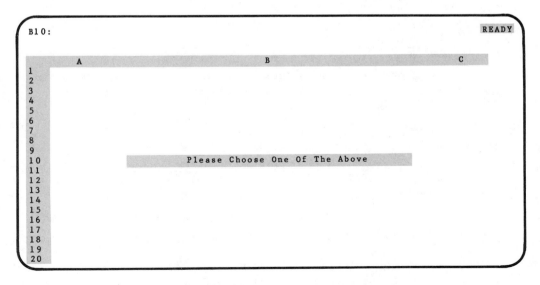

**Screen 3-11. Message with Clear Control panel.**

## Dealing With @DATE

The ability to perform arithmetic on dates is a very strong feature of 1-2-3. But with this added power comes a problem: in order to use date arithmetic, you must enter dates as an @function. Here's an example of how you'd write July 4, 1984: `@date(84,7,4)`.

@Date takes the form: @DATE(year,month,day), an entry many people find cumbersome to use. Not only is it long, but Americans are used to writing dates in the order "month-day-year"—we find 1-2-3's order difficult to remember. You can have the best of both worlds with some simple macro routines to handle the @date functions, while allowing operators to use familiar methods of entering dates.

Macro 3-12 is a routine you can use to make date entries a lot easier.

### Macro 3-12. Date entry macro.

| Name | Macro | Comment |
|------|-------|---------|
| \d | `/xlPlease enter month: ~MONTH~` | Prompted data.. |
| | `/xlPlease enter day: ~DAY~` | ...entry... |
| | `/xlPlease enter year (2 digits): ~YEAR~` | ...sequence. |
| | `@date(` | Begin formula. |
| year | | ...Year... |
| | `,` | Req'd comma |
| month | | ...Month... |
| | `,` | Req'd comma |
| day | | ...Day... |
| | `)~` | Close formula |
| | `/rfd2~/xq` | Format cell |

As always, when you see macro Range Names entered in the names column, your first step is to use the **Range Name Labels Right** command sequence to name the macro cells to their right.

This macro should be used with the cursor positioned on the cell in which the date is to be entered. The routine above uses `/xl` statements to get a date from the user and enter the date numbers in the appropriate locations farther down in the macro. Since the numbers entered in response to the prompts will become part of the macro, they MUST be label entries. Thus, the prompts must use `/xl`, not `/xn`.

The fourth line of the macro begins writing the @DATE formula, using the numbers supplied by the data entry sequence. The tilde at the end of the @DATE sequence enters the formula into the current worksheet cell. The final line of the macro formats the worksheet cell as Range Format Date 2 (Month/Day format). This format is recommended because it can display the date using the standard nine space wide 1-2-3 column width. You could use the Day/Month/Year format (the command for that is **/rfd1˜**), but you'll need to add the macro code **/wcs10˜** to make sure the column width is at least ten spaces to accommodate it.

Another method for writing @DATE formulas may be more helpful when your application requires a lot of them. Instead of using **/xl** commands, this method uses a simple onscreen layout, set up so operators can enter a date in the order they usually use, as shown in the left half of the screen below. A Range Input command can put the entry of the dates under macro control. This would require Range Unprotecting columns A, C, and E.

To clean up the screen, you may wish to place the @DATE functions off the screen entirely, and reference them for your date arithmetic.

```
A3:                                                                 READY

         A      B      C     D     E         F             G              H
 1    Month  /      Day   /     Year
 2    -------------------------------
 3                /            /             @DATE(E3,A3,C3)
 4                /            /             @DATE(E4,A4,C4)
 5                /            /             @DATE(E5,A5,C5)
 6                /            /             @DATE(E6,A6,C6)
 7                /            /             @DATE(E7,A7,C7)
 8                /            /             @DATE(E8,A8,C8)
 9                /            /             @DATE(E9,A9,C9)
10                /            /             @DATE(E10,A10,C10)
11                /            /             @DATE(E11,A11,C11)
12                /            /             @DATE(E12,A12,C12)
13                /            /             @DATE(E13,A13,C13)
14
15
16
17
18
19
20
```

**Screen 3-12. Date screen.**

Now that you can control your screens, it's time to learn more about menus so that you can make effective use of all of your macros. Menus can do more than you suspect, as we show in the next section.

# 3.2  Menu Techniques or How To Get More Mileage From Your Menus

In this section we'll discuss menu design, how to structure systems of menus, how to create oversized menus, and then present some innovative ways menus can be used.

## *Menu Design*

### Worksheet Design

You can make the process of writing custom menus a lot simpler if you do some worksheet formatting for your macros first. This will allow all of your menus and macros to be written in the same columns of the worksheet, making them much easier to understand and edit. Because we are going to vary column widths, select columns for your macros that aren't used by your application. The number of spaces for each column is shown at the top of the example worksheet below:

```
A1:                                                                    READY

            A         B         C         D         E         F         G         H         I    J
 1
 2    column widths:
 3        8         8         8         8         8         8         8         8         7    1
 4
 5
 6    menu choices:
 7    (name         1         2         3         4         5         6         7         8)
 8
 9    menu1     view      data      file      sort      edit      print     help      quit
10
11
12    macros:
13    (name     macro                         comments)
14    \m        /xmMENU1~                      display main menu
15
16
17
18
19
20
```

**Screen 3-13. Worksheet layout for menus and macros (Macro 3-13).**

This format allows eight spaces for the left hand "Name" column, which will require you to keep your range names fairly brief to have them fully displayed. But all eight menu choices can be contained in one screen, with eight characters of each menu choice displayed (the eight spaces only affect the display of the macro code ... it has no effect on how the menu will display when the macro executes).

We made the ninth column seven spaces wide, and the tenth one space. The menu in the ninth column can overwrite that last space to display a choice. The Tenth column is there to help prevent errors. This single space column acts as a "menu buffer". In writing menus using the maximum eight choices, we occasionally ran into unexpected trouble.

If eight menu choices are entered in B3..I3, then any entry in J3 will exceed the allowable limits for menu size. The menu would try to read the entry, and exceed the eight allowable choices. But since J3 would normally be on the next screen, hidden from the menu range in B3..H3, we occasionally made entries there without realizing it would affect the menu. The next time the macro executed the menu, we'd get an "Illegal menu" error message. Keeping column J as a one cell wide "buffer" for the menu range eliminates this problem.

Admittedly, not all of your macros are going to use eight menu choices, but this format will allow you to prevent any problems when they do. Here's a small utility macro that does the formatting for you. Place your cursor in the left column of the screen before executing it.

---

**Macro 3-14. Format menu columns.**

| Name | Macro | Comment |
|------|-------|---------|
| \f | /rncHERE~~ | Set marker |
| | /wcs8~{right}/wcs8~{right} | Format columns |
| | /wcs8~{right}/wcs8~{right} | . |
| | /wcs8~{right}/wcs8~{right} | . |
| | /wcs8~{right}/wcs8~{right} | . |
| | /wcs7~{right}/wcs1~ | for menus |
| | {goto}HERE~/rndHERE~/xq | Return to marker, delete |

---

## Using Menus in Innovative Ways

Section 3.1 showed you how to create custom prompts using the /xm command. In this section we'll present some other unusual ways menus can help improve your macros:

1. You can include a prompt within a menu, and use it to disable the default menu choice, preventing accidental execution of a critical operation (like a Range Erase).
2. Macro menus can totally disable the Escape key, preventing it from causing both macro and menu to "crash".
3. You can build multi-level menus that work in the same manner 1-2-3's command menus work: when you press the Escape key, the previous menu will display.
4. Menus can be used to help the operator in other ways as well. Choices can be executed by number instead of by letter (numbers are easier for non-typists to find on a keyboard), and menus can provide onscreen HELP explanations for more complex choices.

## *Protecting A Critical Choice*

In situations where operators must make a critical decision, such as whether or not to update (save) a file, you don't want any risk that they will accidentally press a key and execute the wrong choice. Usually the most frequently executed choice is placed in the "default" menu position. The default choice is the one farthest to the left, where the menu pointer will automatically rest when the menu is displayed. All that's needed to execute this choice is to press **ENTER**.

One sure way to get into trouble is to place an important choice in the default position. NEVER do this. You are inviting someone to mistakenly execute it by resting a finger on the **ENTER** key.

You could shift an unimportant choice to the default position, but what if EACH CHOICE is an important one? How do you safeguard a menu such as this? The answer is to disable the default choice by making it into a simple prompt, with all the choices in the seven positions to the right. Macro 3-15 is an example.

---

**Macro 3-15. Disabled default menu choice.**

| *Name* | *Macro* | | |
|--------|---------|---|---|
| macro2 | /xmMENU2~ | | |
| | | | |
| menu2 | pause | save | return |
| | please choose | save the file | continue processing |
| | /xgMACRO2~ | /xgMACRO3~ | /xgMACRO4~ |

---

Look at the far left choice "pause" for a moment. If you select it, the macro executes the command /xgMACRO2~, redirecting the flow of control back to the cell containing the command /xmMENU2~. Since /xmMENU2~ will redisplay the menu all over again, it acts as a loop, effectively disabling the default menu choice. The "pause" selection acts not as a menu choice, but a prompt. Since it's the default choice (in the far left position in the menu range) the explanation line beneath it displays automatically, prompting the user to "please choose".

For real caretakers, here's another point. You know any menu choice can be executed by pressing its first letter (if each choice begins with a unique letter). If a menu choice calls another menu, ensure the second menu does not use that same first letter to execute a critical choice. If the operator presses too hard on that letter in the first menu, the second menu's critical choice will execute before it can be stopped.

## *Disabling The Escape Key*

One of the inherent problems of macro menus relates to the **ESCAPE** key; it makes them "crash". Try it. Put up a menu and press the **ESCAPE** key — the macro will end. And if you use the kind of macro design we often use in this book (with the menu text written just below the **/xm** statement), you'll discover another unpleasantry. The macro will try to write the next cell of the macro below the **/xm** statement on the worksheet. And if the cursor happens to be on some data, you'll find the data's been overwritten. Trouble? Relax—here's why that happens and how to fix it.

When a macro reads an **/xm** command, it pauses to display the custom menu. The flow of control has stopped right on the **/xm** command, waiting for the operator to make a choice. If the operator presses the **ESCAPE** key, it makes the macro "jump" the **/xm** command, and continue reading the VERY next thing it comes to—as a macro. If the very next thing it comes to is a blank cell, the macro will terminate. That's the way we've been advising you to write menus until now.

But if you didn't leave a blank space and the next thing the macro reads is the label of the first menu choice (written in the cell below the **/xm** command), the macro will read that text as it would any other text entry. It'll keep reading down the column until it encounters a tilde. The tilde will cause the entire text to be entered on the worksheet as a label (overwriting whatever may have been in the current cell).

Neither of these situations is very desirable, so this is how to disable the **ESCAPE** key completely. Here is a standard menu.

| Name | Macro | Comment | | |
|------|-------|---------|---|---|
| \b | /xmMENU~ | Display custom menu below | | |
| menu | enter | save | print | quit |
| | enter data | save file | print sheet | return |

To disable the Escape key, add a command to the first line of the macro:

### Macro 3-16. Disabled Escape key.

| Name | Macro | Comment | | |
|------|-------|---------|---|---|
| \b | /xmMENU~/xg\b~ | Display custom menu below and disable Escape | | |
| menu | enter | save | print | quit |
| | enter data | save file | print sheet | return |

You already know that when a menu is displayed in the control panel, the macro flow of control has stopped on the **/xm** command. If the operator presses the **ESCAPE** key, the flow of control jumps the /xm command and reads the very next thing it encounters.

In the revised example above, another command has been added to the first line of the macro: /xg\b~. If the operator presses **ESCAPE**, the macro jumps the /xm command and executes the command /xg\b~. This loops the flow of control back to reread the same cell. The macro rereads the instruction /xmMENU~, and the menu displays again.

After instituting this change, you no longer have to place empty cells after the /xm command.

## Using the Escape Key to Call Prior Menus

Just as 1-2-3's menu choice **Worksheet** calls another menu choice, you may have already written custom menus that call other custom menus. You can also make the **ESCAPE** key work the same way in your menus as it does in 1-2-3: to call the previous menu.

Macro 3-17 is an example:

### Macro 3-17. Menu using the Escape key to call prior menus.

| Name | Macro | Comment | |
|------|-------|---------|---|
| \a | /xmMENU~/xg\a~ | Display menu & loop to disable Escape | |
| menu | enter | print | quit |
| | make entries | print reports | end menu |
| | /xgMACRO1~ | /xgMACRO2~ | /xgMACRO3~ |
| macro1 | /xmMENU1~/xg\a~ | Display menu & return to prior menu | |
| menu1 | sales | purchases | expenses |
| | select report | select report | select report |
| | /xgMACRO4~ | /xgMACRO5~ | /xgMACRO6~ |
| macro4 | /xmMenu4~/xgMACRO1~ | Display menu & return to prior menu | |
| menu4 | month | quarter | year |
| | monthly report | quarterly report | annual report |
| | /xgMACRO7~ | /xgMACRO8~ | /xgMACRO9~ |

The instruction to call the top menu is written in the cell named \a.

One of the menu choices, enter, calls the routine macro1, which displays another menu. macro1 contains the command /xmMENU1~/xg\a~. You already know you can use an /xg command right after an /xm command to loop back to the same cell, thereby disabling the **ESCAPE** key. In this case, we're using a variation of that same idea with the command /xg\a~. Instead of looping back to the SAME cell, the instruction loops back to **\a**. **\a** contains the command calling the previous menu.

In turn, the **sales** selection will call MACRO4. The **/xm** command here will display another menu, and it will return to the previous menu, MACRO1, if **ESCAPE** is pressed. Thus, these macros mimic normal 1-2-3 menus by allowing movement up and down the menu structure through use of the **ESCAPE** key.

## Making Life Easier For Non-Typists

If you're writing macros for someone who doesn't type well (could be you), try putting a number in front of every choice. It's a lot easier for a non-typist to find a number along the top row of the keyboard than to find letters on the QWERTY keyboard. See Macro 3-18.

**Macro 3-18. Menu using numbers.**

| Name | Macro | Comment | |
|------|-------|---------|---|
| \a | /xmMENU~/xg\a~ | Display menu, disable Escape | |
| menu | 1. Enter | 2. Print | 3. Quit |
| | make entries | print reports | end menu |
| | /xgMACRO1~ | /xgMACRO2~ | /xgMACRO3~ |

The adjustment you should make with this menu is to capitalize the first letter of each menu choice. You may have noticed that 1-2-3 will capitalize the first character of each menu choice and explanation. Since we've used a number as the first character of each choice, you'll need to capitalize the word that follows.

## Menu Structures

1-2-3's **/xm** command allows a maximum of eight menu choices, but for complex worksheets, that may not be enough. There are two ways you can deal with this:

1.  Have menu choices call other menus.
2.  Create a special large menu without the **/xm** command.

We have just shown how to have menu choices call other menus in the previous segment. Before moving on to showing you large menus, we'd like to clarify a couple of design considerations for this kind of menu.

There are two approaches to adding extra choices to a menu, and 1-2-3's command menus use both of them. The first type of menu displays general subject headings on the first level: choices like Range, File, Graph, Data, and

Print on 1-2-3's main menu. Beneath each of these is a group of related choices pertaining to the main subject heading.

The second method deals with additional choices that are essentially unrelated to one another. In this case, place those options under a menu choice called "More". In 1-2-3's **Print Printer Options** menu, there's a choice like this; it's called Other, and includes several choices unrelated to the other items on the Options menu. The Worksheet command on 1-2-3's main menu functions in this capacity as well. The choices beneath it are essentially unrelated to one another.

With so many menus and menu choices, you may find you can keep the macro routines organized more effectively if you adopt a macro naming convention. In simple macros, it's appropriate to give a routine the name of the menu choice that executes it. Thus, the choice "Sort" executes the command */xgSORT~*, sending the macro to a routine called SORT. Using names like this eliminates any doubt about what this routine does or what menu choice called it.

Complex systems of macros may benefit from a convention where each routine is given a number. In the "Using The Escape Key" section above, consecutive numbers were assigned to each macro. As the system grows, there needs to be a method to keep track of which chain of the system the macro is in, and which menu called it. There are several numbering conventions that can help with this problem.

**Macro 3-19. Macro numbering convention.**

| *Name* | *Macro* | | *Comment* | |
|---|---|---|---|---|
| \a | /xmMENU~/xg\a~ | | | |
| menu | sort | find | report | |
| | sort records | locate records | create reports | |
| | /xgMAC1~ | /xgMAC2~ | /xgMAC3~ | |
| | | | | |
| mac1 | /xmMENU1~/xg\A~ | | | |
| menu1 | ascending | descending | reverse | |
| | order of sort | order of sort | put back in order | |
| | /xgMAC10~ | /xgMAC11~ | /xgMAC12~ | |
| | | | | |
| mac2 | /xmMENU2~/xg\A~ | | | |
| menu2 | sales | purchases | budget | |
| | monthly sales | monthly purchases | budget reports | |
| | /xgMAC21~ | /xgMAC22~ | /xgMAC23~ | |
| | | | | |
| mac23 | /xmMENU23~/xgMAC2~ | | | |
| menu23 | monthly | quarterly | annual | |
| | monthly budget | quarterly budget | annual budget | |
| | /xgMAC231~ | /xgMAC232~ | /xgMAC233~ | |

You can call the macros MAC***, and call the menus the same number as the macro that invoked it, MENU***. For example, the first menu choice of the main menu (MENU) calls the macro named MAC1. MAC1 calls MENU1. Macros called by MENU1 would start with MAC10, then proceed to MAC11, MAC12 and so on. Macros called by MAC10 would start with MAC100 and proceed to MAC101, MAC102, and so on.

The suggested 10 column format for the macro area works well with this method. By placing the macros right under the menus that call them, the structure of the system is visually apparent. Here is a diagram of a typical menu system.

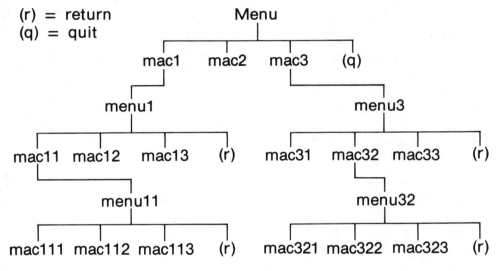

**Diagram 3-1. A menu tree.**

## Returning Back Up Through The Menus

You've already seen how to use the Escape key to return the flow of control from a subsidiary menu back to the main menu. (If your menus are crowded, that may be the only method of returning that you offer to the operator.) But consider at least one other approach: provide a menu choice to execute that function.

Think about 1-2-3's approach to this for a moment. In the **Print Printer Options** menu, the choice Quit will return you from the Options menu to the main Print menu. Pressing **Escape** has the same effect as the Quit choice—but it's helpful to provide this choice when an operator will want to be able to back up, and it will make your menus easier to use.

This is simple to implement. Add a "Quit" or "Return" choice to the menu, and enter the macro command that will call the previous menu macro.

## Creating Large Menus

1-2-3's macros provide other, less obvious ways of displaying menu options to an operator. These methods can't match the elegance of the custom menus created with the /xm command, but they are a more effective way of displaying many more than eight choices onscreen at one time.

The first method, described below, uses /xi commands to test a number (representing the item selected). A user selects the number from a screen of possible choices. The second method is described in Section 4.1, and uses the Data Query commands of 1-2-3. Although it is more complex, it executes much faster. The worksheet for this chapter on the book diskette offers 36 choices on one screen!

A large menu (as we'll call it) requires that you format a screen with remarks describing each menu choice. Since the operator will make selections by entering a number, each menu choice must display a unique number alongside. A sample menu screen showing choices of twelve monthly sales analyses is shown below.

```
A1:                                                              CMD EDIT
Please select a number

        A       B       C       D       E       F       G       H
 1
 2              * * *   M E N U    O P T I O N S   * * *
 3
 4      --------------------------------------------------------------
 5                      -  SALES ANALYSES FOR 1984 -
 6
 7      1)  JANUARY                      7)  JULY
 8
 9      2)  FEBRUARY                     8)  AUGUST
10
11      3)  MARCH                        9)  SEPTEMBER
12
13      4)  APRIL                       10)  OCTOBER
14
15      5)  MAY                         11)  NOVEMBER
16
17      6)  JUNE                        12)  DECEMBER
18
19
20
```

**Screen 3-14. Large menu.**

The top left cell in this screen should be given a range name. In this case, we'll assume the range name "MENUSCREEN" has been assigned to that cell.

Here is the macro to display the screen, prompt the operator for a numeric choice, and execute the choice:

---

**Macro 3-20. Long menu—A.**

| Name | Macro | Comment |
|------|-------|---------|
| \a | `{goto}MENUSCREEN~` | Display menu screen |
|  | `/xnPlease select a number: ~CHOICE~` | Prompt for choice |
|  | `/xiCHOICE=1~/frJAN~` | Process choice... |
|  | `/xiCHOICE=2~/frFEB~` | . |
|  | `/xiCHOICE=3~/frMAR~` | . |
|  | `/xiCHOICE=4~/frAPR~` | . |
|  | `/xiCHOICE=5~/frMAY~` | . |
|  | `/xiCHOICE=6~/frJUN~` | . |
|  | `/xiCHOICE=7~/frJUL~` | . |
|  | `/xiCHOICE=8~/frAUG~` | . |
|  | `/xiCHOICE=9~/frSEP~` | . |
|  | `/xiCHOICE=10~/frOCT~` | . |
|  | `/xiCHOICE=11~/frNOV~` | . |
|  | `/xiCHOICE=12~/frDEC~` | . |
| choice |  | Operator selection |

---

In the macro above the first line displays the menu screen. The second line uses the `/xn` command to display a custom prompt and enter the operator's response as a value in the location Range Named CHOICE. The function of the cell named CHOICE is to store the value so it can be used by subsequent macro commands.

The heart of the macro is the twelve `/xi` commands that follow. Each command tests the cell CHOICE to determine if it holds a certain value. The commands begin by testing for the number one, and work their way up to twelve. If the operator input is not equal to one, the first `/xi` command skips the remaining commands on the same line and passes control to the following line. Line by line, the macro tests the operator input until it finds a match, then executes the routine that follows the `/xi` command. In this macro, the routines retrieve a different file, one for each month. If the operator's input was 3, then the command `/xiCHOICE=3~` will be evaluated as true, and the macro will execute the remaining instruction on that line: `/frMAR~` (File Retrieve the file named MAR).

Since the instruction retrieves a new worksheet file, the macro will terminate when the other worksheet is retrieved. That's why no `/xq` commands are used in the macro. But that poses another problem. What happens if the operator mistakenly enters a number that doesn't match any available choice (such as 13)?

This macro has no provision for handling that possibility. The following example shows that a slight modification to the macro will trap the error.

## Macro 3-21. Long menu—B.

| *Name* | *Macro* | *Comment* |
|--------|---------|-----------|
| \a | {goto}MENUSCREEN~ | Display menu screen |
| | /xnPlease select a number: ~CHOICE~ | Prompt for choice |
| | /xiCHOICE=1~/frJAN~ | Process choice... |
| | /xiCHOICE=2~/frFEB~ | . |
| | /xiCHOICE=3~/frMAR~ | . |
| | /xiCHOICE=4~/frAPR~ | . |
| | /xiCHOICE=5~/frMAY~ | . |
| | /xiCHOICE=6~/frJUN~ | . |
| | /xiCHOICE=7~/frJUL~ | . |
| | /xiCHOICE=8~/frAUG~ | . |
| | /xiCHOICE=9~/frSEP~ | . |
| | /xiCHOICE=10~/frOCT~ | . |
| | /xiCHOICE=11~/frNOV~ | . |
| | /xiCHOICE=12~/frDEC~ | . |
| menu | /xmTRAP~/xgMENU~ | Display message |
| trap | Illegal number entry... Choose only one of the numbers listed Press <ENTER> when ready to proceed. | |
| | /xg\a~ | |
| choice | | Operator selection |

Four lines have been added to the bottom of the main macro routine. In the first cell, Range Named MENU, there's an **/xm** command to display the custom menu contained in the cell below, named TRAP. The **/xgMENU~** command that follows on the same line is a loop to disable the **ESCAPE** key.

The menu written below is a prompt-menu, and it will only display if the operator's input matches none of the numbers in the **/xi** commands above. In this case, the operator has made an illegal number input, and the menu prompt displays telling him so. When the operator is ready, pressing the **ENTER** key will execute the command **/xg\a~**. This is a loop to the top of the routine, redisplaying the prompt for a numeric selection from the menu.

The next section on looping shows the power of 1-2-3. The ability to automate the execution of a macro sequence turns your worksheets from merely being useful, into incredible workhorses.

# 3.3 Looping and Self-Modifying Macros

Much of the power of any computer lies in its ability to automate repetitive tasks. For example, a bank's computer processes hundreds of thousands of checks—basically a simple process of charging an account for the amount of a check and remitting the amount to the payee.

Repetitive operations such as these are accomplished with a process known as a "loop". In the case of the bank operation, the tasks included in the loop might be: (1) The first check is examined for the amount and account. (2) The account is found, and if there is money in it, charged for the amount of the check. (3) The next check is selected. This constitutes one cycle of the loop, which is repeated for each check to be processed. When the computer detects no more checks to be posted, the loop terminates.

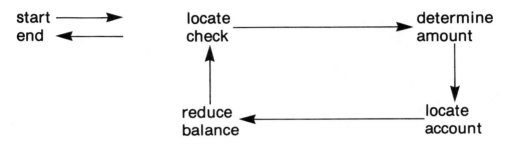

**Diagram 3-2. The activity of a sample loop.**

A loop is a very efficient data processing tool. But loops aren't the sole province of professional programmers. You can and should use them in macros because they are one of the keys to automating a worksheet.

## Creating A Simple Loop

The simplest type of macro loop is also very simple to create. Place an **/xg** command at the end of a macro, redirecting the flow of control back to the beginning of the macro, so it will execute the commands again. Each time it comes to the end and reads the **/xg** command, it'll repeat itself.

This simple posting macro is an example of a loop. The macro pauses for operator input, moves down one cell, and repeats. It allows the use of the numeric keypad while entering data when using an IBM style keyboard.

---

**Macro 3-22. Simple loop.**

| Name | Macro | Comment |
|------|-------|---------|
| \a | {?}~ | Pause for data entry |
| | {down} | Move down to next cell |
| | /xg\A~ | Repeat |

---

The user places the cursor at the top of the column where the items will be posted. The macro will first pause for data entry. Line 2 will move the cursor down to the next cell. Since cursor movement is handled by the macro, the operator can set NUM LOCK on and use the numeric keypad exclusively for data entry. Line 3 redirects the flow of control back to the first cell, named **\a**. The data entry and cursor movement commands will then be repeated. This is an endless loop. There's nothing to stop it built into the macro. It must either be terminated by the operator (pressing **Ctrl-Break** will terminate any macro), or it will continue down the column until insufficient memory causes an error.

While functional, the type of loop described above could be enhanced a great deal with one addition: an **/xi** command. **/xi** tests a logical formula to see if it is true or false, and carries out a set of instructions if it's true. If the formula is false, the set of instructions will be ignored. The macro will continue in the next cell down.

In the example of the bank processing checks, the **/xi** command might test to see if the number of checks left to be processed was greater than zero. As long as the macro finds that formula true, it would execute a loop to process another check. When the formula is found to be false (there are no more checks) then the instruction to loop is bypassed and the macro moves on to another routine.

There are several ways an **/xi** command might be applied to our posting example. We'll present one of them here. Suppose you have ten entries to make at this location on the worksheet. After each loop, we'll use the @COUNT function to count the number of entries made. When that number reaches ten, the macro will terminate. In preparation for using the macro, we'll create a one-column range of ten cells named DATACELLS in which to post the entries. This Range Name will be written into the counting formula. In addition, since the counting formula counts all cells with entries in them, the macro begins with a command to erase the range to be posted to be sure there is no data in the area when it starts.

### Macro 3-23. Loop with test.

| Name | Macro | Comment |
|------|-------|---------|
| \a | {goto}DATACELLS~ | Position cursor to begin |
| | /reDATACELLS~ | Erase range of cells |
| Loop | /xi@count(DATACELLS)=10~{home}/xq | End if complete |
| | {?}~ | Pause for data entry |
| | {down} | Move down one cell |
| | /xgLOOP~ | Repeat lines 3–6 |

The macro is divided into two parts: setup and repeating instructions. We do not wish to repeat the setup portion, so the Range Name LOOP is established at the point where looping is to begin. The /xg command will then bypass the first part of the macro code.

Another enhancement you can make to this macro involves a special feature of the /xl and /xn commands. You already know that these commands are used to display a custom prompt and enter the operator's entry in a designated cell on the worksheet. We'll assume we're dealing with numeric input in this example, so we'll use the /xn command. Its normal format is: /xn[prompt]~[location]~ where [prompt] is a message of no more than 39 characters, and [location] is either a cell address or named range.

However, the command may also use this format: /xn[prompt]~~. In this case, the location for the data to be entered on the worksheet will be the current location of the cursor when the macro executes the command. In order to add a custom prompt to the posting macro, we will use this modified format of /xn. Since the macro moves the cursor down one cell with each loop, the cursor will always be positioned correctly to enter data. Here's the new macro:

## Macro 3-24. Loop with message.

| Name | Macro | Comment |
|------|-------|---------|
| \a | {goto}DATACELLS~ | Position cursor to begin |
| | /reDATACELLS~ | Erase range of cells |
| loop | /xi@count(DATACELLS)=10~{home}/xq | End if complete |
| | /xnPlease enter a number: ~~ | Prompt for data entry |
| | {down} | Move down one cell |
| | /xgLOOP~ | Repeat lines 3-6 |

This macro will work fine for a situation where you know how many items will be entered. What if you are processing different numbers of entries each time? One way to stop the macro is to test the last entry to see if it is a certain value. If so, the macro can quit or perform some other operation. A unique number must be used, or one of your entries will stop the macro! We will use the number .9999 for this next example.

## Macro 3-25. Loop with test.

| Name | Macro | Comment |
|------|-------|---------|
| \a | /rncTEST~~/rndTEST~/rncTEST~~ | Initialize pointer |
| loop | /xnEnter a number (.9999 to quit) ~~ | Prompt for data entry |
| | /xiTEST=.9999~/re~/rndTEST~/xq | If end: erase, delete name |
| | {down} | Move down one cell |
| | /rndTEST~/rncTEST~~ | Set pointer |
| | /xgLOOP~ | Repeat lines 2-6 |

Place the cursor on the first item. Line 1 initializes the pointer by making sure the Range Name TEST does not exist elsewhere on the worksheet. The prompt in line 2 also tells what to enter to stop the macro. If .9999 is entered by the user, line 3 erases the number, deletes the Range Name, and the macro quits. If not, the cursor will move down, the name TEST will be given to the new cell, and the macro loops.

## Using A Counter

The macros shown above are fine for data applications, and they certainly execute rapidly. But some looping macros, such as printing multiple worksheet copies, can't very well count data cells or test entries to know how many times they should repeat. For these applications a counter can be used.

In the example that follows, the macro begins by prompting the operator for the number of copies of a worksheet to be printed. This number is entered in a cell range named LIMIT. Each time the macro prints a worksheet copy, it increments a value in another cell, range named COUNTER. Before each printing operation, an /xi command tests to see if the value in COUNTER is equal to the value in LIMIT. If the formula is false, then the macro prints another copy of the worksheet and increments the COUNTER cell again. When the /xi command determines the value in COUNTER is equal to the value in LIMIT, making the formula true, the macro terminates.

**Macro 3-26. Loop with counter.**

| Name | Macro | Comment |
|---|---|---|
| \a | /reCOUNTER~ | Clear counter cell |
| | /xnPlease enter number of copies: ~LIMIT~ | Get number |
| Loop | /xiLIMIT=COUNTER~/xq | End if limit is reached |
| | /ppcrr | Clear prior print range |
| | A1..H74 | Set print range |
| | ~agpq | Print and advance page |
| | /df | Data fill counter cell |
| | COUNTER~ | Data fill range |
| | COUNTER+1~ | Start value |
| | ~~ | Default step/stop values |
| | /xgLOOP~ | Repeat |
| limit | | Limit value |
| counter | | Counter value |

Since the cell named COUNTER will be incremented to record the number of loops the macro performs, it should start off with no entry. The first line ensures that it does by erasing the range COUNTER.

Line 2 of the macro prompts the user for the number of copies he wishes to print and enters that value in the cell range named LIMIT. Note that an /xn command is used for prompting because the number of printing copies must be entered on the worksheet as a value entry. This value will subsequently be tested by a formula.

Line 3 evaluates a logical formula to determine if it's true or false. That formula, LIMIT=COUNTER, compares the number of times the macro has looped (recorded in COUNTER) with the number of times the operator wanted it to loop (recorded in LIMIT). When the formula is true, the /xi command will direct the flow of control to the remaining commands on the same line: /xq — the macro terminates. If the formula is false, the macro skips directly from the /xi command to the next line of the macro.

Line 4 executes the beginning of the printing routine: clearing any prior print range. Line 5 provides the new range, and line 6 executes the printing operation. As with the earlier examples, the print range has been isolated on its own line so it can be modified easily. In fact, an /xl command added at the top of the macro could easily prompt the operator to supply this range.

Line 7 uses the 1-2-3 **Data Fill** command to increment the COUNTER cell by 1 after each printing operation. This means that every time a worksheet is printed, the number in COUNTER will increase by 1. The **Data Fill** command enters values into a worksheet range according to specific settings, or parameters. Here are those parameters, and the default settings 1-2-3 will give them if you don't specify otherwise:

| *Command:* | *Parameter:* | *Default Value:* |
|---|---|---|
| Data Fill | *Fill range:* the range of wkst cells to be filled with values. | The current cell, or the last fill range used. |
| | *Start value:* the value to be entered in the first cell of the Fill Range. | 0 |
| | *Step value:* that amount to increment each succeeding cell, beginning with the Start value. | 1 |
| | *Stop value:* the maximum value to be entered in the Fill Range. If Data Fill reaches this value before filling the entire range, it will stop. Otherwise, the entire Fill Range will be filled with incremental values. | 2047 |

Now we'll apply that to the command in Lines 7-10:

/df executes **Data Fill**. COUNTER~ specifies the Fill Range as a single cell. The Start Value to be entered in COUNTER will be calculated by the formula COUNTER + 1. Each time this macro loops, it will add one to whatever value was previously entered in the COUNTER cell. That command is the heart of this operation. With each printing loop, the value in COUNTER is increased by one.

In this case, the next two parameters are largely irrelevant. The macro includes two tildes to accept their default values. The Step value increments all cells after the first cell in the Fill Range. Since there's only one cell in the Fill Range, the Step value will never be used. However, the macro must include a tilde to accept the default value or an error will result. The last tilde accepts the default Stop value (2047), since the counter in this operation won't be going over that amount.

This command is a bit tricky. If you have trouble following this explanation, you can clarify the operation by setting up the Range Name COUNTER and executing lines 7-10 of the macro manually.

## Testing For Empty Cells

In the next example, we'll introduce a fourth way to control the number of times a macro repeats itself. This technique employs the @COUNT function. @COUNT reflects how many cells contain entries in a given range. For example, if the range A1..A10 contains six cells with entries and four blank cells, then @COUNT(A1..A10) will return the value 6.

If you are processing a list of numbers with a macro, you can use the @COUNT function to stop the macro at the end of the list, provided one condition is met: the list must have a blank cell beneath it.

To use this function, a Range Name is created at the top of the list that has a range of two cells. If @COUNT finds two entries, there is an entry below the first cell, so the macro can loop. If there is only one entry, the end of the list has been reached and the macro can stop. Each time the macro loops it will move the Range Name, and again set it to contain two cells.

In the example below, the worksheet shows a list of entries to be rounded. The rounded list of data and the macro using the @COUNT function follow.

```
A1:                                                              READY

              A         B         C        D        E        F        G        H
  1
  2
  3               Results
  4                21.432
  5                21.7565
  6               213.752
  7                24.83421
  8               123.739
  9    total     405.51371
 10
 11
 12
 13
 14
 15
 16
 17
 18
 19
 20
```

**Screen 3-15. List of data.**

```
A1:                                                              READY

            A        B        C              D              E        F
  1
  2
  3             Results
  4              21.43   <------   @ROUND(21.432,2)
  5              21.76
  6             213.75
  7              24.83
  8             123.74
  9    total    405.51   <------   @ROUND(@SUM(D4..D8),2)
 10
 11
 12
 13
 14
 15
 16
 17
 18
 19
 20
```

**Screen 3-16. Rounded list of data.**

## Macro 3-27. Looping macro with @COUNT.

| Name | Macro | Comment |
|------|-------|---------|
| \a | /rncPOINTER~~/rndPOINTER~ | 1. Initialize name |
| loop | {edit}{home}@round({end},2)~ | 2. Round entry |
| | /rncPOINTER~{down}~ | 3. Create two-cell name |
| | /xi@count(POINTER)=1~/xgEND~ | 4. Test count range |
| | {down}/rndPOINTER~ | 5. Move down one, delete name |
| | /xgLOOP~ | 6. Repeat |
| end | /rndPOINTER~ | 7. Delete range name |
| | {end}{up}/xq | 8. Return to top of list, quit |

    \a       /rncPOINTER~~/rndPOINTER~        1. Initialize name

This assures that the name does not exist elsewhere on the worksheet.

    loop     {edit}{home}@round({end},2)~     2. Round entry

Since we have moved the cursor to the list before starting the macro, there is an entry in the current cell. Line 2 performs the rounding operation on it.

         /rncPOINTER~{down}~         3. Create two-cell deep
                                        name

Line 3 creates the variable range name. The range name is POINTER, and it will encompass both the current cell and the one directly beneath.

         /xi@count(POINTER)=1~/xgEND~    4. Test count range

Line 4 is designed to see if there's an entry in the cell beneath the current cell. It evaluates the @COUNT value of the range POINTER, made up of the current cell and the one below. We know the current cell has an entry, so if the cell below has an entry in it, the @COUNT value will be 2. But if the cell below is empty (signalling the end of the list), then the @COUNT value will only be 1. For this reason, the /xi command in line 4 tests to see if @Count(POINTER) is equal to 1. If the formula is true, the remaining command on this line will be executed. That command, /xgEND~, redirects the flow of control to a routine to terminate the macro.

         {down}/rndPOINTER~         5. Move down one, delete
                                       name

Lines 5 and 6 will only be executed if the /xi command on the previous line finds the formula false. The implication is that there's another entry in the list in the next cell below. Line 5 moves the cursor down one cell and deletes POINTER.

`/xgLOOP~`                                                6. Repeat

Line 6 redirects the flow of control to the cell named LOOP, which is line 2 of the macro. Since we've already established that the new current cell has an entry in it, line 2 rounds the entry. In Line 3, the macro will recreate POINTER to test the next cell for an entry. When @COUNT returns a value of 1, meaning there is no entry in the cell below, line 4 of the macro will redirect the flow of control to line 7, the routine named END.

end        `/rndPOINTER~`                                7. Delete range name

Line 7 deletes POINTER. Range Names should normally be deleted when a macro is done with them.

`{end}{up}/xq`                                           8. Return to top of list, quit

Line 8 returns the cursor to the top of the list and terminates the macro.

## Summary

In previous examples, you've seen how to use the following ways of automatically terminating a macro:

1.  In the example of rounding an entire list of entries, in Section 2.11, the value @NA was placed at the bottom of the list. The macro tested for the presence of this value and used it as an indicator of when the bottom of the list was reached.

2.  In a data entry example, we established a range for the data entry cells. The range was erased at the beginning of the macro to make sure it was empty. After each entry, the macro used the @COUNT function to count the number of entries made in the range. When the count equalled the specified number of entries, the macro ended.

3.  In another example, the operator entered a number of repetitions a printing macro should perform. After printing each worksheet copy, the macro incremented a counter to keep track of the number of copies printed. Then the macro compared the counter with the operator's input of the number of copies to be made, and terminated when the numbers were equal.

4.  The last example showed how to use @COUNT to stop a macro at the end of a list. This method can also be used to test a data base for entries in a horizontal row. The Address Label Printing Macro in Section 4.4 uses both methods in order to avoid printing blank address lines.

## Self-Modifying Macros

In addition to simple looped repetition of the same instructions, macros are capable of modifying some of their instructions with each loop, adding new flexibility to what you can do with them. For example, if you want a worksheet range to be copied to several different ranges on the worksheet, a macro could make one copy per loop—changing the range it copied TO each time. Here are two additional techniques:

1. Slider Range—a slider is a horizontal range of cells that intersects one line in a macro. Each cell in the slider range contains a different macro instruction. The slider range moves to the left one cell with each loop of the macro, moving a new instruction into the macro each time.

2. Column Range—a column is a vertical range of cells that contains different macro instructions in each cell. With each loop of the macro, a different instruction is copied into a line of the macro.

Each of these techniques can be used in a macro independently or together. The decision of which one to use should be based on how the worksheets are organized and the number of loops the macro is to execute:

- If there are a specific number of loops to perform and the macro performs an identical task each time, the incrementing counter macro is the best method of control.
- If the macro must modify its instructions slightly each time, and the number of repetitions isn't large, a Slider range can be used.
- If the macro must modify its instructions slightly each time, and the number of repetitions is larger, a Column Range should be used. This method usually takes less of your worksheet space and RAM memory, because it runs parallel to your macros on the worksheet. The Slider Range must be entered horizontally.

Since the counter macros have been covered, the following examples will present the Slider and Column Range techniques for modifying macros.

# Working With A Slider Range

A Slider range is a way of modifying a looping routine, allowing the macro to vary its instructions each time it repeats. The method was originally developed to allow a macro to copy one schedule to twelve different worksheet locations—without writing the copying operation twelve times. In the example that follows, we'll show you a simple example of how a Slider range works. The sample macro copies a range (named SCHEDULE in the macro) to six different locations on the worksheet. To make the macro work, you must create this range on your worksheet.

```
 S2:                                                                    READY

         S        T        U       V       W       X        Y       Z     AA  A
  1   \b        /cSCHEDULE~                      1. Copy SCHEDULE to...
  2             A75      R66     C101    D35     B89      AA100~/xgEND~
  3             ~                               3. Complete copy operation
  4             {goto}SLIDER~                   4. Position cursor...
  5             /mSLIDER~{left}~                5. ... and Move Slider left
  6             /xg\B~                          6. Repeat routine
  7             ---------------------------------------------------------------
  8   end       {goto}\B~{down}                 7. Position cursor...
  9             /mSLIDER~~/xq                   8. ...and reset Slider
 10
 11
 12
 13
 14
 15
 16
 17
 18
 19
 20
```

**Screen 3-17. Slider macro (Macro 3-28).**

    **\b**    **/cSCHEDULE~**           1. Copy SCHEDULE to...

The first line of the macro begins a Copying operation. The range "Schedule" is designated as the "Copy from:" range. "Schedule" is a named range containing the original schedule that will be copied into six different worksheet locations. Note that at the end of line 1, the macro is in the middle of a Copy command. The "Copy from:" range has been completed, the "Copy to:" range has not.

  **A75**      **R66**      **C101**      **D35**      **B89**      **AA100~/xgEND~**

Line 2 supplies the "Copy to:" range in the form of a cell address. In the first loop of this macro, this range will be cell A75. Each of the cell addresses shown to the right of A75 is in a different cell. Collectively, these cells make up the named range SLIDER.

           **~**            3. Complete copy operation

Line 3 contains the tilde needed to complete the Copy operation. This could have been included in the slider after each cell address, but since it's the same for every operation, placing it outside the slider allows it to be written once instead of several times.

      **{goto}SLIDER~**        4. Position cursor...

Line 4 positions the cursor in the leftmost cell in the slider range. This step is in preparation for moving the slider range.

      **/mSLIDER~{left}~**      5. ... and Move Slider left

Line 5 moves the entire slider one cell to the left. This positions a new cell address in Line 2. After the macro loops, a new cell address, R66, will be read as the "Copy to:" range for the schedule.

```
/xg\B~                          6. Repeat routine
```

Line 6 redirects the flow of control back to Line 1, creating a loop.

The macro continues copying, moving SLIDER to insert a new location to copy to, and looping, until the final cell of the slider is read: `AA100~/xgEND~`. This cell not only supplies the location to copy to, it provides the tilde to complete the copy operation, and an **/xg** command redirecting the flow of control to a routine named END.

```
end {goto}\B~{down}             7. Position cursor...
```

Line 7 is the first line of the END routine. This routine is used to reset the Slider back in its original position and to end the macro. This line positions the cursor in the second line of the macro, as a preparation for moving SLIDER.

```
/mSLIDER~~/xq                   8. ...and reset Slider
```

Line 8 executes the Move command. The "Move FROM:" range is SLIDER, the "Move TO:" range is the current cell. Line 7 positioned the cursor in the second line of the macro. When a Move command is executed, the "Move TO:" prompt will show the default location as the current cell. By entering a tilde, the macro accepts the default location. When an entire range is Moved, the top left cell of that range is placed at the "Move TO:" location. In this case, the far left cell of SLIDER will be placed in the second line of the macro, with the remaining cells arrayed to its right. That is exactly the position the slider started in, readying it for the next time the macro is used. The last command, **/xq**, terminates the macro.

## General Comments On The Slider Range

A slider range stores all the variable data in an otherwise uniform operation. In the example above, the copying operation is uniform, with the exception of the locations to which the data is to be copied. The locations, which are the variables, are placed in the SLIDER range, while the constant instructions form the main body of the macro.

This macro presents an oversimplified example of a Slider at work, to enable us to concentrate on explaining the technique involved. Generally, the more variables that must be "plugged in" to the main routine, and the longer the main routine of uniform instructions, the more valuable this technique will be to you.

The costs of using a Slider macro are: 1) As you've seen, there are several lines of instructions necessary to move the slider each time, and to reset it at the end of the macro. 2) It also requires room: there must be an equal number of empty cells for the horizontal Slider range to move across, as there are cells in the Slider.

## Working With A Column Range

If you have many different instructions, you may be able to make better use of available worksheet space by using a slightly different technique. A Column range can contain the same information as a Slider range, but it is positioned vertically instead of horizontally, so it parallels the columns used by the macro. For this reason, it can usually make more efficient use of worksheet space: it only uses an adjacent column.

Rather than moving a block of cells through a macro, a Range Name is moved through a column. With each loop of the macro, it copies the currently named cell into the macro, and moves the Range Name to the next cell in the column.

Macro 3-29 will place the average of several test scores into a summary schedule. To prepare the worksheet for this macro, the Range Names must be assigned for the Summary and Test ranges.

### Macro 3-29. Looping macro with column range.

| Name | Macro | Comments |
|------|-------|----------|
| \j | {goto}SUMMARY~ | 0. Position cursor |
| | /rncMARK~~/rndMARK~ | 1. Initialize name |
| loop | /cPOINTER~MACRO~ | 2. Insert information in macro |
| | @avg( | 3. Begin formula to be entered |
| macro | | 4. Cell to be filled |
| | )~{edit}{calc}~ | 5. Convert formula to value |
| | {right} | 6. Move cursor to new position |
| | /rncMARK~~ | 7. Set placemark |
| | {goto}POINTER~ | 8. Move to POINTER in list |
| | {down} | 9. Move to next cell down |
| | /rndPOINTER~ | 10. Delete name |
| | /rncPOINTER~~ | 11. Recreate name |
| | {goto}MARK~ | 12. Move back to place mark |
| | /rndMARK~ | 13. Delete place mark |
| | /xgLOOP~ | 14. Spot where command is placed |
| ------ | ------------------------------ | ----------------------------------------- |
| pointer | TEST1 | 15. Range 1 |
| | TEST2 | 16. Range 2 |
| | TEST3 | 17. Range 3 |
| | TEST4 | 18. Range 4 |
| | TEST5)~{edit}{calc}~/xgEND~ | 19. Range 5, call END routine |

## Macro 3-29. Looping macro with column range (continued).

| Name | Macro | Comments |
|------|-------|----------|
| end | `{goto}POINTER~` | 20. Cursor to Pointer |
| | `{end}{up}{left}` | 21. To pointer label |
| | `/rnlr~` | 22. Reset Pointer name to top |
| | `{goto}SUMMARY~/xq` | 23. Return cursor to start; quit |

Here's the explanation:

| | | | |
|---|---|---|---|
| `\j` | `{goto}SUMMARY~` | 0. | Position cursor |

The first line of the macro positions the cursor on the worksheet where it will begin posting formulas.

| | | |
|---|---|---|
| `/rncMARK~~/rndMARK~` | 1. | Initialize name |

This command sequence makes sure that the variable Range Name does not already exist on the worksheet

| | | | |
|---|---|---|---|
| `loop` | `/cPOINTER~MACRO~` | 2. | Insert information in macro |

Line 2 copies the entry in the cell named POINTER into the cell named MACRO. POINTER is the first cell in the Column range holding the variable code for this macro. The cell named MACRO is the location where these commands will be placed.

| | | |
|---|---|---|
| `@avg(` | 3. | Begin formula to be entered |

Line 3 begins writing an averaging formula.

| | | |
|---|---|---|
| `macro` | 4. | Cell to be filled |

Shown blank now, line 4 will have each of the cells in the column copied into it to supply the argument for the @AVG function.

| | | |
|---|---|---|
| `)~{edit}{calc}~` | 5. | Convert formula to value |

Line 5 closes the @AVG formula and enters it on the worksheet in the current cell (in the SUMMARY range). The formula is then edited, and its value calculated and entered.

| | | |
|---|---|---|
| `{right}` | 6. | Move cursor to new position |

Line 6 repositions the cursor on the worksheet in preparation for the next entry to be made.

| | | |
|---|---|---|
| `/rncMARK~` | 7. | Set placemark |

Line 7 marks the position of the cursor with the Range Name MARK. Since the macro must move the cursor away in the next few steps, it will need a way to return to this cell to make the next entry.

`{goto}POINTER~`     8.    Move to POINTER in list

Line 8 positions the cursor on the cell named POINTER.

`{down}`     9.    Move to next cell down

Line 9 moves the cursor down one cell, to where the Range Name POINTER must be assigned for the next loop.

`/rndPOINTER~`     10.    Delete name

Line 10 deletes the name POINTER.

`/rncPOINTER~~`     11.    Recreate name

Line 11 assigns the range name POINTER to the next cell in the Column range. It will be copied into the macro when the macro loops.

`{goto}MARK~`     12.    Move back to place mark

Line 12 returns the cursor to the Summary file in the location named MARK. MARK was set in line 7 to mark the worksheet location where the next line of data entry is to take place.

`/rndMARK~`     13.    Delete place mark

Now that the cursor has been returned to where it left, the name MARK can be deleted.

`/xgLOOP~`     14.    spot where command is placed

Line 14 returns the flow of control to the cell named LOOP, which is Line 2 of the macro. The macro will continue from this point.

The last line of the Column range will close the formula and convert it to a value. It then redirects the flow of control to the routine named END on line 20.

`end`    `{goto}POINTER~`     20.    Cursor to Pointer

Line 20 positions the cursor on the last cell of the Column range.

`{end}{up}`     21.    To top of Column range

Line 21 moves the cursor to the top cell of the Column range, the first cell to have been named POINTER.

`/rndPOINTER~/rncPOINTER~~`
    22.    Reset Pointer name to top

Line 22 transfers the POINTER to the top cell in the list, ready to start the macro again.

`{goto}SUMMARY~/xq` 23.    Return cursor to start; quit

Line 23 returns the cursor to its starting point on the worksheet and terminates the macro.

Because these techniques require cursor movement into the Slider or Column ranges, they can be a bit sloppy in their screen appearance. Here's a good place to apply what you learned about screen management to hide that activity from the operator. Create a subroutine to Hide the cursor and place it at the beginning of the macro.

Even with the relatively simple macros we've demonstrated so far, you may have noticed that it was not easy to move data about the worksheet. The next section explores this subject, and gives some solutions.

# 3.4 Efficient Worksheets

The goal of increased efficiency, how to achieve results faster and with less cost, is central to the use of macros. This underlies the value of the looping techniques introduced earlier, of macros, and of using 1-2-3 in general.

1-2-3 doesn't introduce any potential that couldn't be achieved with paper and pencil—it merely speeds up the process and makes it easier. As you begin to develop more sophisticated macro applications, their speed and efficiency should be central goals in your planning.

In this section, we'll present some techniques that will help you achieve those goals.

## *Setting Up The Worksheet*

Take some time to plan your worksheet in advance of building your macro. The more operations you can accomplish through existing worksheet structures, the faster your macro will tend to operate. Here's an example.

In a worksheet, four screens show reports that must include a date keyed in by the operator. The date of each report will be the same, but since posting may happen several days after activity, the date will not necessarily be the "system date" (the date entered when you start up the computer). What's the quickest way to enter the date on all four reports? Let's answer the question by evaluating the obvious solution first.

The obvious method is to have a macro move the cursor to the cell to contain the date in the first report, pause for the operator to enter a date with the @DATE function, have the macro format the cell with the range format command, and move to the next report to repeat itself.

There are several problems with this method. First, moving the cursor is a slow operation. Second, the method requires the operator to write the long

@DATE formula. Third, it requires the operator to write the same formula four times. And fourth, it forces the macro to format each cell as it goes along.

How can this operation be speeded up? There are three changes that can be made:

First: As we presented in Section 3.1 dealing with @DATE, you can use a series of **/xn** commands to prompt operators for the numbers used in the @DATE formula. The macro can prompt the operators in the same MONTH/DAY/YEAR order to which they are accustomed:

```
/xnEnter month: ~MON~
/xnEnter day: ~DAY~
/xnEnter year: ~YEAR~
```

The **/xn** commands place the arguments needed by @DATE into named ranges:

```
Range named "YEAR" -->     _____
Range named "MON"  -->     _____
Range named "DAY"  -->     _____
```

An @DATE formula on the worksheet can reference these ranges to pick up the proper arguments and calculate the correct date:

**@DATE(YEAR,MON,DAY)**

Second: Instead of repeating the dating process four times, you will save time by making some entries on the worksheet in advance of running the macro. When you set up your worksheet, enter a cell reference into each cell in which you wish to show the date. If the @DATE formula shown above is in cell A48, then each of the reports will contain a cell with the entry +A48. As soon as the macro inserts the date information into the named ranges, the @DATE formula will calculate the date. Each report will have the same date immediately.

Third: Range Format the cells containing the date references when you create the worksheet. Do NOT have the macro format the date cells each time it runs. Once a cell is formatted, it'll stay that way. There's no need for a macro to perform this one-time operation over and over.

Conclusion: As this example suggests, sometimes the way to make a macro operate more efficiently is to use the abilities of 1-2-3 together with the macro. A cell reference installed on the worksheet when you set it up will transfer numeric data much faster than any other method. If cells must be given Range Formats, do that when you set up the worksheet. It's wasteful to have a macro do things over and over that can be done when you set up the worksheet. It was this type of planning that helped cut the execution time of one large application from nineteen to three minutes.

## Transferring And Transforming Data

While the simple cell references shown above are incredibly useful, they won't solve all your problems. There will be times when you'll need to accomplish more:

1. Occasionally you won't be able to use a cell reference, because you plan to erase the original cell later, or because you plan to edit a copy of the formula, which isn't possible with a cell reference.
2. You may need to transform a formula (or a range of formulas) into a simple number to preserve its current value.
3. You may need to transfer ranges of data including text entries.
4. In special circumstances, such as inter-program data transfer, you may have to transform a label entry containing a number into a value entry.

## If You Must Copy...

If you have the first problem on the list, and must use a macro to make copies of formulas, you are stuck with a very slow process. However, there are some things you can do to improve the situation. First, if you have to copy more than one cell, try to copy an entire range of cells at once, rather than copy each cell individually. The fewer times you have to execute the command, the faster the macro will run. You may have to be creative to arrange the worksheet so all cells to be copied are within a range, but it'll pay off in speed every time you execute the macro.

The second thing you can do is to determine the ranges you must copy from and copy to in advance. If these ranges can be written into the macro, you won't have to rely on moving the cursor to indicate the ranges each time the macro executes. Cursor movement is one of the slowest methods to use in indicating ranges. If you can, create named ranges in advance, and write the named ranges into the copy command in the macro: /cHERE~THERE~ where HERE is the "Copy from:" range and THERE is the "Copy to:" range.

## Transforming Formulas Into Simple Numbers

It's not unusual for an application to require you to maintain a permanent record of its status at one phase of its operation. In our first example, the dates on the worksheet will change if the entries in the named cells change. Simply copying formulas to a separate work area won't do. Even if the formulas are absolute, they'll still change as the original data changes.

What you need is a way to preserve the current value of that formula. There are essentially four ways to do this, each of which transforms a formula into a simple number that will no longer change. Each method has its own special place in an application. Here they are.

## Method 1: Use Edit-Calc

If the application has one or only a few cells to be "frozen" at their current value, you can place the cursor on the cell containing the formula and use the following sequence of commands: **EDIT, CALC, ENTER**. If you want to keep the original formula intact, create a cell reference to the original formula and perform this operation on the cell reference. Since this technique can only be applied to one cell at a time, it's only appropriate for applications where one or a few cells must be converted. It is also hampered by the need to move the cursor to each cell to be converted. The commands would look like this in a macro: {edit}{calc}~.

## Method 2: Use Data Fill

Data Fill is a more powerful way of achieving the same result as that described in Method 1. It can transfer the value of one cell to any other cell, or to any range of cells, and it can be done without moving the cursor to the data entry location. In the following example, cell A2 has been range named TEST1. TEST1 contains a formula that has the value 7. The macro will transfer the value of the formula as a simple number to a range named TEST2 (cell C4).

In the example worksheet shown on page 142, the entry in cell A2 is shown in Text Format to clarify that it is a formula.

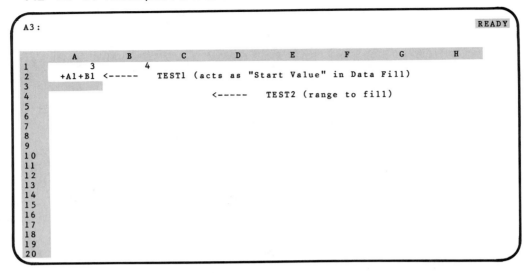

**Screen 3-18. Formula to convert.**

**Screen 3-19. Converted formula.**

**Macro 3-30. Convert formula with data fill.**

| Name | Macro | Comment |
|------|-------|---------|
| \d | /df | Data fill |
| | TEST2~ | Range to fill |
| | TEST1~ | Start value |
| | ~ | Step value |
| | ~ | Stop value |
| | /xq | End macro |

We used the Data Fill command to increment a counter in Section 3.3. This macro is just a variation on that technique. The Data Fill command first requests a Fill range. The macro enters TEST2. This is the cell that will receive the result of the Data Fill command.

The command then asks for the Start value. The value can be a number, a formula, or a cell address. If an address is given, the contents of the cell will be used to determine the value the fill sequence will start from. If a cell with a formula is specified, its value will be entered into the Fill range. The Range TEST1 is given as the Start value. The remaining prompts for Step and Stop have no effect. They determine what will happen in the remaining cells of the range, and there are no other cells.

## Transferring Ranges, Including Text

Both of the above methods are limited in that they cannot transfer any more than one cell at a time, making them unacceptably slow when you have to transfer an entire range on the worksheet. Fortunately, the Data Query Extract function can fill this need. Not only will it transform formulas into simple numbers when it copies the data, but it will transfer text entries within the same range.

Data Query Extract was designed as a means to copy selected records from a data base to an output (report) range. However, if you arrange your worksheet correctly, Data Query Extract can be used to copy any range of data to any other range on the worksheet. Formulas will all be converted into simple numbers. Text entries will be copied as well.

Screen 3-20 is a sample worksheet with formulas to be converted.

```
C10:  @SUM(B4..B8)                                                  READY

              A          B          C         D        E        F        G        H
  1
  2    Quarterly Costs
  3
  4    Sept           2345
  5
  6    Oct            2343
  7
  8    Nov            4391
  9
 10    Total Unit Cost          9079
 11
 12
 13
 14
 15
 16
 17
 18
 19
 20
```

**Screen 3-20. Formula conversion using data query—A.**

The method for using Data Query follows the conventional rules, with some unique twists:

1. The original range of data must be given field names at the top of each column. Don't worry about rearranging the data to look like a data base—that's not necessary. Just make room for a row at the top where you will enter a unique field name at the top of each column. The field names do not have to mean anything, but they must be labels (as opposed to values) and they must be different from one another. Start at the left column and use the letter "a" as the first field name, then continue across the columns with "b", "c", etc. These field names will be used to head up the Data Query Input range later in this operation.

2. Now Copy only the field names to the top of the range where you wish to place the converted data. Use the Copy command to do this so that all field names are reproduced precisely and that they remain in the same order. These field names and the worksheet area beneath them will serve as the Data Query Output range. You must be sure there is sufficient blank space on the worksheet beneath these field names for the original data. Now make a copy of one of the field names and place it just above a blank cell on the worksheet. The sample worksheet below shows the copies of the field names in cells F5..H5. In cell E2 is the extra field name with a blank cell below it.

3. Now you must assign the three Data Query settings needed to perform a Data Query Extract:

| Commands: | Which mean: |
|---|---|
| **/DQI** | Data Query Input-range |
| **A1..C10 ENTER** | Range entered |
| **C** | Criterion-range |
| **E2..E3 ENTER** | Range entered |
| **O** | Output-range |
| **F6..H14 ENTER** | Range entered |
| **Q** | Quit |

Notes:

a.  Make sure that the range of cells designated as the Output range is empty. 1-2-3 erases all data in the output range (with the exception of the field names) when an Extract is performed.

b.  The Criterion range is left blank so that ALL entries in the input range will be copied to the output range.

4.  Now execute the extract with the commands / **Data Query Extract Quit**. The data in the input range will be reproduced in the output range, and all formulas will be converted to simple numbers, preserving their present value. The macro to perform this entire operation, Macro 3-31, is a simple one:

## Macro 3-31. Convert formulas with data query.

| *Name* | *Macro* | *Comment* |
|---|---|---|
| \q | /dqi{bs}{?}~ | Data Query Input-range |
| | c{bs}{?}~ | Criterion-range |
| | o{bs}{?}~ | Output-range |
| | eq/xq | Extract, Quit, End macro |

5.  The output range creates a copy of the original data. If you do not want two copies, you can copy the Output range back to the Input range, and erase the Output and Criterion ranges. This will leave you with just one copy of the original data, but all formulas will have been converted to simple numbers.

```
H14: 9079                                                              READY

              A          B          C      D      E      F        G        H
  1    a          b          c
  2    Quarterly Costs                            a
  3
  4    Sept          2345
  5                                                 a          b          c
  6    Oct           2343                           Quarterly Costs
  7
  8    Nov           4391                           Sept          2345
  9
 10    Total Unit Cost      9079                    Oct           2343
 11
 12                                                 Nov           4391
 13
 14                                                 Total Unit Cost      9079
 15
 16
 17
 18
 19
 20
```

**Screen 3-21. Formula conversion using data query—B.**

## Method 4: Extract Data To Another File

All of the above techniques work within a single file. For those times when you want your worksheet record saved to a different file, you'll want to use 1-2-3's File Extract function. This function allows you to create a new worksheet file that saves a partial portion of the current worksheet. It also provides the option of saving the formulas or converting them into simple numbers. After executing / **File Xtract**, 1-2-3 presents you with a choice between saving Formulas or Values. The option Values (shown in the macro below) will convert all formulas into simple numbers as they are written to the disk file.

**Macro 3-32. Xtract values.**

| Name | Macro | Comments |
|------|-------|----------|
| \x | /fxv | File Xtract Values (converts formulas) |
| | SAMPLE | Name of file to create |
| | ~ | Accept name |
| | A2..F7 | Range of worksheet to be saved |
| | ~/fcce | Combine file |
| | SAMPLE | Name of file |
| | ~/few | Erase file |
| | SAMPLE | Name of file |
| | ~y/xq | End macro |

The new file containing the simple numbers is then File Combined into the current file. If the cursor is on the top left cell of the range that was File

Xtracted, the range will have all of its formulas converted into simple numbers. The next section has more information about this technique.

## Special Needs: Transforming A Label Entry Containing A Number Into A Value Entry

Occasionally you'll be faced with transforming a label entry holding a number into a value entry. When you only have a few of these to deal with, you can easily write a macro to move to each cell, go into EDIT mode, and delete the label alignment character at the front of the entry.

**Macro 3-33. Convert label to value.**

| Name | Macro | Comment |
|------|-------|---------|
| \e | {edit} | Edit mode |
| | {home} | Cursor to beginning of entry |
| | {del} | Delete label alignment character |
| | ~ | Re-enter on worksheet |
| | {?} | Move to next cell |
| | /xg\e~ | Repeat macro |

That's fine for a small number of entries, but it produces unacceptably slow results when you are faced with a large amount of entries to change. Such a situation might occur were you to incorporate data from a dBASE II data base. In one application, a large accounts receivable file was created with dBASE II. The date field had been entered as a character entry, and was formatted as MON/DAY/YEAR. Since dBASE had no date arithmetic function to speak of (a real strength in 1-2-3), extracts of the dBASE file were sent over to 1-2-3 on a monthly basis to age the accounts receivable file ("aging" refers to the process of arranging in groups by age of the original invoice).

However, because the dBASE date field was entered as a character entry, (which would require extensive work to change) the date field came into 1-2-3 as a label entry:

'7/19/84

Not only did this present a problem of changing a large number of label entries into values, we had to get rid of the slashes in the entry and put the numbers in a format that could be used by 1-2-3's @DATE function.

The solution is not as difficult as it might seem. After the data was brought from dBASE II into 1-2-3, the illustration shows how the original worksheet appeared. Keep in mind that all the date entries shown are labels, and the list shown has been abbreviated for this example—you could expect to work with a list of several hundred entries in this application.

```
A11:                                                              READY

         A          B          C      D      E      F      G      H
 1   Invoice    Amount      Date
 2      2423    234.34   02/03/84
 3      4234    472.34   04/16/84
 4      6456    843.32   02/13/84
 5      8654    455.47   03/23/84
 6      5632    543.41   03/27/84
 7      8458    744.45   04/03/84
 8      2634    313.34   04/19/84
 9      7658     90.23   03/30/84
10      4234     34.34   02/23/84
11
12
13
14
15
16
17
18
19
20
```

**Screen 3-22. Converting dBASE dates—A.**

## Before The Macro: Worksheet Formatting

In this case, the first step is to make sure the three columns directly to the right of the date column are empty, because we'll use them later. Step two is to Range Name the very top entry of the date column (column C) START. Then run Macro 3-34.

### Macro 3-34. dBASE conversion—A.

| Name | Macro | Comment |
|------|-------|---------|
| \v | {goto}START~ | 1. Position cursor on first date entry |
| | /pfTEMP~ | 2. Create print file TEMP |
| | cr | 3. Clear any prior print range |
| | r.{end}{down}~ | 4. Set new print range column |
| | oouq | 5. Options, Other, Unformatted, Quit |
| | gq | 6. Create print file and quit print menu |
| | /fin | 7. File import only numbers... |
| | TEMP~ | 8. ...from TEMP print file |
| | /fepTEMP~y | 9. File erase print-file TEMP, (yes) |
| | /xq | 10. Terminate macro |

Screen 3-23 is how the worksheet appears after the macro is finished (each of the entries in columns D, E, and F are now value entries).

```
All:                                                              READY

         A          B          C         D         E       F       G       H
 1   Invoice     Amount     Date
 2     2423      234.34        2         3        84
 3     4234      472.34        4        16        84
 4     6456      843.32        2        13        84
 5     8654      455.47        3        23        84
 6     5632      543.41        3        27        84
 7     8458      744.45        4         3        84
 8     2634      313.34        4        19        84
 9     7658       90.23        3        30        84
10     4234       34.34        2        23        84
11
12
13
14
15
16
17
18
19
20
```

**Screen 3-23. Converting dBASE dates—B.**

Here's how the macro accomplishes that:

\v          {goto}START~          1.  Position cursor on first date entry

Line 1 positions the cursor at the top of the date field.

/pfTEMP~          2.  Create print file TEMP

Line 2 starts to create a print file named TEMP (a standard name for a temporary file, as is this one).

cr          3.  Clear any prior print range

Line 3 clears any prior print range that may have been used with this worksheet.

r.{end}{down}~          4.  Set new print range including date column

Line 4 sets a new print range (which will define the contents of the print file). The period anchors the cursor, {end}{down} expands the pointer to the bottom of the date field, and the tilde enters the print range.

oouq          5.  Options, Other, Unformatted, Quit

Line 5 selects **Print Options Other Unformatted**. The Unformatted print option eliminates all margins and page breaks, which would otherwise be inserted into the print file. Since we want a straight columnar file of data, no margins or page breaks are desired. The Other menu automatically quits back to the Options menu after you select the Unformatted command. You must then include a Quit command to return to the main print menu for the next command.

gq                                  6.   Create print file and quit print menu

Line 6 creates the print file on the disk and returns 1-2-3 to READY mode with the Quit command.

/fin                                7.   File import only numbers...

With the cursor positioned at the head of the date column, Line 7 executes the command to import a print file, but only to import the numbers found in that file. Numbers separated by any alphabetic characters will be treated as separate entries. If you look back at the entries that were saved in the print file, they were in the form 3/4/84. This means that the month entry will be entered in the first column, the day in the second, and the year in the third. The slashes will not be imported.

TEMP~                               8.   ...from TEMP print file

Line 8 names the print file TEMP as the file to import numbers from. The cursor position serves as the top left corner of the range where the imported numbers will be entered in the current file. Since the print file contains three sets of numbers separated by slashes, the numbers imported into the worksheet are entered into three separate columns, side by side.

/fepTEMP~y                          9.   File erase print-file TEMP, (yes)

In line 9, the macro erases the print file TEMP. Note that the "y" (standing for Yes) must follow the command to erase the file. Before erasing a file, 1-2-3 will make you confirm the operation with a final NO/YES menu to protect you from accidental erasures.

/xq                                 10.  Terminate macro

The last line terminates the macro.

To complete this operation, you'll need to provide @DATE formulas (necessary for subsequent date arithmetic operations) that reference the numeric entries generated in the File Import operation just described. In the example worksheet shown below, the @DATE formula is written as: @DATE(E2,C2,D2), and has been assigned the Date 1 Range Format (DD/MM/YY). Note that this format requires at least a ten-space column width setting in order to display. When the formula is copied, the format is copied also.

Here's the way the worksheet looks after the macro provides all the date entries:

```
A11:                                                                    READY

         A          B          C          D          E          F          G
 1    Invoice    Amount     Date
 2      2423     234.34        2          3         84  03-Feb-84
 3      4234     472.34        4         16         84  16-Apr-84
 4      6456     843.32        2         13         84  13-Feb-84
 5      8654     455.47        3         23         84  23-Mar-84
 6      5632     543.41        3         27         84  27-Mar-84
 7      8458     744.45        4          3         84  03-Apr-84
 8      2634     313.34        4         19         84  19-Apr-84
 9      7658      90.23        3         30         84  30-Mar-84
10      4234      34.34        2         23         84  23-Feb-84
11
12
13
14
15
16
17
18
19
20
```

**Screen 3-24. Converting dBASE dates—C.**

Macro 3-35 is used to create the @DATE formulas.

## Macro 3-35. dBASE date conversion—B.

| Name | Macro | Comment |
|------|-------|---------|
| \e | {goto}START~ | Position cursor at top of date field |
| | {right}{right}{right} | Move across 3 columns |
| | @date(E2,C2,D2)~ | Enter date formula |
| | /rfd1~ | Format cell |
| | /c~. | Copy the formula from the top |
| | {left}{end}{down}{right}~ | ...of the column to the bottom |
| | /xq | Terminate macro |

The macro is quite simple, so we won't go through an entire line by line description. It begins by positioning the cursor at the top of the far left date field, named START. Moving across three columns to the right places the cursor in the first blank column, where the macro enters the formula. The macro then copies the @DATE formula down the entire column by anchoring the cursor, and moving it one column to the left, to the bottom of the list, and to the right.

If you wish, the formulas can then be converted to values by using the Data Query or File Xtract methods. The columns containing the month, day, and year can then be deleted to clean up the worksheet.

In the next section we'll look at macro-controlled file operations in more detail.

# 3.5 File Operations Under Macro Control

Macros are a powerful tool for automating the entire spectrum of 1-2-3 File operations, from Saving and Retrieving files to Combining and Extracting them. This section will show you how to deal with the special challenges of writing the routines for these operations.

## Saving Worksheet Files

There are two circumstances under which you might save a worksheet:

1. The first time it's saved, and
2. When you are replacing an existing file.

Here are the commands you'd need to save a file called SAMPLE for the first time (the macro to execute the command is shown to the right):

`/ File Save SAMPLE ENTER`                     `/fsSAMPLE~`

But when a file already exists on the disk, 1-2-3 changes its command structure, and issues a conditional command: Replace. Replace is only presented as a choice on the menu when 1-2-3 detects another file on the disk with the same name. As a result, when you are replacing an existing worksheet file with a file of the same name, the commands and macro must be written this way:

`/ File Save SAMPLE ENTER Replace`            `/fsSAMPLE~r`

The first macro works when the file is new, but won't do the job when the file already exists: it lacks the Replace command needed to overwrite an existing file. And the second macro is no better; the `r` at the end will cause an error if this macro saves a new file, because 1-2-3 issues no Replace command. What we need is one macro that can handle either circumstance. Here it is:

`/fsSAMPLE~r{esc}`

Here's how the last macro works under either condition:

1. When the file is saved for the first time: The File Save command is executed and a file name entered. 1-2-3 returns to READY mode. The macro types `r`, which puts 1-2-3 into LABEL mode. `{esc}` cancels the label and returns 1-2-3 to READY mode.

2. When the file replaces an existing file: The File Save command is executed and a file name entered. 1-2-3 detects an existing file on the diskette and displays the Cancel Replace menu. The macro types `r` to select Replace and returns to READY mode. The macro types the Escape key, which has no effect.

## Graph Files

1-2-3 graphs are printed by saving them to disk in a special file created with the Graph Save command, and that can be a very useful feature to build into a macro. But as with worksheet files, graph file menus are conditional. If 1-2-3 detects an existing file with the same name it displays the Cancel Replace option.

The solution to this situation is not as simple as it was with the worksheet files. The worksheet File Save menu returns you directly to the READY mode. If the operation saves a new file, the **r** is read as a label and the **{esc}** command cancels it. A graph File Save isn't quite so clean. It returns you to the Graph menu, where an extra **r** executes an entirely different command when it doesn't function in the Replace capacity. The macro to deal with it is shown below:

```
/gs{?}~rqq{esc}
```

Here's an explanation of the effect of the macro under each circumstance:

1.  When the file is saved for the first time: The Graph Save command is executed and a name entered. 1-2-3 returns to the Graph menu (still in MENU mode). The macro types **r**, which selects the Reset command and places 1-2-3 in the Reset menu. **q** selects Quit and returns 1-2-3 to the Graph menu. The next **q** selects Quit to return to READY mode. Finally, the macro types **{esc}**, which has no effect.
2.  When the file replaces an existing file: The Graph Save command is executed and a name entered. 1-2-3 displays the Cancel Replace menu, the macro types **r** for Replace, **q** for Quit, and returns to READY mode. The macro types **qq** as a label in the control panel, **{esc}** cancels the entry and returns 1-2-3 to READY mode.

## Relating Saved and Named Graphs

Saving graphs and Naming graphs are separate 1-2-3 operations: naming a graph allows it to be recalled for display from within a worksheet while saving a graph places the graph in a separate file for printing. Since the graphs saved for printing no longer respond to subsequent worksheet changes, there's often a need to resave these graphs to reflect updates to the original data.

But how do you retrace your steps to re-Save a graph file? You've got to recall the original settings. If you haven't named them chances are the settings are long gone and will have to be re-Created. And even if you have named the graph, it's often difficult to relate the File name (used for printing) to the Graph Name (stored with **Graph Name Create**). The solution is to minimize confusion by giving the Graph Name and File the very same name. Macro 3-36 can speed up this operation.

**Macro 3-36. Graph save.**

| Name | Macro | Comment |
|------|-------|---------|
| \g | /xlEnter Graph file name: ~MAC1~ | Prompt user for name |
|    | /cMAC1~MAC2~ | Duplicate name |
|    | /gnc | Name the graph |
| MAC1 |  | (name) |
|    | ~s | Save the graph |
|    |  | ( ) |
| MAC2 |  | (name) |
|    | ~rqq{esc} | Replace option |
|    | /xq | End |

## Print Files

Unfortunately, these routines offer no help for saving print files. Those menus aren't amenable to any of the tricks contained in the macros presented above. Assuming that most of the time you'll be replacing existing files, you'll have to write the macro with the **Replace** option, and before running it for the first time, create a dummy file on the disk to ensure it will work.

## A General Warning About Saving Files

This warning appears in Section 2.7 in the section on protecting your work, but it's worth repeating here. 1-2-3 contains a quirk that could cost you a file if you don't understand it. When you **File Save Replace** one file over an existing one of the same name (such as when you update an existing worksheet), 1-2-3 writes the new file over the old one, destroying it.

Under most circumstances, that's not a problem: you don't want the old version of the file. But if that new file is larger than the space available on the disk, 1-2-3 will not only have destroyed the old file, but it won't have space to save the new one... leaving you with no file at all. So if you ever get a "Disk full" error message when replacing one file with another, be sure to go get another disk or you'll lose your file entirely.

## Combining And Extracting Files

Although 1-2-3's worksheets have great capacity, there will still be times when you will keep related information on separate worksheets, and want to pass data between them. Some examples of this include periodic reports prepared at different times, such as monthly sales summaries that will later be consolidated into quarterly summaries; and reports originating in different parts of your organization, such as a pricing worksheet kept by Finance on a product that will provide input to a sales projection model kept by Marketing. Fortunately,

1-2-3 provides a set of commands to help move data between worksheets, File Xtract and File Combine. Following is a brief summary of their capabilities.

*File Combine:* used for "pulling" data from a file on disk into the current worksheet file (that is, the worksheet in RAM). Options include:

- Combine all or just part of a file into the present file. If combining only part of a file, a named range must be specified to identify the portion of the disk file to be combined.

- Copy, Add, or Subtract incoming data from data already in the current file. The Copy option copies the disk file data into the current file, but differs from the operation of the normal Copy command in one important way. Blank cells in the incoming range of data will have no effect on the corresponding cell in the current file. In a normal Copy operation, a blank cell would erase the contents of the cell to which it was copied.

   The Add option adds the value of the incoming data to the value in the corresponding cell in the current worksheet, and the Subtract option does the reverse. Add is also useful where you are combining data including formulas. If the cells those formulas reference are not also combined into the current worksheet, the formulas will most likely return meaningless values. If you **File Combine Add** the formulas, they will be transformed into simple numbers, bringing a value into the current file instead of the formula.

- The location of the cursor in the current file establishes the location of the top left corner of the range of data being combined. For this reason, correct cursor position is imperative.

- Range names and other worksheet settings are not transferred in with the data being combined.

*File Xtract:* used to "push" all or part of the current worksheet out to the disk.

- File Xtract creates a new file made up of all or part of the current worksheet. Formulas can be extracted intact or be transformed into simple numbers. Data CANNOT be extracted onto an existing file on disk—the Xtract operation can only create a new file, or overwrite an existing one with the same name.

- All range names from the current worksheet are transferred to the extracted file, even if they are located outside the specified extract range. Worksheet global settings and graph settings are transferred as well. Beware: Range Names should be checked in the extracted file—Range Names outside the extract range are sometimes moved to new locations.

The use of macros to control the extracting and combining of worksheets tremendously broadens the scope of possibilities of worksheet applications.

Because a macro precisely defines where each piece of data will be placed, all the variables in this process can be controlled so that no errors are made. When used with custom menus, users can manipulate files without having the slightest idea how 1-2-3 is moving the information.

Among the applications covered in the next section, the Check Register, the Payroll Tax Register and the Mortgage Manager all make use of combining and extracting files.

## The Importance Of Range Names

Range Names make it easy to build and control macros that manipulate files. Any range containing data to be extracted should be range named so it can more easily be used in a macro.

An application of this technique can be found in the Check Register macro presented in Section 4.5. The whole check register has been Range Named ACCOUNT and the summary line within it has been range named TOTAL. In the following routine, the operator specifies a file name in response to a prompt. The macro extracts the entire register (named ACCOUNT) containing the month's transactions to make a separate file:

**Macro 3-37. Xtract portion of file.**

| Name | Macro | Comment |
|---|---|---|
| extract | /xlEnter name of file ~EXT~ | Get file name, put in EXT |
| | /fxf | Make extract |
| ext | | File name |
| | ~ACCOUNT~r{esc} | Range, overwrite file |
| | ~xq | Quit |

Within the Xtracted range ACCOUNT is the range TOTAL, containing the check register totals. When it comes time to consolidate all the monthly totals, another macro can File Combine just the range TOTAL to the consolidation worksheet, as shown in the following routine.

**Macro 3-38. Recombine portion of the file.**

| Name | Macro | Comment |
|---|---|---|
| loop | /xlEnter Name Of File ~FILE~ | Get filename, put in FILE |
| | /fcanTOTAL~ | Combine range TOTAL |
| file | | User specified file |
| | ~{down} | Move to next line |
| | /xgLOOP~ | Continue consolidating |

To do this more efficiently the macro could select the files to be combined by using one of the self-modifying macro techniques presented earlier, such as a Column range or Slider range.

## Dealing With Storage Problems

Applications that make extensive use of external files (such as those described above) may demand more disk storage space than is available on floppy disk systems. To estimate your file storage requirements, use the Disk Manager utility in the Lotus Access System or the DOS **dir** command to keep track of the size of your worksheet files. The size of a file is expressed in bytes.

The Disk Operating System (DOS) 1.X stores roughly 320,000 bytes on a floppy disk, DOS 2.X stores about 360,000. While in DOS, the **dir** command will list the amount of bytes remaining on your disk after listing the files. While using 1-2-3, use the **File List Worksheet** commands to keep track of how much space is available on the disk: it will report the names of the worksheet files and the number of available bytes of storage on the disk.

The most effective solution to disk shortage problems is also the most expensive—buy a fixed disk to expand available storage (most fixed disks, including IBM's XT, offer 10 million bytes of storage). If that's not possible (such a fixed disk costs from $850 to $3000), there are several less expensive options you can evaluate:

1. Make sure you are using at least version 2.0 (or higher) of DOS.
2. Compress your files by having macros specially prepare them before storage.
3. Use a macro disk management system to allow an operator to change diskettes and preview their contents prior to retrieving any files.

Warning: it is possible to remove the 1-2-3 System Disk from the A: drive and place another data disk there, and have a macro switch from one drive to the other (using the / **File Directory** commands). However, we warn you NOT to use this option. Although there is no warning to this effect in the 1-2-3 manual, while the System Disk is out of the A: drive you are susceptible to a program crash that will force you to re-boot your computer (and lose all work you had not previously saved to disk).

Here's the problem. If the operator inadvertently touches the Help function key while the System Disk is out of the A: drive, 1-2-3 will try to access the Help file. Unfortunately, instead of reporting that it can't find it, it will just keep looking. The disk drive light will remain on and the computer will remain locked up until re-booted. While you might think it's unlikely the operator would press the Help function key, on an IBM style keyboard that's extremely easy to do accidentally when reaching for either the EDIT or NAME function keys located to the right and below. Making this sort of mistake was exactly how we learned of this problem (at the cost of two hour's worth of unsaved work).

Here are more details on each of the techniques we do recommend:

**1.    Make sure you are using at least version 2.0 (or higher) of DOS.**

If you are using any version 1.x (such as version 1.1 or 1.25) you can increase your disk storage from 320K to 360K by purchasing version DOS 2.0 or higher. There are several ways to check to see which version you are using. The simplest is to read the label on the original DOS system diskette. Another is to put the DOS diskette in the A: drive (usually located on the left if your drive slots are mounted vertically, or on the top if they are mounted horizontally) and turn the computer on. After responding to the date and time prompts it should print its version number and copyright(s) on the screen. Another method to use if the computer is already running with the A> prompt displayed, is to type the word VER and press the ENTER key. If it responds with a version number, you'll have your answer. If it responds with "Bad command or file name", you can assume you have version 1 DOS (version 1 did not include the VER command, which is why it can't interpret it).

If you do have version 1 and decide to change to version 2, you will need to take some steps before you can take advantage of version 2. (1) Get out Lotus' "Read This First—Getting Started" booklet (or look in the front of the manual in the section entitled "Getting Started") and follow the instructions to install the new version of DOS on your 1-2-3 diskettes. This operation is simple, only takes about 5 minutes, and is ABSOLUTELY necessary. If you were to boot your computer with a version 2 DOS disk, and place a 1-2-3 disk in the drive with the old version 1 DOS on it, Lotus warns you it could cause serious trouble. (2) You must use the new version of DOS to format all the data diskettes you will be using. Reminder: do NOT format a disk with files on it—they will be irrevocably destroyed. If you run out of space on existing diskettes, copy all its files onto a blank data disk that has been formatted with DOS 2. When you do this, you must use the "Copy" command, NOT the "Diskcopy" command. Diskcopy will format your new disk to be the same as your old one.

Here's how to do this copying quickly and easily:

You are in DOS, not 1-2-3 for this operation. You should see the DOS "A>" prompt on the screen. If the original disk is in the A: drive and the blank formatted disk is in the B: drive, the command to transfer the files from A: to B: is...

    `copy *.* b:ENTER`

...where **ENTER** represents pressing the ENTER key.

**2. Compress your files by having macros specially prepare them before storage.**

A macro can prepare blocks of information prior to their being File Xtracted to minimize the space they will occupy on the disk by deleting unnecessary headings and labels. Another macro can restore the formatting when you retrieve the file at a later date.

This can be accomplished with three steps. First, create a standard form which includes all the labels and formulas but excludes the data. Copy the form to a blank area of the worksheet. Range Name the copy MASTER, providing a blank master template that can be used repeatedly. At this stage, the formulas on the template will provide meaningless values or ERR. Don't worry—they are simply waiting for data.

When you are ready to save your data to a disk file, Range Erase all the formulas and labels that are included on the MASTER template. Extract the file, including only the necessary information.

When you are ready to view the data from an Xtracted file, first make a copy of the MASTER template to a location we'll name FORM on the worksheet. Next **File Combine Copy** the extracted file into the FORM. If the cursor is on the top left corner of FORM, the blank spaces in the incoming data will correspond with the labels and formulas in the form so they will recombine perfectly. This technique is used in the Mortgage Manager, in Section A.4.

In the Mortgage Manager example, we have stripped away all the extra information so that we could get as many files as possible on a disk. We need to restore the extra information before we can look at one of the files. A macro to perform this first copies the MASTER template into the working area, then combines the ACCOUNT range of extracted file back into the working area.

**Macro 3-39. Master template with Xtracted file.**

| Name | Macro | Description |
|------|-------|-------------|
| \a | {goto}FORM~ | Move cursor to FORM |
| | /cMASTER~FORM~ | Copy the master template |
| | /xlEnter File Name ~NAME~ | Prompt for name |
| | /fccnACCOUNT~ | Combine sales data from |
| name | | File name |
| | ~/xq | Quit |

**3. Use a macro disk management system to allow an operator to change diskettes and preview their contents prior to retrieving any files.**

A macro-operated disk management system allows you to spread related files over several disks and access each of them under macro control. Such a system includes the following options:

1. Pause to allow the operator to change data diskettes

2. List the files on the disk for the operator to read
3. Retrieve a file from the selected diskette
4. Quit back to the operating system if no diskette is to be used.

The disk management system can be used as a subroutine to any macro, since it is a self-contained unit of instructions. You can set one up with the following steps:

1. Set up a disk management message screen on the worksheet. The message screen will explain each of the choices shown on the disk management custom menu, which will display in the control panel during the operation. The screen is shown below (you may recognize it from the section on Menu Techniques, where it was used as an example of how to provide onscreen messages):

| *Menu Choice:* | *Explanation:* |
|---|---|
| **Pause** | Allows you to change diskettes in the right hand drive prior to reviewing them. |
| **List-files** | Displays a list of worksheet files stored on the current diskette, and shows available space remaining. |
| **Select-diskette** | Selects the current diskette for processing, and presents a menu of files stored there for retrieval. |
| **Exit** | Returns to DOS to use other programs. |

The subroutine used to operate this macro is simple. To get started, assign the Range Name MESSAGE to the top left corner of this screen.

## Macro 3-40. Disk manager.

| *Name* | *Macro* | | | *Comments* |
|---|---|---|---|---|
| \d | /xgDISKMGR~ | | | 1. Call "DISK MANAGER" routine |
| diskmgr | {goto}MESSAGE~ | | | 2. Display explanation screen |
| | /xmMENU1~/xgDISKMGR~ | | | 3. Call menu below |
| menu1 | pause | list-files | select-file | exit |
| | you may now change | list files stored | select files for | exit to DOS |
| | /xgPAUSE~ | /xgLIST~ | /xgSELECT~ | /xgEXIT~ |
| pause | /xgDISKMGR~ | | 7. Loops to disk manager routine | |
| list | /flw | | 8. List worksheet files and pause | |
| | /xgDISKMGR~ | | 9. Return to disk manager menu | |
| select | /fr{?}~ | | 10. File retrieve and pause | |
| exit | /xmMENU2~/xgDISKMGR~ | | 11. Call menu (Esc calls disk mngr) | |
| menu2 | cancel | exit | | |
| | cancel and return | exit to DOSager menu | | |
| | /xgDISKMGR~ | /qy | | |

Here's a line-by-line explanation:

```
\d          /xgDISKMGR~
```
          1. Call "DISK MANAGER"
             routine

Line 1 calls the "Diskmgr" routine.

```
diskmgr   {goto}MESSAGE~
```
          2. Display explanation screen

Line 2 is the beginning of the Disk Manager routine. It sends the cursor to the Range Name MESSAGE, located in the top left corner of the screen describing the menu choices.

```
          /xmMENU1~/xgDISKMGR~
```
          3. Call menu below

Line 3 displays the Disk Manager menu. If **ESCAPE** is pressed during the menu display, the second command, `/xgDISKMGR~`, will cause the routine to start again. Its effect is that of a loop.

```
menu1     pause         list-files      select-diskette   exit
```

Line 4 holds the menu range, containing the selections to display on the top line of the menu.

```
you may now changelist files stored select files for rexit to DOS.
```

Line 5 looks like nonsense because it shows four labels overwriting one another. Each cell on this line holds an explanation line for the menu choice just above it. Although this is how such explanations appear in the macro, the menu displays each explanation. They will display beneath the menu choices when the choices are highlighted, without any overwriting. Here are the actual entries in the explanation line cells, beginning with the one for the far left choice:

| For choice: | The entry in the explanation line reads: |
| --- | --- |
| **pause** | you may now change diskettes in the drive |
| **list-files** | list files stored on this diskette |
| **select-diskette** | select files for retrieval |
| **exit** | exit to DOS |

```
/xgPAUSE~        /xgLIST~        /xgSELECT~        /xgEXIT~
```

Line 6 contains the first line of the macros that will be executed by each of the menu choices. Since there are several choices, we chose to devote this line to `/xg` commands that will redirect the flow of control to routines written else-where. As you've seen in other macros, this is an organizational technique to avoid writing four separate macros side by side.

```
pause     /xgDISKMGR~
```
          7. Loops back to disk manager
             routine

If the operator presses the ENTER key when the cursor highlights the default selection, "Pause", this routine will be executed. "Pause" is meant as a prompt, not as a menu selection. The explanation line for "Pause" informs the operator that he can now insert a new diskette in the drive. Therefore, the "choice" that is executed is a simple loop to redisplay the menu, in effect disabling this choice.

```
list      /flw                        8. List worksheet files and pause
```

Line 8 will be executed if the "list-files" option is selected from the menu. The command **File List Worksheet** will (1) clear the screen, (2) list the worksheet files on the diskette in the B: drive, and (3) specify the space still available on that drive (expressed in bytes). 1-2-3 automatically pauses when this command is executed. The operator must press a key for the worksheet to reappear on the screen (although 1-2-3 displays no message to this effect).

```
          /xgDISKMGR~                 9. Return to disk manager menu
```

Line 9 redirects the flow of control back to the original "Disk Manager" routine. This has the effect of redisplaying the menu.

```
select    /fr{?}~                     10. File retrieve and pause
```

Line 10 executes in response to the choice "select-diskette". After the operator has used the "List-files" selection to locate the proper file on a diskette, this command will execute the File Retrieve command and pause to allow the operator to select a file from the menu of files displayed in the control panel.

```
exit      /xmMENU2~/xgDISKMGR~        11. Call menu below (Esc calls
                                          disk manager)
```

Line 11 executes in response to the "Exit" selection on the menu. It calls another menu designed to prevent the operator from exiting accidentally.

```
menu2 cancel exit
```

Line 12 shows the menu choices that will display as a result of selecting "Exit" from the main menu. To prevent the operator from exiting accidentally, the default choice "Cancel" will return to the main menu.

```
cancel and return exit to DOSager menu
```

Line 13 contains the explanation lines for the menu choices in line 12. They are shown as you'd see them on your worksheet, overwritten. Here they are in more readable form:

| For choice: | The entry in the explanation line reads: |
| --- | --- |
| **cancel** | cancel and return to disk manager menu |
| **exit** | exit to DOS |

```
/xgDISKMGR~          /qy
```

Line 14 contains the choices executed by the menu described in line 13. The default choice, "Cancel" will execute the command **/xgDISKMGR** to return to the main menu. The "exit" choice executes the command "Quit Yes" to leave 1-2-3 and return to DOS.

# 3.6 Managing Memory

As you begin to take advantage of the power of macros with more sophisticated, comprehensive applications, you will doubtless find your worksheets growing in size. At some point, most people will encounter the limits of available memory. When that happens, 1-2-3 will beep, display the error message "Memory full" in the lower left corner of the screen, and prevent the current entry or operation from proceeding. Unless you've already filled your computer to the maximum available memory (this varies by computer, but 640K is the current IBM standard limit), the surest fix is to go down to your computer store and have more memory added.

We recommend adding more memory when your worksheets start outgrowing your computer. You want to spend your time getting jobs done, not in fighting file space. However, if you already have the maximum memory, or if the cost of adding memory chips is too expensive (particularly if you must buy a new board to mount the chips on), this option may not be available.

Fortunately, there are a number of other alternatives, but they are easier to implement if you PLAN for them initially. First, you need to know the four sources of demand on memory when you use 1-2-3:

1. Overall worksheet size.
2. Density of data on the worksheet.
3. Remembered worksheet settings, including range names and graph settings.
4. External factors determined in DOS.

We'll review them one at a time.

**1. Overall worksheet size.**

1-2-3 allocates memory in a manner similar to the way it defines ranges. A range must be rectangular, and 1-2-3 reserves memory in a rectangular block. Cell A1 always defines the top left corner of this block (we'll call it the "active range").

In Diagram 3.3, two entries were made on a blank worksheet, each consisting of the value "1". One entry was made in cell A20 and another in cell H1. With these entries, the active range is A1..H20.

**Diagram 3-3. Large active range.**

You can check the size of this "active range" by pressing the END and HOME keys (in that order). The cursor will move to the bottom right corner of the active range of the worksheet (cell H20 in this case).

Before the entries were made we used the **Worksheet Status** command to check available memory: 144,572 bytes were available. After the entries were made the **Worksheet Status** command shows available memory to be 143,936 bytes (636 bytes were used when these two entries were placed on the worksheet).

In a situation like this, all the empty cells in the active range between the two entries are using memory unproductively. The rectangle could be made smaller (using less memory) if the two entries were placed closer to the "home" position (cell A1).

We executed **Worksheet Erase Yes** to start with a fresh worksheet once again. The Worksheet Status command shows available memory has returned to 144,572 bytes. We made two more entries once more, and again, both consist of the value "1". But this time the entries are placed much closer to the "Home" position (cell A1), in cells A5 and C1. The active range now looks like Diagram 3-4.

**Diagram 3-4. Small active range.**

Another check of **Worksheet Status** shows available memory to be 144,516 bytes. Only 56 bytes were used to make the entries that required 636 bytes before! Simply reducing the size of the active range saved over 1000%.

The implications for worksheet design are obvious: you'll get more mileage from your memory by "compacting" your worksheets into less space. However, there are a few things that aren't obvious about this:

1. A Range Format applied to a cell can also define the outer corner of the active range—even if the cell contains no entry; so can Range Unprotecting a cell.

2. Merely Range Erasing cells containing entries cannot reduce the size of the active range. You must File Save and Retrieve the worksheet before 1-2-3 will release the memory reserved for those entries—even though the entries no longer exist. Keep in mind that if the cell containing the entry had also been Range Formatted, you must not only Range Erase it, but execute the command Range Format Reset as well.

### Notes On Reducing The Size Of The Active Range

If you are trying to reduce the active range of the worksheet, begin by using the **Worksheet Status** command to check how much memory is available. We strongly suggest you use the **File Xtract Formulas** command to create a file containing just the range of the worksheet you wish to retain. Then File Retrieve the new worksheet for use. This will eliminate all stray entries (or empty Range Formatted cells) you may have inadvertently left outside the new active rectangle. After you Retrieve the new file from disk, press END and HOME (in that order) to send the cursor to the new lower right corner of the active range. This last step will confirm you have executed the operation properly and consolidated the worksheet space as much as possible. You can then use the **Worksheet Status** command to check the increase in available memory.

### 2. Density of data on the worksheet.

A more obvious use of memory relates to the density of the data entered within the active range on the worksheet. A simple single digit number entered in a cell will use less memory than a long formula entered in the same cell. A short formula uses less than a long formula. You might apply this understanding in a situation such as the following example.

We'll look at an example of creating percentage calculations. Suppose you have a list of costs, and want to calculate the percentage of total represented by each cost. You might write a formula such as the one shown in cell C4 in the worksheet below (the formulas are shown in Text Format to facilitate explanation). This approach requires the entire formula, @SUM($B$4..$B$13), to be repeated ten times.

```
A2:                                                                    READY

                 A            B            C            D        E
 1  PURCHASES:
 2
 3  ITEM              COST    PERCENT OF TOTAL
 4  Computer        2,899 +B4/@SUM($B$4..$B$13)
 5  Modem             499 +B5/@SUM($B$4..$B$13)
 6  Add on board      439 +B6/@SUM($B$4..$B$13)
 7  Printer           499 +B7/@SUM($B$4..$B$13)
 8  Cables             25 +B8/@SUM($B$4..$B$13)
 9  Monitor           300 +B9/@SUM($B$4..$B$13)
10  Hard disk       1,800 +B10/@SUM($B$4..$B$13)
11  Lotus 1-2-3       495 +B11/@SUM($B$4..$B$13)
12  D.O.S.             60 +B12/@SUM($B$4..$B$13)
13  Training          250 +B13/@SUM($B$4..$B$13)
14
15
16
17
18
19
20
```

**Screen 3-25. Inefficient formulas.**

An alternative is to write the formula @SUM(B4..B13) once in cell B1. Then use the abbreviated formula, +B4/$B$1, to calculate the percentages. This results in a smaller formula being repeated ten times, and is more efficient in both use of memory and execution speed. While such differences are insignificant in an application the size of this example, they make a substantial difference in larger applications.

Here's how you would set up the new worksheet:

```
A2:                                                                    READY

                 A            B        C        D        E        F
 1  PURCHASES:        @SUM(B4..B13)
 2
 3  ITEM              COST    PERCENT OF TOTAL
 4  Computer        2,899 +B4/$B$1
 5  Modem             499 +B5/$B$1
 6  Add on board      439 +B6/$B$1
 7  Printer           499 +B7/$B$1
 8  Cables             25 +B8/$B$1
 9  Monitor           300 +B9/$B$1
10  Hard disk       1,800 +B10/$B$1
11  Lotus 1-2-3       495 +B11/$B$1
12  D.O.S.             60 +B12/$B$1
13  Training          250 +B13/$B$1
14
15
16
17
18
19
20
```

**Screen 3-26. Efficient formulas.**

Copying the formula in cell C4 to the range C5..C13 will produce the formulas to calculate percentages for each item in column B. Since the formula in cell B1 is now only written once, we have a more efficient use of memory.

When a worksheet recalculates slowly, or runs out of memory, check to see if it contains many similar formulas that can be reduced through referencing.

**3. Remembered worksheet settings, including range names and graph settings.**

Both these settings are "invisible factors" in that they don't show up on the worksheet itself, yet use some memory.

Once a graph has been stored with the **Graph Name Create** command, it occupies 461 bytes of memory. Each subsequent graph stored will claim an additional 461 bytes of memory. You should distinguish that from a Graph Saved for printing. The **Graph Save** command doesn't use memory, it writes a file to the disk, and uses disk space instead of the computer's RAM. To reclaim the memory allocated to a Named Graph, you must not only **Graph Name Delete** the graph, but **File Save** and Retrieve the worksheet.

Named ranges can also use memory, but considerably less than a named graph. The amount per Named Range can vary with worksheet conditions, but estimate 32 bytes per name. Unlike named graphs, 1-2-3 will release memory allocated to named ranges as soon as they are Range Name Deleted (without File Saving the worksheet).

**4. External factors determined in DOS.**

Several factors determined in DOS (the Disk Operating System) can have an effect on available memory.

Before we deal with specifics, we want to provide some background to help you understand what will follow. As of this writing, most computers running 1-2-3 use a version of Microsoft's MS-DOS. For example, IBM calls their DOS "PC-DOS", Compaq calls theirs "Compaq DOS", but both are just variations of MS-DOS in disguise. The same goes for the TI Professional, the Wang Professional, the Heath-Zenith Z-100, the Bytec Hyperion, and almost every other machine running 1-2-3. Convergent Technologies' CTOS (and Burrough's clone of CTOS, called BTOS) may be the only exceptions to this.

DOS, or Disk Operating System, does a lot more than operate the disk drives—it runs the computer itself, coordinating all of the computer's components (including keyboard, monitor, disk drives, and ports to send output to a printer or a modem) into an "operating system". For this reason, DOS must be loaded into the computer before running 1-2-3. This is why your 1-2-3 installation instructions tell you how to install DOS on your 1-2-3 System Disk before using it. If you have a hard disk, you won't need to do that, DOS should already be on the hard disk. Since DOS runs while you are using 1-2-3, it uses some of the computer's memory. How much memory? That depends on what version of DOS you have.

Running 1-2-3 with DOS version 1 takes the least memory, leaving more of your installed RAM free to be used for your 1-2-3 worksheets. On a 256K Compaq, DOS 1 left 156,220 bytes of memory once the worksheet was loaded, while DOS 2 left only 144,572 bytes. This gives DOS 1 users an immediate advantage of 11,648 bytes, a significant savings. However, there are other factors to consider in the choice of which DOS to use with 1-2-3. If you are using an IBM XT, IBM Portable Personal Computer, or IBM PCjr.,you must use DOS 2. DOS 2 formats disks with more storage space than DOS 1, and once disks are formatted with DOS 2, they cannot be read with DOS 1. Finally, DOS 2 contains several useful features not found in DOS 1.

For these reasons (even on a floppy drive system that doesn't require it) we favor using DOS 2, although it means giving up a little bit of memory. There are several other factors that affect memory that can be influenced from within DOS.

## Change the Autoexec.bat File

When the computer starts, it scans the disk in drive A: for a file called "Autoexec.bat". If found, the contents of this file will be executed just like a macro. The 1-2-3 System Disk contains an Autoexec.bat file with the commands:

```
date
time
lotus
```

This file prompts you to enter the system date, the time, and then automatically loads the Lotus Access System. However, if you're like us, you rarely use the Lotus Access System for anything... yet it occupies memory if you use it to access 1-2-3. Fortunately, you can access 1-2-3 without using the Lotus Access System. Start your computer with your DOS diskette, then remove it and place the 1-2-3 System Disk in the A: drive. Type "123" (omit the quotes) and press **ENTER**.

You can easily rewrite the original Autoexec.bat file using 1-2-3. Here's how.

First, place the following entries on a blank worksheet:

```
date
time
123
```

With a formatted disk in the data drive, execute the following commands to create an unformatted print file:

| Commands: | Which mean: |
|---|---|
| / | Slash opens command menu |
| pf | Print File |
| AUTOEXEC | File name is "Autoexec" |
| cr | Clear prior print range |
| rA1..A3 | Range: A1..A3 |
| <ENTER> | Confirm range |
| oou | Options, Other, Unformatted |
| ml0~q | Left margin: 0, Quit |
| gq | Go (create file), Quit |
| **(Note: the file has now been written to disk)** | |
| /qy | Leave 1-2-3 to return to DOS |

1-2-3 has created an unformatted print file with the name "Autoexec.prn" on the B: drive. This file contains the commands we want executed when the computer starts: date, time, and load 1-2-3. However, the file must be changed slightly before it will work: the extension ".prn" must be changed to ".bat". We'll do that with the DOS "rename" command, as follows. Note that the "A>" shown to the left of each command is the DOS prompt as you will see it on your screen. Do NOT type it with the command that follows it.

| Commands: | Explanation: |
|---|---|
| A> rename b:autoexec.prn b:autoexec.bat | Rename the file |
| **ENTER** | Confirm entry |
| A> type b:autoexec.bat | Show file's contents |
| **ENTER** | Confirm entry |
| **(the computer will display the contents of the file, as follows:)** | |
| date | File... |
| time | ...contents |
| 123 | |
| A> | DOS prompt returns |

You now have a file named "Autoexec.bat" on the B: drive. There is another file of the same name on the 1-2-3 System Disk in the A: drive (which is the original file that came with 1-2-3). Before you can use the new Autoexec file with 1-2-3, it must be copied to the 1-2-3 System Disk. To preserve the original file, we'll rename it so it won't be overwritten when the copying takes place. Before doing this, you must remove the write-protect tab from your 1-2-3 System Disk so the file can be transferred there.

| Commands | Explanation |
|---|---|
| A> ren autoexec.bat autoexec.bak | Rename the original file |
| **ENTER** | Confirm entry |
| A> copy b:autoexec.bat | Copy new file to the 1-2-3 disk |
| **ENTER** | Confirm entry |

**(Note: the new file is now in place on your 1-2-3 disk. To test this file, just enter the following:)**

| | |
|---|---|
| `A> autoexec` | Run autoexec file |
| **ENTER** | Confirm entry |

This new file will bypass the Lotus Access System whenever you start the computer with the 1-2-3 System Disk in the A: drive, saving you about 600 bytes of memory. More importantly, you now know how to use 1-2-3 to create your own "batch" files. Autoexec.bat is one kind of batch file (that's what the ".bat" extension designates). There are numerous useful appplications for batch files, particularly if you are using a hard disk.

# 3.7   Building a Macro System

As we've moved through the book, you've been introduced to succeedingly more sophisticated macros. In the next chapter, we'll present several "macro systems". A macro system is a group of related macro routines which work together to act as one comprehensive "program". Macro systems are nothing more than many simple macros working together.

While you have the techniques needed to create powerful, effective macros to handle a broad range of needs, you may not have given much thought to the development of more comprehensive macro systems. Aside from the larger size of these macros, the main difference between them and the smaller macros you've been writing is the coordination you must exert in their development.

There are some very useful analogies between the building of a system of macros and the structure of any other kind of organization. You will be able to apply your knowledge of how to plan, organize, and control any type of work to the development of a macro system. Our experience has lead us to favor an approach we call a "development loop", modeled below:

1. Identify the job to be done.
2. Break that down into separate tasks.
3. Write and test a routine to accomplish each task.
4. Link the routines to the rest of the system and test them as part of the system.
5. Test the system as a whole to make sure it accomplishes its purpose.

Step one is concerned with establishing goals. Step two breaks that down into specific tasks that must be performed, and provides specifications for the writing of routines in step three. After a successful test of the routines in step 4, they can be linked into the macro system, and tested again. When all macro routines are finished, the performance of the entire system should be evaluated in step 5 relative to the requirements set in step one. The name "development loop" comes from the fact that step five loops back to step one (as the source of the requirements), as any good planning and control system should. The development cycle works from major objectives, to intermediate tasks, to the detailed steps to accomplish an activity.

What's important about this approach is its ability to organize the development process into discrete steps. As indicated in steps three and four, the effectiveness with which each step is implemented can be verified as the process unfolds, identifying problems as early as possible. This is a key point, because when a problem is detected early in the development of a system, it can be corrected at far less cost than when it is found later in the development work. The work of changing them is easier, requiring less time, and the needed changes affect fewer other things.

## "Driver Routines"

An important aspect of the structured approach advocated above is the use of "driver routines". Just as the driver of a car is in control of the vehicle, a driver routine can be placed in control of a macro system. Another useful analogy is the human body, where the driver routine can be compared with the backbone, and the subordinate routines with the limbs. The limbs do all the work, while the backbone ties everything together properly. Thus the driver routine doesn't accomplish any work directly; it manages all subordinate routines that carry out the tasks of the system (such as printing reports or performing calculations). The advantages of building systems using drivers are that they can be tightly controlled, are extremely flexible, and easily modified.

There are two aspects of using a driver system. First, the task to be done can be broken down into small steps. Second, the driver macros arrange each of the steps in a hierarchical order, so they can be easily used or modified.

Subordinate macro routines are insulated from each other by the main routine. For example, the main routine uses an /xg or /xc command to call a routine to create a graph. When the routine completes its work it returns control back to the main routine with another /xg or /xr command. In this way, the main routine is the only link between subordinate routines, making it very easy to modify routines without having to rework the entire system.

A driver routine can do more than control macros within a single worksheet, it can also be used to call macros located in other worksheets. The macro-controlled file management system presented earlier is an example of a main routine that links to other worksheets.

## *User-Friendly Systems*

The term "user friendly" has been overused by the press and by software vendors. However, the fundamentals of the concept are sound, and should be part of any system you build. Basically, this means that each system should be designed with the end user in mind. Users need guidance in order to know what the system expects them to do. Menu choices should flow naturally from one to the next. At tricky points, additional guidance should be given through on-screen messages.

There are several phases that need to be considered:

1. Entry and exit from the system.
2. Logical menu structure.
3. User prompts.
4. Error trapping.

You must decide how the system will be entered. Will the worksheet be given the name AUTO123 so it will automatically load? Will another worksheet load it from a menu? Or, will you require the user to know which file to load?

When the user is done, the system must provide for the next step. The user can be sent to another worksheet, be given a blank worksheet, or be sent out of 1-2-3. Try to determine the most logical step, or provide several choices.

The menu structure needs to be organized around the main functions of the system. Each menu level should be grouped in a logical arrangement with the preceding and following menus. The user must be able to easily move between the menus in order to find the desired task.

At all times the user needs to know what the system expects as the next keyboard input. This involves the use of prompts, messages, and on-screen directions. While designing the macros, be alert to areas that may be confusing or complicated. Often a task may be broken up into smaller steps that are easier to follow.

There may be times when the system must receive data in a prescribed form. Values may need to fall within a range, or you may wish to restrict the type of input a user may make. There are three basic methods to error trap (catch an error before it is entered): 1) provide selections from a menu, 2) use 1-2-3 commands, and 3) test the value of an entry that is made.

Using regular or long menus (covered in Section 3.2) is the way to force a choice among predetermined tasks or entries. This is very inflexible, because all the possible variations must be built into the menu. The user does not have the option of allowing for an unusual occurrence.

Use of the Range Input command (covered in Section 3.1), and the **/xn** command (covered in Section 2.9) are two ways to have 1-2-3 control what may be entered onto the worksheet. Range Input will restrict the users to cells that have been set aside for input. The user cannot move into any other cells. However, there is no control over what is placed in the cells. The /xn command forces a number to be placed into a cell. However, it does not place any size limits on the number.

A value can be tested after it is entered into the worksheet by the /xi command. The test value is predetermined or entered through a menu choice. The steps the macro must make are:

1.  Place a number from the user into the current cell.

    ```
    loop 1 /xnEnter a number~~
    ```

2.  Range Name the cell that holds the entry.

    ```
    /rndENTRY~/rncENTRY~~
    ```

3.  Test the value of the cell against the limit with the /xi command, and loop back to have the entry made again if it does not meet the test.

    ```
         /xiTEST<ENTRY~/xmREDO~
    redo                          The number is too large.  Please try again.
         Press the SPACE bar to continue
         /xgLOOP1~
    ```

Another /xi command can be written to test for a lower limit. While these commands do allow any entry on the worksheet to be tested, the additional macro code will slow down the execution of the task.

An effective way to see if your system is user friendly is to have someone try it who knows little about the task. If they can get through it with little or no coaching, you have done a good job.

Now that you are developing systems, you may need to work with different computers that will run your macros. The next section deals with how fast different computers run, and how easy it is to move data between them.

# 3.8 Computer Speeds and Compatibility

If you are developing macros and systems for other people, and you are using a different computer than they are, you should be aware of the relative speed of execution between the machines. We used a Wang PC to develop several of the systems shown in this book. We found it to be one of the fastest and easiest computers to use of the ones we tested. The systems worked just fine on the Wang. But when we tried them on the much slower IBM and compatibles, some of the programs became unacceptably slow.

During the course of our research for this book, two things became apparent: 1) There were large differences in the time it took different computers to process information, and 2) Lotus had done an incredible job of making 1-2-3 appear to be identical on the different computers.

## Differences in Speed

In order to develop a basis to compare the machines, a benchmark test was developed. As the basis for it is in the book, you can easily test your own machine!

Computers have two major tasks. One is to transfer data between the memory storage device (floppy, hard, or RAM disk) and the active memory of the computer. The other is to process the data itself. The test was divided between these tasks.

The Mortgage Manager keeps its files in stored memory, and works on one file at a time in active memory. The UPDATE function goes out to memory storage to access each file, gets the summary data, and places it into a list in active memory. The list is then copied, sorted and processed with the Data commands.

The Create function of the Mortgage Manager was used to create 35 files. The files were put on each of the computers, and their floppy, hard, and RAM disks were tested. The Update function was used to see how long it took the different computers to retrieve and process the data. The procedure was timed from the pressing of "U" , to initiate the UPDATE macro from the main menu, to the reappearance of the menu.

We were suprised by the results. The IBM hard disk did not save nearly as much time as we thought it would, and the Wang hard disk was almost as fast as using a "ram" disk on the Wang.

## Comparisons of 1-2-3 on Other Computers

As we moved the files from computer to computer, we were also surprised by the ability of the machines to pass data files. All the computers could exchange MS DOS 1.1 files, and many could read MS DOS 2.0 files. Exceptions to this were the two Hewlett-Packard computers and the Victor, which had to have the files transferred to their special disks.

The screens, commands, and functions were identical on all the machines. The only differences were the placement of the individual keys. Sometimes different combinations of keys were necessary to invoke or stop a macro. (The two Hewlett-Packard machines had fewer rows on the screen.) The following table is a summary of test results.

## Test Results

| Computer | floppy disk | | hard disk | | ram disk | |
|---|---|---|---|---|---|---|
| | min | sec | min | sec | min | sec |
| Wang | 3 | 16 | 1 | 33 | 1 | 21 |
| Radio Shack 2000 | 3 | 52 | 1 | 17 | | |
| Texas Instruments | 4 | 48 | | | | |
| Compaq | 4 | 52 | | | | |
| Compaq Plus | 4 | 54 | 3 | 21 | | |
| Victor | 5 | 26 | 3 | 0 | | |
| Hewlett-Packard 110 (portable) * | 5 | 42 | | | 3 | 27 |
| Hewlett-Packard 150 (touch screen) ** | 7 | 22 | 6 | 14 | | |
| Zenith | 7 | 27 | 5 | 24 | | |
| IBM XT | 8 | 15 | 6 | 31 | | |
| IBM PC | 8 | 17 | | | 2 | 37 |
| DEC Rainbow | 9 | 14 | | | | |

* The portable could not hold all the files internally for the RAM test. This number was calculated from the files it could hold to give a comparison. The double-sided floppy diskette (3¼″) did hold all the files.

** The single-sided floppy diskettes (3¼″) did not hold all the files for the test. This number was calculated for comparison purposes.

# 4

# Advanced Macro Applications

# What's In This Section

Following on the heels of Techniques For Macros, this chapter shows macros at work in four advanced applications.

# Introduction

As we described in the introduction of this book, the macro systems found in this section are included as a means to teach you the important concepts for designing and developing large systems. Due to the extensive worksheet formatting associated with large macro applications such as these, we will concentrate on showing you the important techniques contained in each application, rather than try to reproduce the details of each application in its entirety. If you have purchased the diskette, you will be able to see each macro at work, but this isn't necessary in order to benefit from the principles this section will teach.

# 4.1   The Macro-Directory: A File Access System

The Macro-Directory is similiar to the Lotus Access System menu. It provides access to the files of a diskette. It's designed for use when you want to control access to diskette files through a macro, and is especially useful in applications for people who don't know how to use 1-2-3. But it also adds a very polished front end to any multiple worksheet application. Not only does it provide simple to use menu prompting as a way to access files, but it also traps errors effectively.

Underlying this macro is another very useful tool: the ability to offer your user more choices than can be placed on a macro menu. The MACRO-DIRECTORY in this example has twelve choices, four more than a conventional custom menu. More choices could have been easily added.

1-2-3's abilities can be put together in new ways by a macro to accomplish a task. This macro uses the /xn command to get a numeric response from the user. The numbers correspond to tasks that the operator may perform, and they are displayed on a message screen. The response is put into a criterion range. The macro then uses the Data Query commands in a data base that matches the numbers to cells containing macro code. A Data Query Extract command will extract the code, and place it into the macro. In this macro, the code will be used to retrieve a file.

The AUTO123 file uses a timer consisting of 230 spaces and an ESCAPE in a macro to display a copyright screen and instructions. The MENU file is then retrieved which displays the screen reproduced on page 180.

```
B2:                                                          CMD EDIT
Please enter the number of your choice:

          A                    B                         C
 1                       MACROS   FROM
 2               -* THE HIDDEN POWER OF LOTUS 1-2-3 *-
 3    == SECTION ============================================= NUMBER ==
 4        Two     The Basics Of Macros (All Macros)           1
 5    ---------------------------------------------------------------
 6        Three   Techniques For Macros                       2
 7    ---------------------------------------------------------------
 8        Four    Memo-Writer: A 1-2-3 Word Processor         3
 9                Address Manager: A Personal Address List    4
10                Label Writer: An Address Label Printer      5
11                Check Register: A Multi-Purpose Check Record 6
12                Pay Day: A Payroll Tax Register             7
13                Mortgage Manager: A File Management System  8
14    ---------------------------------------------------------------
15    Other Operations:         Special ACCII Characters      9
16                              View These Macros             10
17                              Blank worksheet               11
18                              Leave 1-2-3                   12
19                              Disk Back-up Instructions     13
20    ===============================================================
```

**Screen 4-1. Directory screen.**

When the macro executes, a prompt will ask users to enter a number. Here's the routine that does it:

`/xnPlease enter the number of your choice:~CRIT1~`

A number is selected from the right column, corresponding to the file to be retrieved. The files are described to the left of each number. The /xn prompt will automatically screen out anything but a number from being entered. If the user types the number as a word ("one" instead of "1"), or types an "L" as a "1" (as many typists do), 1-2-3 will beep and display the error message "Illegal number input". The user must press ENTER or Esc and try again, but the macro will not "crash" (a nice feature of the /xn command).

The number input is used by the macro to select the file to be retrieved—but in an innovative way that effectively traps any illegal responses. Although the /xn command traps any non-numeric entries, the user still may enter a number that's not on the list of choices.

The /xn command enters the number on the worksheet in a location called CRIT1, which is the second row in a criterion range. The third and bottom row of that range is occupied by the number zero permanently. Here's the criterion range and the input range it selects from:

```
===========================================================================
 - Input Range -             :------------------:
code        routine          :         code     :         <-- Crit Range
         1 /frMAC2~           :crit          10 :         <-- Crit Range
         2 /frMAC3~           :              0 :         <-- Crit Range
         3 /frWORDPRO~        :------------------:
         4 /frAD_MGR~
         5 /frLABELS~
         6 /frCHECK~
         7 /frPAYROLL~
         8 /frMORTGAGE~
         9 /frASCII~
        10 {goto}INDEX~/xq
        11 /wey
        12 /qy
         0 /xgMAC~        <--Note: this MUST be last choice in Input
                             Range for macro to work properly.
===========================================================================
```

The output range for this Data Query operation is located in a macro routine. The field name sits above two cells of output space. The first cell is named MAC3. Here's the code you saw above put back in context:

```
===========================================================================
\0        {goto}C~{goto}D~
mac2      /xnPlease enter the number of your choice:~CRIT1~
          /dqeq
          /xgMAC3~
          ---------------------------------------------------------------
          routine  <--- Output range
mac3               <--- Output range
                   <--- Output range
          ---------------------------------------------------------------
mac4      /xmMENU4~/xgMAC4~
menu 4       INVALID CHOICE: Please select one of the listed numbers.
          Press the space bar to proceed.
          /xgMAC2~
===========================================================================
```

Now let's describe the macro in action:

1.  The user responds to the prompt with a number.
2.  The macro enters the number in the second line of the criterion range. On the third line is the number 0.
3.  The macro performs a Data Query Extract from the input range to the output range. The first line of the output data is located in a cell called MAC3.
4.  An /xg statement transfers flow of control of the macro to MAC3. The macro reads whatever was extracted there and executes it.

5. If the user's entry was a valid choice, there will be two records extracted to the output range. The output range only has one field, with the field name "routine". Each record in the "routine" field in the input range is a line of macro code, as shown in the model. The extract will be two lines of macro code.

6. Since the position of a record in the input range is reflected in its position in the output range, and the record containing the "0" is last in the input range, the macro code for the criterion "0" will always be listed second. However, the macro code on the first line always executes an operation that self-terminates (such as a file retrieve), so in this case, the second line of code will never be read.

7. If the user enters a number not contained in the input range, the only record extracted to the output range will be the macro code matching the criterion "0". The record matching the criterion "0" is **/xgMAC4~**. Since it is the only record extracted to the output range, it will occupy the first line of the output range this time, instead of the second as before.

8. The instruction **/xgMAC4~** transfers the macro flow of control to a menu that acts as a prompt. The menu prompt states that an invalid choice has been made, and gives the instruction to press the space bar to proceed. The menu only has one choice to activate: it executes the instruction **/xgMAC2~**. This command transfers flow of control back to the routine that displayed the original user prompt to enter a number.

9. With this step, the macro has completed a cycle of trapping the user's error of the invalid number entry, advised the user of the problem, and looped back to re-prompt the user for another choice.

This simple method can be revised to handle any number of choices that exceed the eight-choice limit of a 1-2-3 number menu, and control errors just as effectively. With the number of file choices often exceeding eight, this method is very helpful as a disk manager.

Now that you've seen how to organize a system of macros on a diskette with a macro-operated diskette directory, we'll explore some of the macro systems the directory can provide access to.

# 4.2 Memo-Writer: A 1-2-3 Word Processor

Memo-Writer is an excellent example of the power of macros to organize and simplify the use of a group of 1-2-3 commands. Memo-Writer takes just those commands useful for word processing in 1-2-3, organizes them into groups of useful command sequences (to do things like indent and justify text), and makes them accessible through simple menus.

Memo-Writer demonstrates how a complete system of macros can be developed from numerous simple routines. As you look at some of the routines that make up the word processor in this chapter, notice that none of them are complex. In fact, each is a complete routine you could File Combine into another worksheet and use independently of the rest of the macro system.

Now we'll turn our attention to the design of the macro and review its structure. This will help you understand how to undertake a macro writing project and enable you to modify this one to suit your specific preferences.

Since the number of choices in any one menu is limited to eight, you must make some decisions about what should be included in each menu. The main challenge in developing Memo-Writer was to structure the menus properly. The most frequently chosen selections needed to be on the first menu, and succeeding levels of menus logically organized so users would have no trouble finding the functions desired.

## Word Processor Macro Routines

An outline of the menu structure is shown below. The names assigned to each menu within the macro are listed in the left column. The options contained in that menu are shown in the middle column. Brief explanations of each option are shown in the right column. More detail will follow this overview listing:

| Menu Name | Menu Options | Brief Explanation |
| --- | --- | --- |
| **menu1** | write | write on the current line |
| | paragraph-break | skip a line for a paragraph break |
| | up | move up one line and return to menu |
| | down | move down one line and return to menu |
| | indent | call menu6 |
| | erase | erase a portion of the memo |
| | options | call menu2 |
| | quit | return to entry menu |
| **menu2** | edit | edit text using edit keys |
| | indent-edit | call menu8 |
| | justify | justify paragraph |
| | line-edit | call menu7 |
| | up-fast | move up 20 lines |
| | down-fast | move down 20 lines |
| | save | save the current document |
| | print | call menu3 |
| **menu3** | range | to adjust print range |
| | align | set top of form and reset page numbers |
| | print | Print, call menu4 |
| | header-text | Place text you specify at the top of page(s) |
| | number-pages | Number page(s) at the bottom |
| | line-advance | Advance paper one line through the printer |
| | options | call menu4 |
| | return | return to menu1 |

| | | |
|---|---|---|
| **menu4** | top-of-form | move paper to the top of the next page |
| | print | print an additional copy of the document |
| | clear-settings | call menu5 |
| | return | return to menu1 |

| | | |
|---|---|---|
| **menu5** | all-clear | clear all printer settings, reset print range |
| | header-clear | clear the header text |
| | page-numbers-clear | remove page numbering |
| | range-clear | clear the current range setting |
| | range-reset | reset print range to one page (60 lines) |
| | return | return to menu3 |

| | | | | | | |
|---|---|---|---|---|---|---|
| **menu6** | indent | A | B | C | D | E | F |

choose indentation position from left margin, aligned under the letter specified, BEFORE writing text

| | | |
|---|---|---|
| **menu7** | insert-line | insert lines in the text |
| | delete-line | delete lines from the text |
| | return | return to menu1 |

| | | | | | | |
|---|---|---|---|---|---|---|
| **menu8** | indent | A | B | C | D | E | F |

choose indentation position from left margin, aligned under the letter specified, for EXISTING text

Now that you have a sense of the structure of Memo-Writer, here is more detail on the options and the macro routines they execute. The menu names are listed in the left column. Following each menu name, the center column contains descriptions of the choices it offers. Directly below each choice is the macro routine that choice executes.

For the sake of clarity we have omitted most of the **/xg** statements that transfer the flow of control from one routine to another. Therefore, the following does not comprise a complete listing of the macro. Rather, it is an attempt to focus on the functional routines. At this point, you should have no trouble providing the **/xg** commands to link these routines in whatever way suits you best.

| *Code:* | *Menu Option:* | *Explanation:* |
|---|---|---|
| **Menu1** | This is the main menu for the macro. | |

*Write:* allows you to write a line of text. When you press **ENTER** it will move to the next line below and present the main menu again. A more efficient way to use this command is to press the Down arrow at the end of each line of text. This avoids pressing the **ENTER** key, allowing you to move to another line of text without returning to the menu. When you do press **ENTER**, since this choice is located in the default menu position (far left), all that's needed to repeat it is to press **ENTER** again. The routine starts with the left alignment label character so numbers can be typed directly as labels, and ends with a {down} command to position the cursor on the next line automatically.

`'{?}~{down}`

*Paragraph-break:* press this when you've finished writing a paragraph and Memo-Writer will skip a line and wait for you to begin writing. You can edit the code of this routine to insert an indentation at the beginning of the paragraph easily.

`{down}'{?}~{down}`

*Down:* moves the cursor down one line.

`{down}`

*Up:* moves the cursor up one line.

`{up}`

*Indent:* allows user to select from a menu of indentation settings prior to writing a new line on the worksheet (indenting existing entries is handled in the next menu, because that involves an editing operation). The menu consists of selections lettered A through G to match the column headings at the top of the worksheet. The letter selected will indent the text to the column indicated. In the sample code here, the `{?}` is indented several spaces, which will align the entry under the "A" in the top border. Each menu choice aligns under the next column letter. This choice calls menu8.

---

**Menu2**   This menu allows existing entries to be changed.

*Edit:* editing of an entry

`{edit}{?}~`

*Indent-edit:* indents an existing entry through edit mode by calling menu8.

`/xgMACRO8~`

*Justify:* rejustifies, user selects number of lines to justify

`/rj{right}{right}{right}{right}{right}{right}{right}{down}{?}~`

*Line-edit:* allows user to select insertion or deletion of a line. This menu choice executes an **/xg** command to call menu7 making up the "Line-edit" function.

`/xgMACRO7~`

*Up-fast:* move up one page at a time

`{pgup}`

*Down-fast:* move down one page at a time

`{pgdn}`

*Save:* save the report under a file name

`/fs{?}~r{esc}`

*Print:* access to printing routines

`/xgMACRO3~`

**Menu3** This menu provides the major printing selections.

*Range:* the default range is already set to one page, longer reports can be printed by extending the range with this choice.

`/ppr{?}~q`

*Align:* align printer at top of form

`/ppaq`

*Print:* commence printing, then call menu4

`/ppagq`

*Header-text:* enter header text to print at top of each page

`/ppoh{?}~qq`

*Number-pages:* automatically prints page numbers at bottom of page

`/ppof1{esc}!- # -~qq`

*Line-advance:* advance paper one line through printer

`/pplq`

*Options:* offers more printing choices

`/xgMACRO4~`

*Return:* return to main menu (also available by pressing Escape)

`/xgMAC1A~`

**Menu4** This menu offers several more print operations, and is presented automatically after printing a report.

*Top-of-form:* advances paper through printer to top of next page

`/pppq`

*Print:* prints another copy of the report

`/ppagq`

*Clear-settings:* offers another set of choices for resetting print settings

`/xgMACRO5~`

*Return:* returns to prior menu (also available by pressing Escape)

`/xgMAC1A~`

**Menu5** This menu provide the "Clear-settings" options

*All-clear:* clears all print options

`/ppcarA35.H90~q`

*Header-clear:* clears header text

`/ppoh1{esc}~qq`

*Page-numbers-clear:* eliminates page numbering

`/ppof1{esc}~qq`

*Range-clear:* clears print range

`/ppcr`

*Range-reset:* sets print range to original one page size

`/ppcrrA35.H90~q`

*Return:* returns to menu3 (also available through pressing Escape)

`/xgMACRO3~`

---

**Menu6**   This menu consists of indentation choices described earlier. The code used to indent is a number of blank spaces followed by a pause, and a down command to move to the next line. These menus are the first three choices.

```
{?}~{down}
        {?}~{down}
                {?}~{down}
```

---

**Menu7**   This menu handles row insertion and deletion.

*Insert-line:* insert a row at the current location

`/wir{?}~`

*Delete-line:* delete the current row

`/wdr{?}~`

*Return:* returns to menu2 (also available by pressing Escape)

`/xgMACRO2~`

---

**Menu8**   This menu offers the same indentation choices as Menu6, but will indent EXISTING entries, whereas the other menu is used to indent prior to writing a line. The code for this is a little different than the prior indent, shown for the first three menu choices:

```
{edit}{home}{del}  ~
{edit}{home}{del}        ~
{edit}{home}{del}              ~
```

Here's an explanation of these lines:
The `{edit}{home}` brings the cursor to the beginning of the text entry, `{del}` removes the label character, followed by the spaces. The `{del}` could be replaced by `{right}`, which would skip over the label character instead of deleting it. After the macro deletes it, inserts the spaces, and re-enters it on the worksheet, 1-2-3 will automatically insert a new label character.

### Using The Macro

Have fun with the Memo-Writer, it was a fun macro to write. Not only is it useful as is, but you can extract and modify individual routines to suit your needs. The library of word processing routines presented earlier evolved from the Memo-Writer, and we use them constantly. Once extracted and stored in a library file, you can also use any of the Memo-Writer routines to assist you when writing on existing 1-2-3 spreadsheets. You'll find macros can be modified and used over and over to suit a wide variety of situations.

## 4.3   Managing A Data Base

Macros are the best solution to simplifying and organizing 1-2-3's powerful data management functions. For example, a macro can emulate the data entry form approach used in Lotus' Symphony, transferring data from the form to the data base and adjusting the size of the input range automatically. Under macro control, anyone can use 1-2-3's data base functions effectively.

In this section, you'll learn how to customize your own data management macros by examining a system that manages an address list data base. The principles shown here will allow you to set up any type of data base. The system, called the Personal Address Manager, includes the following functions:

**Find:**   Find any entry or entries in the data base matching specified criteria. Criteria are entered in response to a prompt.

**List:**   Same as above, except creates a report of the entries. The report can be printed as well.

**Browse:**   Browse through the data base.

**Maintain:**

   **Add:**   use a form to add records to the list

   **Delete:**   remove records from the list

   **Change:**   free form editing of the list

   **Sort:**   sort the list on any of several fields

**Save:**   Save the latest update of the data base to disk

**Quit:**   Assume manual control of the worksheet.

Criterion range? Input range? Output range? Sort Data-Range? Where are these functions? The user of this macro never sees a criterion range. Query criteria are requested through custom prompts and automatically placed in the proper cells. All Data Query ranges are redefined automatically whenever records are added or deleted. The same is true with the Sort Data-Range. With these things out of the way, the macro allows 1-2-3 to act as if it were a small dedicated list management program. Furthermore, the macro uses a forms data entry routine emulating Symphony's forms data entry.

With so much power, you might think this would have to be a very sophisticated macro. Actually, macros like this only consist of a number of simple, modular routines coupled together. In the following sections, we'll break those routines apart and reveal how each works. This type of building block design not only lets you expand your macros one step at a time, but you can also re-use the individual routines in other macros, making even more use of them.

## *Opening Operations*

The macro opens with a custom menu and screen. The menu is a full line prompt telling the user to make sure the CAPS LOCK key is on. The explanatory line of the menu tells the operator to press the Space Bar when ready to proceed. On the screen is the title of the macro, the Personal Address Manager, and an explanation of why the CAPS LOCK key is requested (it ensures uniform data entry and retrieval). 1-2-3's Data Query function is "case sensitive", meaning it will discriminate between the letter "j" and the letter "J". A criterion range containing the entry "jones" in the last name field will not find a record in the input range with the last name "Jones". Placing the CAPS LOCK on means all data entry and retrieval will use capital letters, removing one source of potential problems in retrieving data from the list.

The initial menu is designed as a prompt, not a menu. Here's the first subroutine of the macro:

| *Name* | *Macro* | *Comment* |
|--------|---------|-----------|
| scr1 | {goto}OPEN1~ | Set position to form window |
|  | {goto}OPEN2~ | Set position to form window |
|  | /wwv | Window screen |
| scr1a | /xmMENU0~/xgSCR1a~ |  |
| menu0 | Please Engage The ""CAPS LOCK'' Key | |
|  | Press the space bar when ready to proceed... | |
|  | /xr | |

The first two lines are always used when setting up a "hide" window onscreen: they position the screen properly. OPEN1 is the top left corner of the window, OPEN2 is the bottom right corner. Once the screen and cursor have been positioned, the window is created with the next line. This particular window hides nothing, rather it gives a nice balance to the title screen of the macro.

Next is the custom menu command **/xmMENU0~**. The menu is a long label in the first cell of the menu range, extending for approximately 75 characters. This displays as one long prompt to the user. Pressing ENTER or the Space Bar will execute the macro. This type of menu is an excellent way of getting a message to the user. The combination of this with an onscreen message is a good way to begin any custom macro.

Note that the custom menu command, **/xmMENU0˜**, is followed by the usual loop to trap the Escape key from crashing the menu. When a macro reads a menu, the flow of control pauses on the **/xm** command and displays the menu. If the Escape key is pressed during menu display, the macro flow of control jumps the **/xm** statement and reads the next thing following as a macro. With the **/xg** command following, it merely loops back to the **/xm** command again.

The macro then presents its initial menu of choices for use:

```
          ----------------------------------------------------------------
macro0    /xmMENUA˜/xgMACRO0˜
          find    list    browse   maintain   save   quit
          find an extract  browse thAdd  Deletesave anReturn to manual contr
          /xgMAC1˜/xgMAC2˜ /xgMAC3˜ /xgMAC4˜ /xgMAC5˜ /xgMAC6˜
          ----------------------------------------------------------------
```

This menu contains the primary operations for the macro, called the "main menu". After any operation is completed, this is the menu that is displayed for further choices. Another subroutine helps standardize the display of menus. It displays a blank screen below the menu with the message "Please choose one of the above".

What follows will be a description of how to handle the main problems encountered in automating this type of data base operation through macros.

## Range Redefinition

Every time a record is added or deleted from the data base, both Data Query Input and Data Sort Data-Range settings must be adjusted. There are two major ways to accomplish this: (1) inserting rows in the existing range, and (2) redefining the range using the border column and rows.

### Method # 1: Inserting Rows

By inserting a new row somewhere within the data base, the Input and Data-Sort ranges will automatically expand to include the new entry. In the following example, the Range Name INPUT has been assigned to the top left corner of the data base. That cell will contain the name of the first field.

| | |
|---|---|
| {goto}INPUT˜ | Position cursor at top of data base |
| {down}{down} | Move into Input & Data-Sort ranges |
| /wir˜ | Insert new row for new entry |

This method is easy to write, but has limited utility due to the following problems:

1. Any time you use the Worksheet Insert Row command, you insert a row across the entire worksheet, not just the Input range. You will have to

design your application to ensure no other data will be affected, and you may end up wasting quite a bit of space to do this.

2. You cannot insert the row after the last entry in the data base because it won't be included in the current ranges. In order to include the new entry in the Input and Data-Sort ranges you must insert it somewhere within the data base. Entries added this way will not be in sequential order (because we are inserting the new record above some of the current ones).

3. As soon as your data base begins to grow, the execution speed of this command begins to slow down. If a row must be entered for each record, the length of time the macro takes will become unacceptable.

## Method # 2: Border column/row definition issues

It's possible to define the data base input range by anchoring the cursor, expanding it across the top row; and then up/down an outside column. The {end} command used with the directional commands (such as {down}) can do this. In advance, Range Name the first field name in the data base INPUT. This will be the top left corner of the data base. Have the macro position the cursor there to begin the process:

```
{goto}INPUT~        cursor to top corner of data base
```

Now set the Data Query range:

```
/dqi{bs}            cancel prior input range
.{end}{down}        anchor cursor, extend down column
{end}{right}~       extend across rows
```

These lines reset the Data Query range after the addition or deletion of a record. The next range to be redefined is the Data Sort Data-Range, which differs from the Query Input range because it excludes the field names at the top of the data base. Here's the routine:

```
{goto}INPUT~        cursor to top corner of data base
{down}              exclude field names
/dsd{bs}            cancel prior datasort range
.{end}{down}        anchor cursor, extend down column
{end}{right}~       extend across rows
```

In line two, the {down} statement moves the beginning of the range to the first record, just below the field names.

This method of setting the range raises an issue: how can you guarantee there will be a consistent range of entries along the left column and bottom row of the data base? If the operator skips an entry in a field when entering a new record this method won't work. The {end} movement will stop upon reaching the blank cell, and the range definition will be incomplete. Two changes can deal with this problem.

1. We know there will always be field names across the top of the data base. That gives us one unbroken row of entries we can use to define the horizontal perimeter of the data base.
2. If we knew that either the first or last field (column) in the data base had consistent entries all the way down the column, we could use the {end}{down} command to define the vertical perimeter. But there's no way of guaranteeing the operator will always place an entry in either the first or last field of a record to create a consistent column. We'll have to let the macro deal with that. Here's how.

## Numbering Entries

If the data base happens to be a numeric data base, perhaps the last column is a TOTALS column, and we can simply have the macro create a total there. But this is an address list, so that's out. What we can do is create a new field in the left column called "No.". Prior to any data entry, the macro will automatically number the record in this field. Numbering records is a feature found in most data management programs, and gives the macro the consistent range of entries in the leftmost column needed to define the vertical perimeter of the data base. Here's how to number the entries:

| | |
|---|---|
| {goto}INPUT~ | 1. Cursor to top corner of data base |
| {end}{down} | 2. Down to last record |
| {down} | 3. Down to next row for new entry |
| +{up}+1~ | 4. Add 1 to number of prior record |
| {right}{?}~ | 5. To next field; pause for entry |

Line 1 moves the cursor to the top left corner of the data base. Since the far left field is the "No." field, the cursor is also at the top of this field.

Line 2 moves the cursor down to the last entry in this field.

Line 3 moves the cursor down one more row to bring it to the first open row for a new record to be entered.

In line 4, the macro adds one to the number in the record above to produce the record number. Since this data entry routine is used with every record, the first field will always be filled, creating a consistent column to define the vertical perimeter of the data base. This method has some other advantages which we'll explore later. For now, let's see how to use it to redefine the necessary ranges.

With the conditions described above, we know two things that can help us:

1. The field names will provide a consistent row across the top of the data base.
2. The number entries in the first field will provide a consistent column of entries along the left side of the data base.

Here's a routine that can take advantage of those entries to redefine the Query Input range.

```
/dqi{bs}            cancel prior input range
.{end}{down}        anchor cursor, extend down column
.{end}{right}~      change anchor, extend across rows
q                   quit to return to ready mode
```

Line 1 cancels the prior Data Query Input range so a new one can be entered.

Line 2 starts with a period to anchor the cursor. {end}{right} expands it down the left column containing the field entries, to include every record in the data base.

Line 3 begins with a period as well, but it serves a different function here. The period redefines the anchor point, placing it back on the top row of the data base. The {end}{right} commands that follow expand the range across the data base, using the consistent row of field names to travel across. If you haven't encountered this feature of changing the anchored cell in a range definition, try it. On a blank worksheet place your cursor in cell C5. Execute the commands / **Range Name Create** Test **ENTER . RIGHT RIGHT DOWN DOWN DOWN ENTER**. Make sure you press the period between **ENTER** and **RIGHT**. The range for this name is C5..E8.

Now execute / **Range Name Create** Test again. You'll see the current range definition highlighted. If you press the down arrow key, the range expands from row 8 to row 9, making the new range C5..E9. If you press the down arrow again, it expands the range to C5..E10. Now press the up arrow key twice to shrink the range back to its original size, C5..E8. Watch the range definition shown in the control panel, and press the period key once. Did you see the range change from C5..E8 to E5..C8? This means the anchor cell has changed from E8 to C8. Press the down arrow key and watch the range shrink from the top border downward to E8..C7. It is this same method by which you can change the anchor cell from the last number entry in the data base to the first entry. With the next command, {end}{right}, the data range is defined.

The method for redefining the Data Sort Data-Range is very similar with one small change.

```
/dsrd               Clear prior data sort range,
.{end}{right}       Anchor and move across field names
.{end}{down}        Change anchor, down No. column
.{down}~q           Change anchor, exclude field names
```

This routine follows the Data Query Input range routine shown above. The cursor is still positioned on the top left field name of the data base. Line 1 eliminates (Resets) the old Data Sort Data-Range, and prepares to define a new one.

Line 2 anchors the cursor and expands across the field names in the top row of the data base.

Line 3 changes the anchor and expands the range down the No. column along the left side of the data base. The macro is the same as the Data Query Input range macro so far.

Line 4 changes the anchor again and executes the {down} command. The "." contracts the range from its top, excluding the row containing the field names from the range. This final step is necessary because the Data Sort Data-Range always excludes field names.

## Renumbering Records

A numbering method automatically renumbers all records after a Data Query Delete removes records. It also renumbers records to reflect their new order after the data base has been Sorted. Every entry in the list must use this formula, starting with the very first entry, which adds one to the label entry above it (the field name must be a label entry, giving it the value 0) to create the number one.

It's not always desirable to have the records renumber themselves after a Sort. If they do not renumber themselves automatically, you can use the "No." field to Un-Sort the records back to their original order. We've reproduced the original routine below:

| | |
|---|---|
| `{goto}INPUT~` | 1. Cursor to top corner of data base |
| `{end}{down}` | 2. Down to last record |
| `{down}` | 3. Down to next row for new entry |
| `+{up}+1~` | 4. Add 1 to number of prior record |
| `{right}{?}~` | 5. To next field; pause for entry |

To "freeze" the numbers so they do not automatically change, remove the tilde from line 4. Then insert the new line 5 shown below:

| | |
|---|---|
| `{goto}INPUT~` | 1. Cursor to top corner of data base |
| `{end}{down}` | 2. Down to last record |
| `{down}` | 3. Down to next row for new entry |
| `+{up}+1` | 4. Add 1 to number of prior record |
| `{edit}{calc}~` | 5. Convert formula to simple number |
| `{right}{?}~` | 6. To next field; pause for entry |

`{edit}{calc}~` will convert any formula into a simple number. Once the formula has been converted to a number, it will no longer change based on the value of the number above it. Therefore, when a Sort is executed, the numbers of each record will remain unchanged. Another Sort on the No. field will then place the records back in their original order.

If you decide to freeze the values of each number, you will need a way to renumber the data base records when you want them to remain in the new order. The same is true when you delete records, you'll need a way to renumber them to fill in the gaps left by the records that were removed.

Here's a quick routine you can use to renumber the records when desired; it uses the Data Fill command:

```
{goto}INPUT~{down}       Cursor on first record number
/df{bs}.{end}{down}~     Reset data fill range
1~1~2047~                Start, step, stop values
```

Before we leave the subject of numbering, we'd like to emphasize that numbering is only one of several possible solutions to the need for having a column of consistent entries. You should understand that you can substitute any other entry in place of a number in this first column and still achieve the consistent column of entries needed for range redefinition. One possibility: have the macro enter a vertical line ( ¦ ) in either the first or last column of the data base.

## Defining Print Ranges

These methods are also used to create printed reports of the Query extracts. Just set up a similar field name structure across the top of the output range, placing the No. field in the far left column:

```
{goto}OUTPUT~      Cursor to top corner of data base
/ppcrr.            Clear prior range and redefine
.{end}{right}      Anchor cursor, extend across rows
.{end}{down}~      Anchor cursor, extend down column
agpq               Align;go;page;quit
```

## Managing The Criterion Range

The next step toward simplifying the Query functions is to remove the need to deal with the Criterion range. Set up a criterion range with a blank row beneath the field names, and define the range manually. The range will not vary.

The first step to manage this operation begins with the main menu we saw earlier. The FIND and LIST options are the **Query Find** and **Extract** functions. After selecting one of these two choices, a menu of the field names we want to be able to Query by is presented (only part of the menu is shown):

```
------------------------------------------------------------------
prompt1   /xmMENU1A~/xgPROMPT1~
menu1a    first name        last name          company        city
          Search by first name Search by last name Search by company Sear
```

The user selects one of the field names to search by, and is then prompted via the /xl statement to enter the particular entry to search for (wild cards can still be used):

```
/xlPlease enter first name: ~FIRST~
/xr
                   /xlPlease enter last name: ~LAST~
                   /xr
                                      /xlPlease enter company
                                      /xr
------------------------------------------------------------------
```

Each of the criterion field names has been used as a label for the cell below it in the criterion range. The /xl statement places the user entry in the criterion range in the proper field before performing the Query operation. The /xr following each indicates the operation is a subroutine: the /xr returns control to the main routine for the Find or Extract operation.

Here's the Extract routine:

```
macro2       /xcPROMPT1~
             /dqeq/reCRITERIA~     Extract records, erase criteria
```

We've already seen PROMPT1 above. All we have to add to that is the actual Data Query Extract commands shown above. Following that the macro erases the entries placed in the criterion range. The entire entry row in the Criterion range has been named CRITERIA, so it's very easy to clear that out each time. If the range isn't erased, we'll have trouble the next time we try to do a Query and have an old entry left in one of the fields.

The next logical step in the Extract operation is to display the Extract for the user to see and possibly print:

```
         {goto}OUTPUT2~            Display output from extract
macro2a  /xmMENU2A~/xgMACRO2A~
         browse          print            quit
         review output   print report     return to main menu
         /xgMAC22~        /xgMAC23~        /xgMAC24~
```

(The print operation was described above.)

## Data Query Find Operation

With the Find operation, things are a little different. A pause is necessary in the macro code after the Find command to allow the user to review the "found" records before proceeding. That looks like this:

```
/dqf{?}~q
```

A quirk occurs when the find is unsuccessful (no records match the entry in the criterion range). Here's what happens: at the pause, the Find locates no records and returns 1-2-3 to the **Data Query** menu; the {?}~ then forces the macro to pause while 1-2-3 displays that menu. The user of the macro is left looking at an unfamiliar menu (the 1-2-3 **Data Query** menu) with no idea what to do. Here's how to deal with the problem:

1. Place an extra empty row below the existing criterion range. In the space under the field heading "Number" (the far left field) place the following entry: (end of entries). This is NOT currently in the criterion range, it is one row beneath.

   CRITERION RANGE (consists of two rows only):

   | No. | First Name | Last Name | Company | City |
   |-----|-----------|-----------|---------|------|
   
   (end of entries)

2. Rewrite the macro code for the Find operation as follows (explanations below):

   | | |
   |---|---|
   | /dqc{down}~ | Expand crit. range to include new entry |
   | i{down}~q | Expand input range one row; quit |
   | {goto}INPUT~ | Goto top left of data base |
   | {end}{down}{down} | To empty row at bottom |
   | /rncEND~~ | Name cell "END" and... |
   | '(end of entries)~ | ...enter label there. |
   | {goto}INPUT~ | Return to top of data base |
   | /xcMAC1A~ | Prompt user for Find criteria |
   | /dqf{?}~q | Find entries and pause |
   | /reCRITERIA~ | Erase user criteria from crit range |
   | /reEND~ | Erase label at bottom of data base |
   | /rndEND~ | Delete range name |
   | /dqi{up}~ | Shrink input range to exclude blank row |
   | c{up}~q | Shrink crit. range |

## Explanation

The problem with the Find command explained above can be remedied by ensuring the operation will ALWAYS find something. Then the pause command works as intended. The criterion range has had an entry placed beneath it in the "No." field; a label: "(end of entries)". For the Find operation, the first step the macro takes is to expand that criterion range one row downward, to include this entry as a criterion in the No. field.

| | |
|---|---|
| `/dqc{down}~` | Expand crit. range to include new entry |

The next step is to expand the Query Input range one row downward as well.

| | |
|---|---|
| `i{down}~q` | Expand input range one row; quit |

This new empty row in the Input range will contain the label "(end of entries)". This label becomes a record that ANY Find operation will locate. It also serves to indicate the end of the data base when using the down arrow key to review the "Found" records. Here's how the macro inserts the new record in the data base:

| | |
|---|---|
| `{goto}INPUT~` | Goto top left of data base |
| `{end}{down}{down}` | To empty row at bottom |
| `/rncEND~~` | Name cell "END" and... |
| `'(end of entries)~` | ...enter label there. |

`{end}{down}{down}` takes the cursor from the top left corner to the row beneath the last entry. The range name END is created there, and the label `(end of entries)` entered on the worksheet.

Notice the label must be preceded by an apostrophe in the macro to force it to be entered as a label (otherwise the leading parenthesis will be interpreted as beginning a value entry).

The next step is to call the prompting subroutine (shown earlier) used to get the criterion from the user and place it in the criterion range. The actual Find operation follows that:

| | |
|---|---|
| `/xcMAC1A~` | Prompt user for Find criteria |
| `/dqf{?}~q` | Find entries and pause |

Finally, the user input criterion is erased from the criterion range, the label `(end of entries)` is erased, and all ranges are readjusted to their original settings:

| | |
|---|---|
| `/reCRITERIA~` | Erase user criteria from crit rng |
| `/reEND~` | Erase label at bottom of data base |
| `/rndEND~` | Delete range name |
| `/dqi{up}~` | Shrink input range to exclude blank row |
| `c{up}~q` | Shrink crit. range |

Could the `(end of entries)` label be left at the bottom of the data base? Yes, but some special arrangements would have to be made to reenter it each time a new record was added to the data base. That is another possible approach, but we won't cover it here.

# Data Entry

Macros offer you several ways of managing the data entry process:

1. Free Form Entry: moving the cursor to the row of the data base for data entry, and restricting entry to that row.
2. Automatic Cursor Movement: moving the cursor field by field through data entry.
3. Custom Prompts: using messages to help the operator to place the correct data in each field.
4. Data entry through a custom form: using a form to enter the data, and letting the macro put it in a data base.

## Method # 1: Free Form Entry

This method moves the cursor to the new row where the next record is to be placed and allows the operator to fill in the data.

```
{goto}INPUT~              Goto top left of data base
{end}{down}{down}         To empty row at bottom
+{up}+1~{right}           Number entry
/rncENTRY~                Create name for row...
.{right}{right}           ...and...
{right}{right}              ...define...
{right}{right}~               ...range
/ruENTRY~                 Unprotect entry row
/riENTRY~                 Restrict data entry to row
/rpENTRY~                 Protect entry row
/rndENTRY~                Delete name
```

The macro moves to the blank row beneath the bottom record, creates a Range Name ENTRY for the row (there are seven fields in the data base), uses the name to Range Unprotect the row, and uses the name as the target range for the Range Input command. Range Input restricts cursor movement to unprotected cells within the specified range. The method is simple to write, and similar to the next method.

## Method # 2: Automatic Cursor Movement

This method moves the cursor for the operator at the end of each entry, eliminating the need to use the cursor control keys:

```
{goto}INPUT~              Goto top left of data base
{end}{down}{down}         To empty row at bottom
+{up}+1~{right}           Number entry
{?}~{right}               Pause...
{?}~{right}                  ...to enter data...
```

```
{?}~{right}                    ...and move to next field
{?}~{right}
{?}~{right}
{?}~{right}
{?}~
{goto}INPUT~          Return to top of data base
```

The limitation of this method is its lack of editing flexibility. If a mistake is made there's no way to reverse it after pressing ENTER. But it's a nice method for repetitive data entry because it moves the cursor, speeding up the work. The ideal solution is to present a menu at the end of the operation for the operator to confirm the entry and proceed, or edit it. If editing is needed, the Range Input routine described above is used for free-form editing. This combines the advantages of both methods.

## Method # 3: Custom Prompts

Custom prompting with the /xl command can help the operator keep track of what to enter in each field, and eliminates the need to put label alignment characters in front of zip codes and telephone numbers. Here's how to modify the above routine to add both the custom prompting and the editing option at the end of the routine:

```
          {goto}INPUT~                         Goto top left of data base
          {end}{down}{down}                    To empty row at bottom
          +{up}+1~{right}                       Number entry
          /xlEnter first name: ~~{right}                Prompted..
          /xlEnter last name: ~~{right}                 ...data...
          /xlEnter address: ~~{right}                   ...entry...
          /xlEnter city: ~~{right}                      ...sequence
          /xlEnter state: ~~{right}
          /xlEnter zip code: ~~{right}
          /xlEnter phone number: ~~{right}
mac20     /xmMENU2~/xgMAC20~
menu2     proceed                              edit
          entries are correct                  change entries
          /xgMAC21~                            /xgMAC22~

mac22     {end}{left}{right}                   Second field in entry
          /rncENTRY~                           Create name for row...
          .{right}{right}                      ...and...
          {right}{right}                          ...define...
          {right}{right}~                         ...range
          /ruENTRY~                            Unprotect entry row
          /riENTRY~                            Restrict data entry to row
          /rpENTRY~                            Protect entry row
          /rndENTRY~                           Delete name
```

## Method # 4: Data Entry Through A Form

Data entry through a custom form gives 1-2-3 the look of a standard data base management program.

1. Create the form on the worksheet (sample below). In this example, the column-widths are adjusted so there are only two columns onscreen; one for each column of entries:

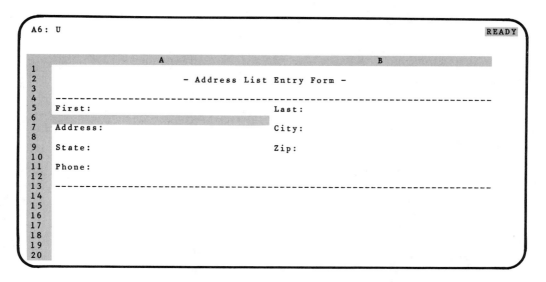

**Screen 4-2 Data entry form.**

2. Range Unprotect just the cells where the data is to be entered on the form (the cell below each field name on the form). All other cells on the form must be Range Protected (which is the default worksheet setting for cells).
3. Give the entire form the Range Name FORM. Give the first entry cell (just below the heading "First") the name START.

Now the following macro code will prompt the user, fill in the form, and allow editing afterward:

```
{goto}FORM~                              Display form on the screen
{goto}START~                             Cursor to first entry
/xlEnter first name: ~~{right}                    Prompted...
/xlEnter last name: ~~{down}{down}{left}          ...data...
/xlEnter address: ~~{right}                       ...entry
/xlEnter city: ~~{down}{down}{left}
/xlEnter state: ~~{right}
/xlEnter zip code: ~~{down}{down}{left}
/xlEnter phone number: ~~
```

```
mac20      /xmMENU2~/xgMAC20~
menu2      proceed                      edit
           entries are correct         change entries
           /xgMAC21~                    /xgMAC22~

mac22      {end}{left}                  To beginning of entry
           /riFORM~                     Edit entry cells only
```

The use of Range Input for editing works well here. The cursor is restricted to moving between the input cells only, skipping the protected field names (this does not require Global Protection to be Enabled).

Transferring the data from the form to the data base is handled by copying the data from a set of range names on the form to the proper fields in the data base.

Create a range name for each row on the form containing data. This range is two cells wide, containing both data entries on each row. Name them ROW1, ROW2, etc.

The macro to do the transfer uses many of the same lines shown earlier; instead of entering them directly, the macro copies them, and then resets the Input and Sort ranges to include the new data:

```
{goto}INPUT~                 Goto top left of data base
{end}{down}{down}            To empty row at bottom
+{up}+1~                     Number record
{right}                      Move right one cell
/cROW1~~{right}{right}       Copy first and last names
/cROW2~~{right}{right}       Copy street and city
/cROW3~~{right}{right}       Copy state and zip
/cROW4~~                     Copy phone
/dqi{down}q                  Reset query range
dsd{down}~q                  Reset sort range
```

Now use the range names to clear the form for future entries:

```
/reROW1~                     Erase...
/reROW2~                     ...entries
/reROW3~
/reROW4~
```

A custom menu should be presented to the user following entry of the last data item on the form. The menu offers the following options:

1. **Continue**   Enters data on form into data base and presents blank form for next record.
2. **Finish**   Enters data on form into data base and returns to main menu for other choices.
3. **Edit**   Free-form editing of the entry on the form with the Range Input routine.

4.  **Erase**  Erases data on the form without making an entry to the data base; return to main menu.

The routines that carry out these choices have already been described. The continue option makes a loop to continue data entry. It is the default choice to allow the operator doing a lot of data entry to just press ENTER when this menu appears to continue entering data.

## Controlling Field Name Display

When working with data in columns, the forms look better if there is a space between the headings and the data. 1-2-3 requires a Data Query Input range to have field names in the row directly above the first record of the data base. However, there are methods that allow you to have a space or a line between the field names and the first record:

1.  **First Record Blank**
    Make the first record blank. This works fine until you sort the data base in descending order and end up with the blanks at the bottom of the data base. To remedy that, begin the Sort Data-Range with the second record of the data base. The only other trouble with this method is the Output range. You cannot get the blanks to show up in your report. If you leave a blank row in the Criterion range, you'll get all the records, not just the blank row. The solution is to enter a space in each cell in this blank record, and keep a row in the Criterion range devoted to an entry with a space so that the blank line will be included in the report as well.

2.  **Field Names As Blanks**
    Make the leftmost field name a space by pressing the spacebar once. Move to the next cell to the right and enter two spaces, move right and enter three spaces, and so on until all fields are given a successively larger number of spaces. The Query function will recognize them as unique field names, because of the different number of spaces.
    Enter the descriptive field names ("First, Last, Address...) above these spaces as labels. Define the Data Query Input range starting with the row of blanks. The names above remain as descriptive labels, but are not used by 1-2-3 to identify fields, as they are not in the Input range. Copy the blanks to the Criterion and Output ranges so you reproduce them precisely.

3.  **Field Names As Lines**
    The technique for lines as field names is the same as method number 2 except that you replace the blanks with a backslash and a horizontal line (\-). In each field to the right, increase the number of lines by one (\--). Thanks to the repeating label character, each field name will display as a

solid line, but 1-2-3 will recognize them as being unique because of the different number of line characters each contains.

## Screen Management

The final ingredient to this system is the addition of screen management routines to mask some of the macro activity. Their description at the end of this section reflects the stage at which you should incorporate them into your macro: last. Once you've written the macro and are satisfied with its performance, the screen management routines are the icing on the cake. If you put them in before you've tested and debugged the macro, they'll obscure operations you need to observe.

It's up to you to select what things to show the user. The screen management techniques described in Section 3.1 give you all the control you need to determine just how the macro will look to users when it's done. You want to hide things like the transfer of data from the form to the data base; no one needs to see that. Put a message on the screen asking the user to "Please wait while processing" and hide the operation.

Since these procedures can be used by numerous macro operations, they should be placed in SUB-routines accessed via the /xc command. Once this has been done, all any routine needs to do is call the particular subroutine it wants:

/xcSCREEN1˜     "Please wait" routine

Here's what SCREEN1 might look like:

{goto}SCR1˜     Position top of screen
{goto}SCR2˜     Position cursor for windowing
/wwv/wwu        Create screen window
{window}        Move cursor out of window
/xr             Return to calling routine

## Summary

In summary, data bases can be made much easier to use through macros. The seeming complexity of the macro breaks down into manageably sized tasks when a structured, "building block" approach is used to develop one routine at a time. The principles presented here can be adapted to automate any data management application.

# 4.4  A Label Printing Macro

How do you format information extracted from a 1-2-3 database in order to write invoices, produce customer mailings and form letters, or mailing labels? 1-2-3's Data Query Extract function lacks a report formatting function such as that found in dBASE II, and can only produce reports in list format. But macros provide a ready solution to these needs.

The macro presented in this section formats and prints mailing labels and can be easily adapted to produce reports for other purposes. (We'll provide some tips for doing that at the end of this chapter.) In its present form, you can use it to print labels directly from a data base Input range, or to print just those addresses Extracted to an Output range.

After the extensive treatment given the automation of data bases in the previous chapter, we won't deal with issues related to setting up or using the data base here. We'll assume you have a list arranged in data base format, one listing per row, with field names at the top. That list could either be the original Input range or a portion of it Extracted to the Output range.

The macro will need to have two Range Names established on the worksheet. LABEL will be a blank area, and the range will be three columns and seven rows. LIST is assigned to the first field name above the first record in the data base.

A sample address list, located in columns A-F on the worksheet, looks like the one shown in Screen 4-3.

```
A5:                                                                    READY

           A            B            C            D          E        F     G
1    NAME 1        NAME  2      ADDRESS 1    ADDRESS 2   CITY       ST    ZIP
2    Jim Smith                  10 Maynard Ave PO Box 1  Springfield WA    76543
3    Big Corp.     Fred Jones   18 May St    Suite 4     Boston     MA    33445
4    Sally Black                9 Hill Rd                New York   NY    99999
5
6
7
8
9
10
11
12
13
14
15
16
17
18
19
20
```

**Screen 4-3. Address list.**

As shown across the top row, this database has seven fields (categories) of address information: Name 1, Name 2, Address 1, Address 2, City, State, and Zip Code. If the record lacks either a Name 2 entry, an Address 2 entry, or both, the macro will exclude the unneeded line(s) from the label, and move the following lines up to avoid blank spaces. As a result, the labels will be from three to five lines long.

Here's an example of a label formatted address entry with both a Name 2 and an Address 2 field included:

```
=============================================================

Big Corp.
Fred Jones
18 May St
Suite 4
Boston     MA      33445


=============================================================
```

As the label below shows, when the label lacks either (in this case, both) of those fields, the macro consolidates the label upward to avoid blank spaces.

```
=============================================================

Sally Black
9 Hill Rd
New York     NY     99999


=============================================================
```

The printing of the labels is designed for a continuous label form that is eight lines from the top of one label to the top of the next. If your label form is a different size, merely change the number of rows included in the printing range (this macro sets the size of that area through the use of the Range Name LABEL).

This macro uses three "pointers" (PTR, CEL, and ROW) to copy information from the data base. A pointer is a Range Name assigned to help a macro keep track of its work. As the macro finishes processing in one location, the pointer is moved to the next area on which to work, following the principles of looping described in Section 3.3.

| | | To print labels |
|---|---|---|
| macro | /xcFREEZE~ | 1. Freeze screen |
| | {ooto}LABEL~ | 2. Cursor to printing area |

|  | | |
|---|---|---|
| | `/rncPTR~~/rndPTR~/rncPTR~~` | 3. Initialize label pointer |
| | `/ppcrrLABEL~oouqq` | 4. Set print specs |
| | `{goto}LIST~{down}` | 5. Goto first field |
| | `/rncCEL~~/rndCEL~/rncCEL~~` | 6. Initialize cell pointer |
| | `/rncROW~~/rndROW~/rncROW~~` | 7. Initialize row pointer |
| Loop | `/reLABEL~` | 8. Erase label area |
| | `/rndCEL~/rncCEL~~` | 9. Set cell pointer |
| | `/rndROW~/rncROW~{down}~` | 10. Set row-pointer |
| | `/xi@count(ROW)<1~/wwc/xg\m~` | 11. Test end of file: quit |
| | `/xcCOPY~` | 12. Get name: subroutine |
| | `{right}/rndCEL~/rncCEL~{right}~` | 13. Set cell-pointer |
| | `/xi@count(CEL)=2~/xcCOPY~` | 14. Test name2: get name2 |
| | `{right}/xcCOPY~` | 15. Get address: subroutine |
| | `{right}{right}` | 16. Position cursor to... |
| | `/rndCEL~/rncCEL~{right}~` | 17. ...reset cell pointer |
| | `/xi@count(CEL)=2~/xcCOPY~` | 18. Test address2: get address2 |
| | `{right}/c{right}{right}~PTR~` | 19. Copy Cty,ST,Zip to label |
| | `/ppgq` | 20. Print |
| | `{goto}LABEL~/rndPTR~/rncPTR~~` | 21. Reset label-pointer |
| | `{goto}ROW~{down}/xgLOOP~` | 22. Goto next row, loop |

--------------------------------------------------------------------- subroutine: get label info

|  | | |
|---|---|---|
| copy | `/c~PTR~` | 23. Copy cell |
| | `{goto}PTR~{down}` | 24. Move to next label line |
| | `/rndPTR~/rncPTR~~` | 25. Set pointer to nextline |
| | `{goto}CEL~/xr` | 26. Goto cell-pointer, return |

## Explanation

`macro   /xcFREEZE~`                                    1. Freeze screen

Line 1 calls the FREEZE subroutine to hide the activity of the cursor from the operator during the macro. This is explained at the end of these comments.

`{goto}LABEL~`                                    2. Cursor to printing area

Line 2 moves the cursor to the label printing area, Range Named LABEL. LABEL is a range three cells wide and seven cells deep on a blank area of the worksheet. The width of this range is set to accommodate the width of the last line of the label, which includes three fields: City, State, and Zip Code. The number of lines in the range reflects the depth of standard mailing label stock.

`/rncPTR~~/rndPTR~/rncPTR~~`                      3. Initialize label pointer

Line 3 initializes a Range Name called "PTR", which will be used to position each element (Name 1, Address 1, City, etc.) of the address in the label prior to printing. At this stage of the macro, it's set to where the Name 1 field will be placed—the top left corner of the label. The macro uses the safety technique described earlier to initialize the pointer by first creating, then deleting, then creating the Range Name again. Whether or not the Range Name already existed from a prior operation, this routine will work.

> `/pprLABEL~oouqq`                          4. Set print specs

Line 4 sets the printing specifications, including the range to be printed (using the range LABEL), and the Options Other Unformatted setting to suppress page breaks, which are not needed when printing on label stock. This could be set later, when the printing is done, but there's an advantage to setting it here. Lines 1-7 are outside the looping part of the macro, and will therefore only be performed once. If this instruction was placed inside the loop, it would have to be read once for every label, slowing the macro down unnecessarily.

> `{goto}LIST~{down}`                         5. Goto first field

Line 5 moves the cursor to the top left field name of the address LIST, and then down one row to the first field of the first record, ready to begin transferring data to the Label range. By placing the Range Name LIST above the address entries (on the top left field name), you will avoid it being accidentally invalidated if an operator were to use the Move command to enter more data into the first record.

> `/rncCEL~~/rndCEL~/rncCEL~~`       6. Initialize cell pointer
>
> `/rncROW~~/rndROW~/rncROW~~`     7. Initialize row pointer
>
> loop    `/reLABEL~`                              8. Erase label area

As in Line 3, CEL and ROW must be initialized. Line 8 Range Erases the label printing area, clearing any prior label entry from it. This line is also Range Named LOOP, meaning that it is the first cell of the loop that will be repeated to print each label.

> `/rndCEL~/rncCEL~~`                        9. Set cell-pointer

CEL is a Range Name used to determine the portion of the address to be copied into the label form. It now points to the first record in the Name 1 column . As the macro progresses, this pointer will move across the row, "pointing to" the cells to copy into the label printing range.

> `/rndROW~/rncROW~{down}~`        10. Set row-pointer

"ROW" is a Range Name used to point to the row of the address list the macro is processing. Note that the range extends down one row: that'll be used in the next line of the macro to test to see if the end of the list has been reached. At the very end of the loop, the macro will return the cursor to this location and move down one row. The next time it loops and reads this instruction, the pointer will be set to the next row down.

> `/xi@count(ROW)<1~/wwc/xg\m~`    11. Test end of file: quit

Line 11 tests to see if the end of the address list has been reached. If the @COUNT function is less than one (zero), then there is nothing in the first field of either this row or the one below it, meaning the end of the list has been reached. Note that this requires each address to have an entry in the first field. Otherwise, the macro might end prematurely.

```
/xcCOPY~                              12. Get name: subroutine
```

Line 12 calls a subroutine to copy the first field to the label printing area of the worksheet (see line 21).

```
{right}/rndCEL~/rncCEL~{right}~      13. Set cell-pointer
```

The subroutine call was at the end of line 10, so the macro picks up again at line 13. The cursor moves one field to the right, and the pointer CEL is deleted and recreated, in order to point to the next field to be copied into the label form. But the new Range Name CEL is two cells wide, covering not only the Name 2 field, but the Address 1 field. In the next line, CEL will be Counted to determine if there is a Name 2 entry.

```
/xi@count(CEL)=2~/xcCOPY~             14. Test name2: get name2
```

Line 14 tests the two cell wide Range Name CEL to determine if there are one or two entries in it. If the @COUNT value is equal to two, there are two entries, and the macro branches to the subroutine COPY to copy the current field, Name 2, into the label printing range. If the @COUNT value is not equal to two, then there is no entry in the Name 2 field and the macro moves directly to line 15 to process the next field to the right, Address 1. Note that this assumes there will always be an Address 1 entry for each address. If there were no Address 1 entry, there could be an entry in the Name 2 field and the @COUNT would still be less than two, causing the macro to skip the field inappropriately.

```
{right}/xcCOPY~                       15. Get address: subroutine
```

Since there will always be an entry in the Address 1 field, the macro moves the cursor into that field and calls the subroutine to copy it into the label printing range. No testing is required.

```
{right}{right}                        16. Position cursor to...
/rndCEL~/rncCEL~{right}~              17. ...reset cell pointer
```

Line 16 positions the cursor so Line 17 can reset the cell pointer into the next field to be copied. Line 17 recreates the Range Name CEL, making it two cells wide, enabling the next line to test for an Address 2 entry.

```
/xi@count(CEL)=2~/xcCOPY~             18. Test address2: get address2
```

Line 18 performs a test on the two-cell wide range CEL, testing to see if there's an Address 2 entry. If there is, it branches to the Copy routine.

```
{right}/c{right}{right}~PTR~          19. Copy Cty,ST,Zip to label
```

Line 19 copies the last three fields, City, State, and Zip Code, to the label form all at once. These three fields can be copied as one line because they share the last line of the label.

```
/ppgq                                 20. Print
```

Line 20 prints the label. The print settings were taken care of earlier, outside the loop. Since the Unformatted mode of printing we're using doesn't issue page breaks, no Align command is needed to set Top Of Form. All that's needed is to print and quit.

```
{goto}LABEL~/rndPTR~/rncPTR~~         21. Reset label-pointer
```

Line 21 moves the cursor to the Label printing range, and deletes the Range Name PTR. PTR was set to the last line of the label just printed. It's now time to set it back to the top of that range in preparation for copying the next label.

```
{goto}ROW~{down}/xgLOOP~              22. Goto next row, loop
```

Line 22 moves the cursor back to the first field in the first row of the address list. It then moves down one row, and branches to line 6 of the macro. Later in the loop, the Range Name ROW will be reset to point to line 2. At the end of each loop, the cursor returns to the ROW and moves down one to continue processing the address list.

```
copy    /c~PTR~                       23. Copy cell
```

This is the first line of the subroutine "Copy". It copies from the field where the cursor is positioned in the address list, to the location in the label printing range currently assigned the Range Name PTR. In the first execution of the subroutine, the Range Name PTR points to the top line in the label printing range.

```
{goto}PTR~{down}                      24. Move to next label line
```

Line 24 moves the cursor from the address list to the line of the label printing area where the first field was copied. Then it moves down one line, in preparation for reassigning the pointer PTR to the next line of the label.

```
/rndPTR~/rncPTR~~                     25. Set pointer to nextline
```

Line 25 deletes the Range Name PTR and assigns it to the Label printing line where the cursor is currently positioned. When this subroutine is repeated for the next field of the address, that field will be copied to this new location of PTR, one line below where the last line was copied.

```
{goto}CEL~/xr                         26. Goto cell-pointer, return
```

Line 26 repositions the cursor from the label printing area to the address list. The cursor goes to the Range Name CEL, which is the field just copied into the label printing range. This prepares the macro to move to the next field and repeat the copying process. The /xr command returns control to the main routine.

With so much cursor movement, this macro is an ideal candidate for screen management techniques. Here's the routine named "Freeze" called in the first line of the macro above:

```
======================================================================
----------------------------------------------Freeze screen
freeze   {goto}UL~{goto}BR~              Prepare to window
         /wwv/wwu                        Create and unsynch window
         {window}/xr                     Move cursor out, Return


======================================================================
```

The message screen displayed while the macro is processing is shown below. The top left cell in the screen is named "UL" (Upper Left) and the bottom right cell "BR".

```
======================================================================
                      A                                              B



          Processing Labels...

          Please Wait One Moment



----------------------------------------------------------------------
!!!!!!!!!!!!!!!!!!!!!!!!!!!!!!!!!!!!!!!!!!!!!!!!!!!!!!!!!!!!!!!!!!!!!!!!
======================================================================
```

## Adaptation Tips

The macro can be adapted to suit your needs quite easily.

*Label Types:* If you are using a different size label than the one we've used in this example, simply adjust the dimensions of the Range Name LABEL used in our example. You'll recall LABEL was used to define the print range, so changing it will change the print range automatically. You may need it to be several lines longer or shorter, depending on the spacing of the labels you are using, and the number of lines of data you wish to print.

*Type Of Form:* The information is copied from the address list into the mailing label area one field at a time, through the use of several moving pointers. You can change the locations these pointers move to, in order to accommodate the changes in design of your form. Alternatively, you might also assign each entry in the form a different Range Name. As you move across the data base with the CEL pointer used here, you could simply copy each field from the data base to the proper Range Name in the form. When the form is complete, print it, erase it, and loop to the next entry until you reach the end of your list.

*Selective Printing:* If you wish to select only certain records from a data base to be printed on forms, simply Extract those records to an Output range. Then proceed to use your Output range as the data for your label.

# A

# Appendix

# What's In This Appendix

We have included here the documentation of three additional systems contained on the optional book diskette. We felt these three should be separated from the rest of the book.

These three systems are complex. The documentation helps you understand how they work, but it would be difficult to duplicate them without the diskette. However, you should read through these chapters even if you do not have the diskette, because they explain more fully several points from the book.

We tried to make the diskette a "value added" component of the book. It is not necessary in order to learn the concepts presented in the book, but it should prove to be extremely useful in its own right.

# A.1 How to Use the Optional Diskette

## *Requirements*

**Hardware:** Minimum of 256K RAM. Single double-sided double-density disk drive.

**Software:** DOS Version 1.1 or higher. Lotus 1-2-3 Version 1A.

## *Instructions*

**NOTE:** To save yourself time, review these instructions once before proceeding with the actual operation.

### For Dual Floppy Disk Drive Systems

1. Remove the diskette from its package, exercising care not to handle the shiny surface of the diskette exposed by the cover slot. The disk should be placed in the "B" disk drive. If you don't know which that is, follow these instructions:

   A. (1) For a computer with side by side mounted disk drives, such as an IBM Personal Computer, the disk should go into the RIGHT hand disk drive. (2) When you open the drive door, observe on which side the drive door is hinged. This is the side toward which the diskette label should face. (3) Insert the diskette so the edge with the exposed slot goes in first.

   B. For a computer with disk drives mounted one over the other, such as a Texas Instruments Professional Computer, the disk should go into the LOWER of the two drives.

   Close the disk drive door securely. Failure to close the door completely will prevent the computer from reading the diskette.

2. Place your 1-2-3 System Disk in the "A" drive. It is the opposite drive from the one described above. Close the drive door securely. Your 1-2-3 System Diskette should have been configured according to the instructions contained in the "Getting Started" booklet accompanying your Lotus 1-2-3 manual. Consult your dealer or Lotus Support if you have difficulties with this process. It must be done correctly.

3. Turn on the computer.

4. Follow the normal start-up prompts displayed by your computer. Usually these prompts will ask for a date and time, requiring that you enter them in specific format and press ENTER after each entry. Consult your com-

puter manual or call your dealer for details on your particular computer if you have trouble with this step.

5. After responding to the date and time prompts, the Lotus Access System will load itself into the computer. When you see the first menu on the screen, press ENTER to select 1-2-3.

6. When the 1-2-3 copyright notice displays on the screen, press any key to proceed. At this point, "Using Macros" MACRO-DIRECTORY worksheet will automatically load itself and display on the screen. Simply press the space bar to proceed past the copyright notice. When you see the prompt requesting a number, select one of the numbers displayed in the right column of the screen. Type the number and press ENTER. The macros you selected will load themselves. Consult Section Four and this Appendix for descriptions of each system. Also included are the macros from Section 2 and 3.

7. If your computer was already running 1-2-3 when you placed the "Using Macros" diskette in the drive, type the following:

| Keys to press: | Explanation: |
| --- | --- |
| / | Activates 1-2-3's command menu |
| f | File |
| r | Retrieve |
| **auto123** | Name of file to retrieve |
| **ENTER** | Press the ENTER key |

This will take you to step 6. Continue with those instructions.

## For Hard Disk Systems And Single Floppy Disk Drive Systems

1. Turn on the computer and respond to the normal prompts for date and time. Enter the date and time in the prescribed format and press ENTER after each entry. If you have trouble with this operation, consult your computer manual or computer dealer.

2. Place the 1-2-3 System diskette in the "A" drive (the floppy disk drive) and close the disk drive door securely. Failure to close the drive door completely will prevent the computer from reading the diskette. The 1-2-3 System diskette must have been configured according to the instructions in the "Getting Started" manual accompanying your 1-2-3 manual. If you have difficulties with that process, consult your dealer or Lotus Support.

3. The Lotus Access System will load itself into the computer. If it has not loaded, type **LOTUS** and press **ENTER**. When you see the first menu on the screen, press ENTER to select 1-2-3.

4. When the 1-2-3 copyright notice displays on the screen, press any key to proceed. When you see a blank worksheet on the screen, remove the 1-2-3 System Diskette from the drive and place it in its protective cover. Remove "The Hidden Power Of 1-2-3" diskette from its package and place it in the floppy disk drive. Close the disk drive door securely.

5. Execute the commands listed below to begin:

| Keys to press: | Explanation: |
|---|---|
| / | Activates 1-2-3's command menu |
| **f** | File |
| **d** | Directory |
| **a:\** | Directory name |
| **ENTER** | Press the ENTER key |
| / | Activates 1-2-3's command menu |
| **f** | File |
| **r** | Retrieve |
| **auto123** | Name of file to retrieve |
| **ENTER** | Press the ENTER key |

6. "The Hidden Power Of 1-2-3" MACRO-DIRECTORY worksheet will load itself and display on the screen. Simply press the space bar to proceed past the notice. When you see the prompt requesting a number, select one of the numbers displayed in the right column of the screen. Type the number and press ENTER. The macros you selected will load themselves. Follow the prompts and menus from there.

7. If your computer was already running 1-2-3 when you started, begin with step 5.

## Additional Notes

Be sure to make a backup of the diskette. Put the original in a safe place so you can restore any files that are modified.

Each macro file has its own menus to work from. When you first retrieve a file, you will get a choice between Viewing the Macros and Returning to the MACRO-DIRECTORY to choose another file.

You will also have a choice to execute the macro directly. However, all the macros are designed to be used in conjunction with the explanatory text in "The Hidden Power Of 1-2-3". Use the appropriate sections of the book to learn what each macro does and how it is designed.

One effective use of the diskette is to extract sections of the macros into your own worksheets for your own use. The macros from Chapters 2 and 3 of the book have each been given the names used in the book to allow you to **File Combine** them directly into your worksheets.

## A.2 Check Register: A Multi-Purpose Check Record

This check register template has been designed to be powerful and as easy as possible to use, yet also to be flexible. In this way it takes advantage of 1-2-3's strengths. The basic design of the system is a "driver" worksheet, for each account, with subsidiary files containing the monthly information.

These are some of its features:

- creates new accounts
- creates new monthly registers, bringing the balances forward
- all information only entered once
- multiple allocations available for any check or deposit
- unlimited number of checks or deposits per month
- produces summaries of any specified months
- easily adapts to any business or home use

The Check Register was included not only as a learning tool, but also as a template that would be useful as an office tool. It uses several unique methods to manipulate the data, and to speed up its processing. Many check register templates we have seen have to compromise on size, speed, or flexibility. We feel this register gives all three.

The following are its major functions:

**VIEW**—This allows the user to go to the current monthly register or the consolidation. The files can be edited or printed by the user. Each check or deposit can be noted for the month it cleared the bank, aiding in reconciling the account.

**INSERT**—This function is used to insert each check or deposit. The sub-menu will keep returning until the user chooses to quit. The macro then saves the updated monthly register and returns to the main menu.

**SAVE**—If editing is done on the worksheet, this will save the monthly information or the current worksheet.

**RETRIEVE**—This provides for the retrieval of any monthly register.

**CONSOLIDATE**—The user can consolidate the totals of any group of monthly registers in order to produce monthly, quarterly, semi-annual, or annual reports.

**NEW**—This function produces a new monthly register, with the headings and balances carried forward. Or, it will produce a new check register for another account.

**QUIT**—This will take the user out of the system.

NOTE: No print menu is provided in this template for two reasons. First, it is very easy to use 1-2-3's print commands. Second, the number of variables in how the files would be printed on each printer are too great, as the files are wider than normal paper.

## Instructions To Use The System

After the template is loaded, the Main Menu waits for instructions from the user.

## Create a new check register

NEW and ACCOUNT are used to create a new check register. The worksheet is prepared, and the user is asked for the following information: Account Name, the number of the first monthly check register (i.e. 3 = March), The Fiscal Year End, The Name of the bank used, the Account Number, and the Beginning balance.

The user is then asked for file names for the Check Register and the first Monthly Register. These must conform to the demands of the computer system. They can be no longer than eight characters, and may not have spaces or any punctuation. If the company name was Smith Enterprises, a suggested file name is SmiEnt84. This name allows a new register to be created merely by changing the year.

To help identify the monthly register, a combination of the name, month, and year should be used. A suggestion for March of 1984 would be SmEn384. Notice that only four characters were allowed for the name. This makes room for the later two digit months.

The INSERT menu is then called so that transactions can be entered. When RETURN is selected from this menu, the entries to the monthly file are saved and the Main Menu will appear.

## Create a new monthly register

NEW and MONTH are selected to create the register for the next month. Make sure that the most recent register is in the worksheet, as the balance will be brought forward and all the transactions deleted. The user will be asked for the number of the month of the register (i.e. 4 = April), and then for the new file name (see comments on file names above). This should be consistent with the previous month's file name. For April this would be SmEn484.

The new file is saved, and the INSERT menu then appears for entry of transactions. When RETURN is selected from this menu, the entries to the monthly file are saved and the main menu will appear.

## Work with a prior monthly register

RETRIEVE is used to get a register from a prior month. The list of registers for the account will be displayed, with the instruction to enter the number corresponding to the desired file. After entering the number and pressing **ENTER**, the file is retrieved from the disk. The main menu will appear so that the user may insert additional transactions, view the register, or edit it.

## View or Edit a register

VIEW moves the screen to the current monthly register or the summary file. Any information on the file may be edited, such as noting returned checks or correcting entries. Note that if an amount is changed, the current register will be automatically updated but any later registers will not. Make a note of the new ending balance. This must be manually inserted in any later registers.

## Insert transactions into a register

INSERT will enter transactions into the current register. Note that dates must be entered in a label format.

CHECK records charges to the check register. A line will be inserted and the cursor will move to the Date column of the Check field. Type in the check or bank charge information, using the arrow keys to move to the next column. First enter the date, check number, and payee information. Place the amount of the check in the appropriate expense column.

If the check covers more than one type of expense, place the proper amount in each column. The total of the check will be accumulated from each of these entries. The INSERT menu will return after **ENTER** is pressed.

DEPOSIT records receipts. A line will be inserted and the cursor will move to the Date column of the Deposit field. As indicated above, use the arrow keys instead of the **ENTER** key to enter the data. Enter the Date and where the receipt came from. The amount of the receipt may be split between the categories, and the total will be recorded as the deposit. The INSERT menu will return after **ENTER** is pressed.

The RETURN selection will save the transactions and return to the main menu.

## Save changes after editing

SAVE is used to save changes to either the monthly register or the account worksheet.

ACCOUNT will save changes made to the FORM of the check register. This would include changes to headings or columns that have been added or deleted. (Be sure to change the summary columns as well!)

MONTH will save changes made to the CONTENT of a monthly register, such as a spelling that has been corrected, an amount changed, or a transaction added.

## Select monthly registers to consolidate

CONSOLIDATE will post the totals from any specified months to the summary file. The user is asked to enter the number of the first and last file of the group to be consolidated. The total line from each file in the range is placed in the summary file, and the screen moves to the file.

## Changes to the Check Register

This template was designed to be as flexible and easy to modify as possible. The main points to remember when making changes are:

1.  Any change made to the check register must also be done to the summary file.
2.  Columns should only be inserted inside the check or deposit groupings so the formulas will include them.
3.  For each inserted column, the corresponding cell in the "formula" row (Range Named R) must be Range Unprotected to allow the INSERT function to work properly.
4.  Changes to the register structure should only be made to a newly created account. Otherwise the summary file will mix the categories from previously created unmodified registers.
5.  For easy movement, the register area is Range Named A, the summary file is Range Named S, and the formula row Range Named R. Just press the **GOTO** function key, the letter, and **ENTER**.
6.  There are just as many columns in the summary file as in the register— but the unneeded ones such as dates and names are set to be only one space wide.
7.  After inserting a column in the register, the entries in an adjacent column should be copied into it. This will capture all the necessary formulas and cell formats.
8.  Make the columns match in the summary file. The contents of the adjacent columns can be copied into the new columns. The title row of the

register can then be copied to the summary file title row and the unneeded entries erased to keep them from being displayed.

9. Be sure to SAVE the new account!

One of the changes needed will be to separate this system from the book diskette. This requires three steps. First, erase the menu macro Range Named MENU. Second, change the macro instructions for the Quit choice of MENU1. This could be a variety of functions, depending on your needs. /wey would erase the current worksheet. /qy would leave 1-2-3, and /fr{?}˜ would allow a different worksheet to be selected. Third, the \0 macro needs to have BLANK changed to BLANK1, and MENU changed to MENU1.

## Worksheet Design

This is the layout of the information on the worksheet:

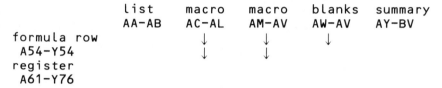

```
                list      macro     macro     blanks    summary
                AA-AB     AC-AL     AM-AV     AW-AV     AY-BV
formula row               ↓         ↓         ↓
  A54-Y54                 ↓         ↓
register
  A61-Y76
```

The register is placed below the rest of the worksheet so that the INSERT function will not interfere with anything else.

## Menu Design

The menus are organized into a main menu and one layer of submenus. Some of the macros are called by both a menu selection and other macros.

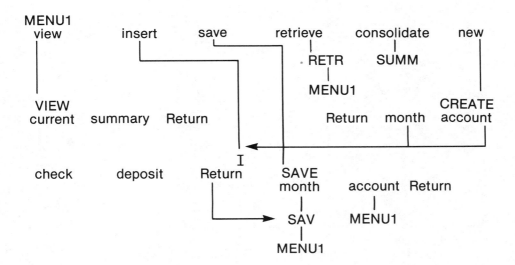

**Diagram A-1. Check Register menu organization.**

## System Macros

The menus are spread out so they can be read. To work properly, they must be in the menu format.

The Main Menu runs the system. It includes each of the major functions that will be performed.

```
menu1    view     insert  save   retrieve  consolidate new quit
```

(view)     to see the files
           /xmVIEW~/xg\M~

(insert)   to record a transaction
           {goto}A~                     move to file
           /xmI~/xg\M~              display Insert menu

(save)     to save the monthly check register
           /xmSAVE~/xg\M~

(retr)     to retrieve another month
           /xgRETR~

(consol)   to produce a consolidation of designated check registers
           /xgSUMM~

(new)  `to create new check registers`
     `/xmCREATE~/xg\M~`

(quit)  `to leave the Check Register`
     `/xmMENU~/xg\M~`

The access macros display the Entry Menu and the Main Menu.

```
--------------------------------------Display Entry Menu
\0       {goto}BLANK~/xmMENU~/xg\0~
--------------------------------------Display Main Menu
\m       {goto}BLANK1~/xmMENU1~/xg\M~
```

The subsidiary macro is called by other macros. `freeze` will display a screen while a macro is running.

```
------------------------------------FREEZE SCREEN
freeze  {goto}UL~                move to upper left corner
        {goto}BR~                move to lower right corner
        /wwv/wwu                 create window
        {window}/xr              move cursor out, start macro
```

The system macros do the actual work of the template. The View menu moves the cursor to the monthly register or the summary file.

(view)  `current summary RETURN`

(cur)  `to see the current check register`
    `{goto}A~/xq`

(summ)  `to see the yearly summary`
     `{goto}S~/xq`

(return) `to return to the main menu`
    `/xg\M~`

The I menu inserts transactions into the monthly register. It is written as compactly as possible to minimize execution time. The entries are repeated in the second line of the menu macro so that the command lines will always remain the same when the menu is displayed. After a transaction is entered, the macro loops back to redisplay the I menu, ready for the next transaction.

- The Formula row (Range Named R) also contains the cell formats. This includes cells that must be Range Unprotected for the Range Insert command to work.
- Range Names could not be used at the bottom of the file to control cursor movement because each register would have a different number of transactions. This would put the Range Names of each register in different cells, so they could not be used as reference points as different registers are brought into the system. Instead, the vertical and horizonal lines in the

register control cursor movement using the **{end}** commands. These move the cursor until a break in the line is found.
- When RETURN is selected, the SAV macro is called.
- The cursor is at A when the macros start.

```
i         check    deposit RETURN
(check)   enter a check  Enter a deposit  Save and Return to the main menu
          {end}{down}{up}{up}              move to insert location
          /wir~/cR~~                       insert row, copy formulas
          {goto}A~{goto}T~/wtb             set titles
          {goto}C~{end}{down}              move to check file
          /ri{end}{right}{up}{up}~         set insert range, insert
          /wtc{goto}A~                     clear titles, move to A
          /rp{end}{down}{end}{right}~      protect new row
          /xmI~/wwc/xg\M~                  loop

(dep)     enter a check  Enter a deposit  Save and Return to the main menu
          {end}{down}{up}{up}              move to insert location
          /wir~/cR~~                       insert row, copy formulas
          {goto}A~{goto}T~/wtb             set titles
          {goto}D~{end}{down}{down}{right} move to deposit file
          /ri{end}{right}{up}{up}~         set insert range
          /wtc{goto}A~                     clear titles, move to A
          /rp{end}{down}{end}{right}~      protect new row
          /xmI~/xg\M~                      loop

(return)  enter a check  Enter a deposit  Save and Return to the main menu
          /xgSAV~                          execute save macro
```

The SAVE menu allows either the monthly ledger or the entire worksheet to be saved to disk.

```
save      month      account RETURN
```

(month)  to save changes to monthly transactions
         /xgSAV~

(accnt)  to save changes made to account worksheet
         /fs~r/xg\M~

(return) to return to the main menu
         /xg\M~/xg\SAVE~

Because the monthly registers vary in length, the TOTAL line must be Range Named each time the file is saved. The file name is copied to this macro by the macros that retrieve or create files, so that it always contains the correct name.

```
          ----------------------------------------To save monthly register
sav       {goto}A~{end}{down}{up}/rndTOTAL~       delete  name
          /rncTOTAL~{down}{end}{right}{up}~       name range
          {goto}A~/fxf                            save  month
```

```
fil       Chek384                              file name
          ~{end}{down}{end}{right}~r           set area
          /xg\M~                               return to menu
```

The RETRIEVE macro uses the list of registers created by the CREATE macros to find the desired monthly registers and place them on the worksheet. The macro first obtains the file name by moving the cursor to the cell with the Range Name of the number specified by the user (3). The file name (Chek384) is then copied to both this macro and the SAV macro. The area to be erased must be defined, because each file could be a different size.

```
          --------------------------------------Get monthly register
retr      {goto}BLANK2~                         go to list of registers
          /xlPlease enter number of desired file ~NUM~{goto}
num       3                                    get file name
          ~/c~FL~/c~FIL~                       copy file name
          {goto}A~/re{end}{down}               erase area
          {end}{right}~/fcce                   get file
fl        Chek384                              file name
          ~/xg\M~                               return to menu
```

The SUMM macro uses three pointers:

- **PTR**—is used to name the first file in the range specified by the user. The macro will move it down the list of numbers.
- **LST**—is the name given to the last file in the range. When PTR is moved down to LST by the loop, the macro will stop.
- **PT**—is used to place the totals lines in the correct row of the Summary file.

Each cell containing a file name has been given the Range Name of the number beside it. The macro uses the number to test for the end of the specified group and uses the file names to retrieve the total lines from each file.

Each time the macro loops, it:

1. Copies the file name into the macro.
2. Resets the summary file pointer for placement of the next total line.
3. Gets the total line from disk memory and puts it in the summary file.
4. Tests for the end of the user specified group.
5. Resets the list pointer to get the next file name.

```
          -----------------------------------Produce summary
summ      {goto}BLANK2~                         display list
          /xlEnter number of first month for summary ~FS~
          /xlEnter number of last month for summary ~LS~
          /xcFREEZE~                            freeze screen
          {goto}                                goto
fs        1                                    month location
          ~{left}/rndPTR~/rncPTR~~{goto}        set pointer, goto
ls        3                                    month location
```

```
        ~{left}/rndLST~/rncLST~~          set pointer
        {goto}SUM~/rndPT~/rncPT~~         set summary pointer
        /reSS~{goto}PTR~                  erase file, goto name
loop    {RIGHT}/c~SM~                     get file name
        {goto}PT~{down}/rndPT~/rncPT~~    reset pointer
        /fcanTOTAL~                       get Total line
sm      Chek384                           register name
        ~/xiPTR>=LST~/wwc{goto}S~/xq      test for last month
        {goto}PTR~{down}/rndPTR~/rncPTR~~ reset pointer
        /xgLOOP~
```

The CREATE macros will produce either a new monthly register or a new account. RETURN is placed first in the menu to help prevent accidents.

```
create   RETURN  month   account
(return) to return to the main menu
         /xg\M~
(month)  to create a new monthly register for this account
         /xgMONTH~
(accnt)  to create a register for a new account
         /xgACCOUNT~
```

The MONTH macro creates a new register by bringing the balance forward, inserting the new month, erasing all the transactions, and saving the new register with a user defined file name.

NN and TT are temporary Range Names. NN is used to get the balance forward from the ending balance. TT is used to determine if there have been any transaction rows inserted into the register. If so, they are deleted.

The cursor is then moved to the listing of register file names. The user is asked for the name of the new register. After the new register file name is entered into the list, it is copied into the macro and to the SAV macro. The pointer for the next register file name is then moved down one cell.

The Total line is Range Named and the new monthly register is saved to disk. The worksheet is also saved to record the new pointer position. The INSERT macro is called to allow entry of transactions.

```
        -------------------------------------Create new Monthly register
month   {goto}A~{end}{down}{up}{right}/rncNN~~   name current balance
        /dfBALFD~NN~~~/rndNN~/reMNTH~            get balance, erase date
        {goto}C~/rncTT~{end}{down}~             set name
        /xi@count(TT)>2~{down}/wdr{end}{down}{up}~ test for entries
        /rndTT~{goto}A~                          erase name
        /xnPlease enter number of the new MONTH ~MNTH~   get month
        {goto}C~{down}{down}{right}/cMNTH~~     copy month
        {goto}BLANK2~                            go to list
        /xlPlease enter MONTH file name ~MR~     get month name
        /cMR~FLNM~/cMR~FIL~                      copy file name
```

```
                    {goto}MR~/rndMR~{down}/rncMR~~              reset pointer
                    {goto}A~{end}{down}{up}/rndTOTAL~           delete name
                    /rncTOTAL~{down}{end}{right}{up}~           name range
                    {goto}A~/fxf                                save file
          flnm      Chek384                                    file name
                    ~{end}{down}{end}{right}~r{esc}            set area
                    /fs~r{goto}A~/xmI~/wwc/xg\M~               save account, input data
```

ACCOUNT is similar to MONTH, with the difference that all the current data is erased and the worksheet prepared for a new account. After the new account information is entered, it is copied to the total line and the Summary file.

The list of file names for the account is displayed, and the user asked for the new file names for the account and monthly register. The pointer is reset, and the file names given by the user are inserted into this macro and SAV. After the Total line is Range Named, the monthly register and new account are saved to their new file names. The INSERT macro is called to enter transactions.

```
          -------------------------------------Create new check register
account   /reNAME~/reMNTH~/reYEAR~/reBANK~/reACCT~        erase entries
          /reBALFD~/reCR~/reLIST~/reSS~
          {goto}C~/rncTT~{end}{down}~                     set name
          /xi@count(TT)>2~{down}/wdr{end}{down}{up}~       test for entries
          /rndTT~{goto}A~                                 erase name
          /xlPlease enter the new account NAME ~NAME~     insert new data
          /xnPlease enter number of the first MONTH~MNTH~
          /xlPlease enter the FISCAL YEAR END ~YEAR~
          /xlPlease enter the new BANK ~BANK~
          /xlPlease enter the new ACCOUNT #~ACCT~
          /xnPlease enter the new BALANCE ~BALFD~
          {goto}C~{down}{down}{right}/cMNTH~~             copy dt,name,yr
          /cNAME~NM~/cYEAR~YR~{goto}BLANK2~
          {goto}LIST~/rndMR~/rncMR~~{goto}blank2~         set pointer
          /xlPlease enter CHECK REGISTER file name ~CR~   get account name
          /xlPlease enter MONTH file name ~MR~            get month name
          /cCR~FLNAM~/cMR~FILNM~/cMR~FIL~                 copy file names
          {goto}MR~/rndMR~{down}/rncMR~~                  reset pointer
          {goto}A~{end}{down}{up}/rndTOTAL~               delete name
          /rncTOTAL~{down}{end}{right}{up}~               name range
          {goto}A~/fxf                                    save monthly register
filnm     Chek184                                        month name
          ~{end}{down}{end}{right}~r{esc}/fs             save new account
flnam     Check                                          acct name
          ~r{esc}{goto}A~/xmI~/xg\M~                      enter data
```

These are the Range Names used on the worksheet that are not macro names or set up by macros.

| Name | Address | Name | Address |
|------|---------|------|---------|
| 1 | AB7 | A | A61 |
| 2 | AB8 | AA | A71 |
| 3 | AB9 | ACCT | J66 |
| 4 | AB10 | BALFD | B71 |
| 5 | AB11 | BANK | I65 |
| 6 | AB12 | BLANK | AW41 |
| 7 | AB13 | BLANK1 | AW61 |
| 8 | AB14 | BLANK2 | AA1 |
| 9 | AB15 | BLK | AW1 |
| 10 | AB16 | BR | AX40 |
| 11 | AB17 | C | G71 |
| 12 | AB18 | CR | AB5 |
| | | D | T71 |
| | | LIST | AB7..AB18 |
| | | M | AC1 |
| | | NAME | I62 |
| | | NM | BF1 |
| | | R | A54..Y54 |
| | | S | AY1..BW20 |
| | | SETUP | B60..I71 |
| | | SS | AY7..BW18 |
| | | SUM | AY6 |
| | | T | C71 |
| | | UL | AW21 |
| | | YEAR | I64 |
| | | YR | BF3 |

These are the messages in the "blank" areas:

**FREEZE**   This screen is shown when the screen is "frozen" (AW1..AX20)

```
Please be patient
```

```
The macro will be done soon
```

```
!!!!!!!!!!!!!!!!!!!!!!!!!!!!!!!!!!!!!!!!!!!!!!!!!!!!!!!!!!!!!!!
```

**BLANK**   This is the screen seen upon entry to the system. (AW21..AW40)

```
Check Register
```

```
Please make a selection
```

**BLANK1**   This is seen when the main menu is displayed. (AW41..AW60)

```
            Please make a selection


        Press ALT M to return to this menu
```

**BLANK2**   This screen shows the files used by the account. (AA1..AB20)

```
These are the files for this account

    CHECK REGISTER:
    Check
    MONTHLY REGISTERS:
  1 Chek184
  2 Chek284
  3 Chek384
  4
  5
  6
  7
  8
  9
 10
 11
 12

    Note: a file name is limited to 8 characters of numbers and letters
```

These are the column widths, formulas, and formats used by the worksheet:

| column width | cell address | format, formula | cell address | format, formula |
|---|---|---|---|---|
| ------- | ------- | -------- | ------- | -------- |
| Formula row: | | | Monthly register, totals line: | |
| 1 | A54: | '¦ | A75: | '¦ |
| 10 | B54: | +E54-C54+B53 | B75: | +$BALFD-C75+E75 |
| 10 | C54: | @SUM(K54..R54) | C75: | @SUM(C71..C74) |
| 3 | D54: | | D75: | |
| 10 | E54: | @SUM(W54..X54) | E75: | @SUM(E71..E74) |
| 3 | F54: | | F75: | |
| 1 | G54: | (G) '¦ | G75: | |
| 6 | H54: | U | H75: | (G) 3 |
| 6 | I54: | (G) U | I75: | |
| 22 | J54: | (G) U | J75: | |
| 10 | K54: | U | K75: | @SUM(K71..K74) |
| 10 | L54: | U | | |
| 10 | M54: | U | Summary file, totals line (each | |
| 10 | N54: | U | cell uses a relative address) | |
| 9 | O54: | U | BL20: | SUM(BL8..BL19) |

```
10      P54: U
 8      Q54: U
 9      R54: U
20      S54: (G) U
 1      T54: ';
 6      U54: U
21      V54: (G) U
 9      W54: U
 9      X54: U
16      Y54: (G) U
```

CHECK REGISTER

```
NAME: Checks, Inc.
MONTH:        3
FISCAL YEAR END:Dec 84
BANK: FB
ACCOUNT #:  11 11 111
```

CHECKS

| BALANCE | CHECKS ret | DEPOSITS ret | DATE | CHK # | PAYEE | INVENTORY | SUPPLIES | OFFICE | SALARIES | UTILITIES | RENT | MAINT |
|---|---|---|---|---|---|---|---|---|---|---|---|---|
| 1504.86 | BALANCE FORWARD | | | | | | | | | | | |
| 1204.86 | 300.00 ap | | 3/5 | 115 | Lease Inc | | | | | | 300.00 | |
| 2204.86 | | 1000.00 ap | | | | | | | | | | |
| 2204.86 | 300.00 | 1000.00 | 3 | | | 0.00 | 0.00 | 0.00 | 0.00 | 0.00 | 300.00 | 0.00 |

DEPOSITS

| MISC | DESCRIPTION | DATE | SOURCE | INCOME | OTHER | DESCRIPTION |
|---|---|---|---|---|---|---|
| | | 3/15 | National Bank | 1000.00 | | 10000 checks |
| | | | | 1000.00 | 0.00 | |
| 0.00 | | | | | | |

SUMMARY     NAME: Checks, Inc

YEAR: Dec 84

| BALANCE | CHECKS | DEPOSITS | DATE | # | CHECKS | | | | | | | | DEPOSITS | |
|---|---|---|---|---|---|---|---|---|---|---|---|---|---|---|
| | | | | | INVENTORY | SUPPLIES | OFFICE | SALARIES | UTILITIES | RENT | MAINT | MISC | INCOME | OTHER |
| 2304.86 | 8200.00 | 10000.00 | | 1 | 8000.00 | 0.00 | 0.00 | 0.00 | 0.00 | 200.00 | 0.00 | 0.00 | 0.00 | 10000.00 |
| 1504.86 | 800.00 | 0.00 | | 2 | 0.00 | 0.00 | 0.00 | 500.00 | 0.00 | 300.00 | 0.00 | 0.00 | 0.00 | 0.00 |
| 2204.86 | 300.00 | 1000.00 | | 3 | 0.00 | 0.00 | 0.00 | 0.00 | 0.00 | 300.00 | 0.00 | 0.00 | 1000.00 | 0.00 |
| TOTALS | 9300.00 | 11000.00 | | | 8000.00 | 0.00 | 0.00 | 500.00 | 0.00 | 800.00 | 0.00 | 0.00 | 1000.00 | 10000.00 |

# A.3 Pay Day: A Payroll Tax Register

This macro system is designed to help with many of the repetitive tasks of producing quarterly and annual payroll reports. These are some of its features:

- A file is kept of each employee's name, social security number, and address.
- After each quarter's payroll is entered, the taxes are computed and the year-to-date figures are posted.
- Annually the W-2s are printed for all employees.
- Each file can be printed to be used with various reports.
- New employees can be added at any time.
- All the tax rates and maximum levels are kept in a separate file. These may be changed at any time, and the formulas will automatically include them.
- New payroll worksheets may be created at any time from a current worksheet. (Just make sure you have saved your current work first.)

These are the main functions of the system:

**view**   This function allows the user to view the different files of the system.
**enter**   This allows entry of data into any of the four quarters.
**print**   The files and W-2 forms are produced by this function.
**save**   This function saves any entries that are made to the worksheet.
**insert**   This is used to insert a new employee.
**create**   Use this to create a new payroll worksheet. To start a new year, it is better to modify the current worksheet.
**rates**   If the tax rates change, this will modify all the formulas.
**quit**   This is used to leave the payroll system.

## Specific Instructions

After loading the worksheet, a menu will be displayed showing the main functions. Be sure to use the arrow keys when entering information. This will both insert any keyed information, and move to the next available cell. Press **ENTER** to return to the menu. (If the READY flag is displayed, press ALT-M.)

**view:** This will display a menu showing the six files of the system. The first four are the quarterly summaries. The fifth is the year-to-date totals, and the last is the address file. By using this function, any information in the files may be edited.

**enter:** This allows the user to make payroll entries into one quarter at a time.

**print:** To print any of the files, just select the one desired. Note that the files are wider than a page. (This system is designed for an Epson-type printer, which allows condensed print. The print command can be modified for other printers. Check your manual for the needed codes.) To print the W-2s, one form at a time can be printed until the paper is properly aligned in the printer. The spacing is designed for the 1983 forms. If the forms change, it is easy to change the location of the entries by moving their placement on FORM. Note that the Range Name of each item is the same as its number on the W-2 form. (Columns and rows can also be modified.)

**save:** After you have made any entries to the worksheet, this function will save the new worksheet and return to the menu.

**insert:** To add an employee to the file, use this command. A new row will be created and the formulas copied into it. You enter the employee information into the address file. This will include name, social security number, and address. The macro will then enter the name and s.s. # into each of the other files. (If you don't have the s.s. #, it will need to be entered manually into all six files later.)

**create:** When a new payroll worksheet is needed, use this function. Make sure that you have saved any changes you have made, because the current worksheet will be modified to make the new one. (This will not affect the saved worksheet.) Every entry on the worksheet will be erased. You will be asked to insert the new year, company name, company address, and company federal and state tax numbers. If you do not have them, they will need to be entered manually into the five payroll files later. This information will be copied into each of the files. You will be asked to name the new worksheet, as it is being saved. You may then enter information into the new worksheet.

If you have become familiar with 1-2-3, you can update a year-end worksheet so it can be used for the next year. This avoids reentering all the current employees. There are five steps to take: 1) Copy the formulas back into the year-to-date file that were turned into values by the W-2 macro (use a formula from an adjacent cell); 2) Erase the entries made to each quarter for each employee; 3) Delete the rows containing employees that are no longer with the company; 4) Change the date in each file; 5) SAVE the new file.

**rates:** If the tax laws change, you will need to enter the new tax rates or maximum taxable income levels into the worksheets. This function allows changes to the FICA, FUTA (Federal Unemployment Tax), and SUTA (State Unemployment Tax) tax levels. (See page 244 for currently used tax rates.)

**quit:** This selection allows the user to leave the system.

## Change the System

As with any of these examples, it is easy to change the macros to meet your own individual needs. One of the changes needed will be to separate this system from the book diskette. This requires three steps. First, erase the menu macro Range Named MENU. Second, change the macro instructions for the Quit choice of MENU1. This could be a variety of functions, depending on your needs. **/wey** would erase the current worksheet. **/qy** would leave 1-2-3, and **/fr{?}~** would allow a different worksheet to be selected. Third, the **\0** macro needs to have BLANK changed to BLANK1, and MENU changed to MENU1.

## Design

The worksheet is laid out like this:

```
1st qtr 2nd qtr 3rd qtr 4th qtr  ytd   addresses  rates macros blanks W-2
  A-M     N-Z     AA-AM   AN-AZ   BA-BM   BN-BY     BZ-CG CH-CQ  CR-CS CT-CZ
   ↓       ↓        ↓       ↓       ↓        ↓               ↓      ↓
   ↓       ↓        ↓       ↓       ↓        ↓               ↓
```

## Macros

The menu macros and system macros are shown below. The menu macros have been shown so that they can be read. Of course, they must be entered into the worksheet in the menu format to work.

MENU1 is the main menu. It directs all the main functions of the system. By using submenus, the user is directed to the necessary tasks, and then brought back to the main menu. The system enables the ESCAPE key by including commands to return to the original menu.

```
menu1 view enter print save insert create rates quit
```

(view) to view the entries for each quarter
   /xmVIEW~/xg\M~

(enter) to enter payroll information for a quarter
   /xmENTER~/xg\M~

(print) to print payroll information
   /xmPRINT~/xg\M~

(save) to save all changes to the worksheet
   /fs~r/xg\M~

(insert) to insert a new employee
   /xgINSERT~

(create) to create a new payroll worksheet
   /xmCR~/xg\M~

(rates) to change the tax rates used to compute the taxes
   /xgRATE~

(quit) to leave the payroll system
   /xmMENU~/xg\M~

VIEW takes the user to each of the files. The macros terminate, so ALT-M must be pressed to return to the main menu.

Note: The following three menus are displayed on two lines but would be written on one line.

```
view    1st Quarter    3rd Quarter    Yr-to-Dt  RETURN ⎫ one
               2nd Quarter    4th Quarter        address ⎬ line
```

(1st q) to view the first quarter payroll
   {goto}FIRST~

(2nd q) to view the second quarter payroll
   {goto}SECOND~

(3rd q) to view the third quarter payroll
   {goto}THIRD~

(4th q) to view the fourth quarter payroll
   {goto}FOURTH~

(ytd) to view the year-to-date payroll
   {goto}YTD~

(addr) to view the address file
   {goto}ADDRESS~

(return) to return to the main menu
   /xg\M~

**ENTER** is used to put the quarterly payroll data in the schedules. Although the macros are a bit longer than the other menus, they are almost identical. After debugging one macro, the information was copied across the columns to complete the menu. To make the operation faster, Recalculation is set to manual, and then reset after the entries are made. The Title function is used to help data entry for long payrolls.

```
enter    1st Quarter       3rd Quarter      RETURN ⎫ one
                2nd Quarter      4th Quarter         ⎬ line
```

(1st q) to enter payroll data for the first quarter
   /wgrm/xcTITLES~      man calc,set titles
   /ri1ST~              insert data
   /wgra{calc}/wtc      auto calc,clear titles
   /xg\M~

(2nd q) to enter payroll data for the second quarter
   /wgrm/xcTITLES~      man calc,set titles
   /ri2nd~              insert data
   /wgra{calc}/wtc      auto calc,clear titles
   /xg\M~

(3rd q) to enter payroll data for the third quarter
   /wgrm/xcTITLES~      man calc,set titles
   /ri3rd~              insert data
   /wgra{calc}/wtc      auto calc,clear titles
   /xg\M~

(4th q) `to enter payroll data for the fourth quarter`
   `/wgrm/xcTITLES~`     man calc, set titles
   `/ri4th~`             insert data
   `/wgra{calc}/wtc`     auto calc, clear titles
   `/xg\M~`

(return)`to return to the main menu`
   `/xg\M~`

PRINT produces all the reports from the system. As in the previous example, each of the choice is nearly identical.

NOTE: Print setup is for condensed print on an Epson-type printer.

```
print  1st Quarter  3rd Quarter  Yr-to-Dt  w-2  RETURN ) one
       2nd Quarter  4th Quarter  address               ) line
```

(1st q) `to print the first quarter payroll`
   `/pprFIRST~q`      set range
   `/xgCOND~`         goto COND submenu to print

(2nd q) `to print the second quarter payroll`
   `/pprSECOND~q`     set range
   `/xgCOND~`         goto COND submenu to print

(3rd q) `to print the third quarter payroll`
   `/pprTHIRD~q`      set range
   `/xgCOND~`         goto COND submenu to print

(4th q) `to print the fourth quarter payroll`
   `/pprFOURTH~q`     set range
   `/xgCOND~`         goto COND submenu to print

(ytd) `to print the year-to-date payroll`
   `/pprYTD~q`        set range
   `/xgCOND~`         goto COND submenu to print

(addr) `to print the address file`
   `/pprADDRESS~q`    set range
   `/xgCOND~`         goto COND submenu to print

(W-2) `to print W-2s`
   `/xmW-2~`

(return)`to return to the main menu`
   `/xg\M~`

The Main Menu is called by the **\M** macro. It displays a message and the menu.

─────────────────────────────────────────  Display main menu

`\m`        `{goto}BLANK1~/xmMENU1~/xg\M~`

These three macros are subroutines called by other macros. `freeze` locks in a screen with a message while the macro is moving the cursor around the worksheet. This helps avoid confusion. `titles` locks in the upper portion of the worksheet during data entry, so that the user will know what information is needed. `cond` prints the designated range in condensed print.

| freeze | `{goto}UL~` | Freeze screen |
| | | move to upper left corner |
| | `{goto}BR~` | move to lower right corner |
| | `/wwv/wwu` | create window |
| | `{window}/xr` | move cursor out, return to macro |
| | | |
| titles | `{goto}ADDRESS~` | Set titles |
| | | move to top of file |
| | `{goto}TT2~` | move to row beneath titles |
| | `/wth/xr` | set titles, return to macro |
| | | |
| cond | `/ppos{esc}\015~qagp` | Print condensed print |
| | | set printer, print |
| | `os{esc}\018~qq` | reset printer |
| | `/xg\m~` | return to menu |

`insert` puts employees into the payroll system. Recalculation is set to manual to speed the process. A row is inserted above the total line, and all the formulas are copied into it from a template named `row`. The area for entering the employee information is defined and the titles set so that the data can be correctly entered. The name and social security number is then copied to each file.

| insert | `/xcFREEZE~` | Insert new employee |
| | | freeze screen |
| | `/wgrm{goto}NEW~/wir~` | man. calc, insert row |
| | `/rndEMP~/rncEMP~{right}` | set insert range |
| | `{right}{right}{right}{right}` | |
| | `{right}~/rndNM~/rncNM~{right}~` | set name & ss range |
| | `{goto}fst~{up}/cROW~~` | copy in the formulas |
| | `/wwc{goto}TT1~{goto}TT2~/wth` | set titles |
| | `/ruEMP~/riEMP~/rpEMP~/wtc` | set range, fill in, clear |
| | `/xcFREEZE~` | freeze screen |
| | `{goto}FST~{up}/cNM~~` | copy name & ss to each file |
| | `{goto}SEC~{up}/cNM~~` | |
| | `{goto}THD~{up}/cNM~~` | |
| | `{goto}FOR~{up}/cNM~~` | |
| | `{goto}YD~{up}/cNM~~` | |
| | `/wgra{calc}` | auto. calc |
| | `/wwc/xg\m~` | clear screen, return to menu |

The W-2 menu provides an opportunity to print one W-2 at a time until the forms are correctly aligned in the printer. Then all the forms can be produced.

---

W-2 menu

w-2    one    all    **RETURN**

(one)    to align printer by printing one W-2

  `/xgONE~`

(all)    to print all the W-2's

  `/xgALL~`

(return) to return to the main menu

  `/xmMENU1~/xmW-2~`

The **all** and the **one** macros are identical except for the looping feature which has been eliminated from **one**. The first portion of the macro sets up the worksheet for printing. The cursor is sent to the first employee, the payroll amounts are converted from formulas to numbers (see Section 3.7 on moving data), the printer is set, and the company information copied to the W-2 form.

The looping portion moves the pointer down the list. On each loop the pointer is tested to see if it has reached the end. If so, the **quit** functions of resetting the printer and clearing the screen are performed.

The payroll information of each employee is then copied into the W-2 form. The number Range Names refer to the numbered blocks on the W-2 form itself. If the form changes, it will be easy to rearrange the placement of each block. After all the information is copied, the form is printed, and the macro loops.

---

Print w-2's

| | | |
|---|---|---|
| all | `/xcFREEZE~` | freeze screen |
| | `{goto}LIST~` | go to top of list |
| | `/fxvPRL~LIST~r{esc}` | extract ytd values |
| | `/fcc~PRL~` | combine values to same location |
| | `/pprFORM~os{esc}\018~ouqq` | set printer:norm prt,unformatted |
| | `/cCOMPANY~/cSTATE~19~1~` | copy company information |
| loop | `{down}/rndP~/rncP~{down}{down}~` | set pointer |
| | `/xi@count(P)<3~/xgQUIT~` | if at end: goto quit |
| | `/c~10~{right}/c~9~{right}` | copy to form:   gross, fwt |
| | `/c~17~{right}/c~11~{right}` | swt, fica |
| | `{right}{right}/c~13~{right}` | fica wage |
| | `{right}{right}{right}{right}` | |
| | `/c~12~{right}/c~8~{right}` | name, s.s. # |
| | `/c~15a~{right}/c~15b~{right}` | street1, street2 |
| | `/c{right}{right}~15c~` | city, state, zip |
| | `/ppgq` | print form |
| | `{goto}P~/xgLOOP~` | to loop |
| quit | `/ppoofqq/fewPRL~y` | reset printer, erase file |
| | `/wwc/xg\m~` | clear screen,return to main menu |

```
----------------------------------------Print one w-2
one     /xcFREEZE~                      freeze  screen
        {goto}LIST~                     go  to  top  of  list
        /fxvPRL~LIST~r{esc}             extract  ytd  values
        /fcc~PRL~                       combine  values  to  same  location
        /pprFORM~os{esc}\018~ouqq       set  printer  to  normal  print
        /cCOMPANY~/cSTATE~19~1~         copy  company  information
        {down}/rndP~/rncP~{down}{down}~ set  pointer
        /c~10~{right}/c~9~{right}       copy  to  form:    gross, fwt
        /c~17~{right}/c~11~{right}                         swt, fica
        {right}{right}/c~13~{right}                        fica  wage
        {right}{right}{right}{right}
        /c~12~{right}/c~8~{right}                          name, s.s.  #
        /c~15a~{right}/c~15b~{right}                       street1, street2
        /c{right}{right}~15c~                              city, state, zip
        /ppgq                           print  form
        /ppoofqq/fewPRL~y               reset  printer, erase  file
        /wwc{goto}BLANK1~/xmW-2~        clear  screen, return  to  w-2  menu
```

The CREATE menu helps to prevent the worksheet from being erased unintentionally. **create** must be chosen twice to start the CREATE macro.

```
                                        ── Create menu
   cr       RETURN   create
(return)to return to the main menu
        /xg\M~

(create)to ERASE this worksheet and create a new payroll
worksheet
        /xgCREATE~
```

CREATE produces a blank payroll worksheet, using the current worksheet as the source for all the formulas, formatting, and screen display. The macro first erases the current company information, and deletes all the current rows holding employee information. The Range Name **DEL** must be manipulated a bit. This is because it must extend beyond the insert range when new employees are being set up (so it will expand to include them), and it must be reduced to delete only the rows including employee data.

The areas to insert the new year and company information are then established. After this data is entered, the areas are protected again before the data is copied to each of the files.

The user is then requested to enter a name for the new file, and it is saved. Notice the use of entering an A and then backspacing over it. When any of the 1-2-3 commands produce a "suggested" prompt containing information that you wish to suppress, the prompt can be erased by this method. Our use of it here prevents any current files from being displayed or written over, which might happen if {esc} was used to eliminate the prompt.

```
------------------------------------------To create a new payroll worksheet
create   /xcFREEZE~                        freeze screen
         /wgrm/reYR~/reCOMPANY~/reSTATE~   man. calc, erase heading
         {goto}ST~{down}/rncDEL~{up}~      set row delete area
         /wdrDEL~/wir~/rncDEL~.{down}~     delete data, reset DEL
         /ruYR~/ruADR~/ruFED~/ruSTE~/ruSTATE~   set entry areas
         /wwc/riY-T-D~{goto}UL~            insert new data, reset screen
         /rpCOMPANY~/rpSTATE~/rpYR~        reset protection
         /cY-T-D~FIRST~/cY-T-D~SECOND~     copy to each quarter
         /cY-T-D~THIRD~/cY-T-D~FOURTH~
         /wgra{calc}                       reset for auto. calc
         {goto}BLANK2~/fsA{bs}{?}~/xg\m~   save new worksheet, quit
```

The **rate** macro is for changing the tax rates used by the system. Recalculation is turned off to speed entry of new data.

```
------------------------------------------  To set rates and maximums
rate     /wgrm/riRATES~                     insert rates
         /wgra{calc}/xg\M~                  return to menu
```

These are the Range Names used by the system that are not created by macros:

| Name | Address | Name | Address |
|------|---------|------|---------|
| 1 | CT18 | FORM | CT18..CZ40 |
| 8 | CT24 | FORMULAS | A26..BM26 |
| 9 | CV24 | FOURTH | AN1..AZ19 |
| 10 | CW24 | FST | A18 |
| 11 | CY24 | FUTA MAX | CC10 |
| 12 | CT26 | FUTA RATE | CC9 |
| 13 | CW26 | LIST | BC12..BI18 |
| 14 | CY26 | M | CH1 |
| 15A | CT28 | NEW | BN18 |
| 15B | CT29 | P | BC14..BC16 |
| 15C | CT30 | RATES | BZ1..CC12 |
| 17 | CW30 | ROW | A26..BM26 |
| 19 | CZ30 | SEC | N18 |
| 1ST | A12..F18 | SECOND | N1..Z19 |
| 2ND | N12..S18 | ST | BA12 |
| 3RD | AA12..AF18 | STATE | BF1 |
| 4TH | AN12..AS18 | STE | BF4 |
| ADDRESS | BN1..BT18 | SUTA MAX | CC12 |
| ADR | BA4..BA7 | SUTA RATE | CC11 |
| BLANK | CR39 | THD | AA18 |
| BLANK1 | CR59 | THIRD | AA1..AM19 |
| BLANK2 | CR79 | TT1 | BN10 |
| BR | CS38 | TT2 | BN12 |
| COMPANY | BA4..BF7 | UL | CR19 |
| DEL | BA13..BA18 | Y-T-D | BA1..BF7 |
| FED | BD4 | YD | BA18 |
| FICA MAX | CC8 | YR | BD1 |
| FICA RATE | CC7 | YTD | BA1 |
| FIRST | A1..M19 | | |
| FOR | AN18 | | |

These are the "blank" areas used by the system to guide the user:

FREEZE:

```
                    Please be patient
              The macro will be done soon
```

```
!!!!!!!!!!!!!!!!!!!!!!!!!!!!!!!!!!!!!!!!!!!!!!!!!!!!!!!!!!!!!!!!
```

BLANK:

```
              Please make a selection
```

BLANK1:

```
              Please make a selection
```

```
          Press ALT M to return to this menu
```

BLANK2:

```
Please enter a name for the new payroll worksheet and press return
```

This is the W-2 form produced by the system (to be printed on continuous W-2 forms):

```
XYZ Company                  992658877        5533289
123 Colman Rd
Suite A
Boston, MA 02155
```

387-94-8856                    800.00           8000.00           640.00


Chipman, Nancy                                  8000.00


c/o Mr. Smith
554 Verndale
Hyde Park      MA   02136                        700.00                    MA

This is the RATES file where the tax amounts are kept:

```
These rates and maximum taxable amounts are used to compute the taxes
              FICA RATE       0.1340
              FICA MAX     37800.00
              FUTA RATE       0.0080
              FUTA MAX      7000.00
              SUTA RATE       0.0400
              SUTA MAX      7000.00
```

The formulas shown below are all those of the payroll system. The displayed line of the worksheet shows the formulas that all the other lines also use. Only the line numbers change. This also holds true for the line Range Named ROW, which is used to copy the formulas and formats into a new line by the macro.

The formulas to compute the taxable income are complex but not complicated. They consist of a series of three tests. If any test is met, the formula quits. First, if the taxable income received in the preceding quarters exceeds the maximum taxable income for the tax in question, the taxable amount for this quarter is zero. Second, if the tax for the previous quarters plus this quarter's income exceed the maximum taxable income, the taxable amount is the maximum tax less the income earned in the previous quarters. Third, the income for this quarter is the taxable amount.

```
Cell Format Formula
--- --      -------
A17: 'Chipman, Nancy
B17: '387-94-8856
C17: U 2000
D17: U 200
E17: U 175
F17: U 160
H17: +C17-D17-E17-F17
I17: @IF(C17>=$FICA MAX,$FICA MAX,C17)
J17: @IF(C17>=$FUTA MAX,$FUTA MAX,C17)
K17: +$FUTA RATE*J17
L17: @IF(C17>=$SUTA MAX,$SUTA MAX,C17)
M17: +$SUTA RATE*L17
N17: 'Chipman, Nancy
```

```
O17:  '387-94-8856
P17:  U 2000
Q17:  U 200
R17:  U 175
S17:  U 160
U17:  +P17-Q17-R17-S17
V17:@IF(C17>=$FICA MAX,0,@IF((C17+P17)>=$FICA MAX,($FICA MAX-C17),$P17))
W17:@IF(C17>=$FUTA MAX,0,@IF((C17+P17)>=$FUTA MAX,($FUTA MAX-C17),$P17))
X17:  +$FUTA RATE*W17
Y17:@IF(C17>=$SUTA MAX,0,@IF((C17+P17)>=$SUTA MAX,($SUTA MAX-C17),$P17))
Z17:  +$SUTA RATE*Y17
AA17:  'Chipman, Nancy
AB17:  '387-94-8856
AC17:  U 2000
AD17:  U 200
AE17:  U 175
AF17:  U 160
AH17:  +AC17-AD17-AE17-AF17
AI17:  @IF((C17+P17)>=$FICA MAX,0,@IF((C17+P17+AC17)>=$FICA MAX,($FICA
          MAX-C17-P17),$P17))
AJ17:  @IF((C17+P17)>=$FUTA MAX,0,@IF((C17+P17+AC17)>=$FUTA MAX,($FUTA
          MAX-C17-P17),$AC17))
AK17:  +$FUTA RATE*AJ17
AL17:  @IF((C17+P17)>=$SUTA MAX,0,@IF((C17+P17+AC17)>=$SUTA MAX,($SUTA
          MAX-C17-P17),$AC17))
AM17:  +$SUTA RATE*AL17
AN17:  'Chipman, Nancy
AO17:  '387-94-8856
AP17:  U 2000
AQ17:  U 200
AR17:  U 175
AS17:  U 160
AU17:  +AP17-AQ17-AR17-AS17
AV17:  @IF((C17+P17+AC17)>=$FICA MAX,0,@IF((C17+P17+AC17+AP17)>=$FICA
          MAX,($FICA MAX-C17-P17-AC17),$AP17))
AW17:  @IF((C17+P17+AC17)>=$FUTA MAX,0,@IF((C17+P17+AC17+AP17)>=$FUTA
          MAX,($FUTA MAX-C17-P17-AC17),$AP17))
AX17:  +$FUTA RATE*AW17
AY17:  @IF((C17+P17+AC17)>=$SUTA MAX,0,@IF((C17+P17+AC17+AP17)>=$SUTA
          MAX,($SUTA MAX-C17-P17-AC17),$AP17))
AZ17:  +$SUTA RATE*AY17
BA17:  'Chipman, Nancy
BB17:  '387-94-8856
BC17:  +C17+P17+AC17+AP17
BD17:  +D17+Q17+AD17+AQ17
BE17:  +E17+R17+AE17+AR17
BF17:  +F17+S17+AF17+AS17
BG17:  +G17+T17+AG17+AT17
BH17:  +H17+U17+AH17+AU17
```

```
BI17: +I17+V17+AI17+AV17
BJ17: +J17+W17+AJ17+AW17
BK17: +K17+X17+AK17+AX17
BL17: +L17+Y17+AL17+AY17
BM17: +M17+Z17+AM17+AZ17
B19: 'TOTAL
C19: @SUM(C12..C18)
```

Page 247 shows a quarterly worksheet.

PAYROLL REGISTER

YEAR 1984 STATE MA

COMPANY
XYZ Company
123 Colman Rd
Suite A
Boston, MA 02155

FED ID # 992658877
ST ID # 5533289

FICA TAX 8214.20
FWT 13068.65
--------
TOTAL 21282.85

FIRST QUARTER
=============

| Name | S.S. # | Gross | FWT | SWT | FICA | Other | Net | FICA WG | FUTA WG | FUTA | SUTA WG | SUTA |
|---|---|---|---|---|---|---|---|---|---|---|---|---|
| Baker, Joseph N. | 032-22-3665 | 40000.00 | 8000.00 | 5000.00 | 6000.00 | | 21000.00 | 37800.00 | 7000.00 | 56.00 | 7000.00 | 280.00 |
| Keogh, Keith | 122-34-3017 | 18000.00 | 4437.95 | 855.54 | 1195.42 | | 11511.09 | 18000.00 | 7000.00 | 56.00 | 7000.00 | 280.00 |
| Murphey, Joanne | 092-59-9933 | 3500.00 | 430.70 | 179.06 | 301.50 | | 2588.74 | 3500.00 | 3500.00 | 28.00 | 3500.00 | 140.00 |
| Chipman, Nancy | 387-94-8856 | 2000.00 | 200.00 | 175.00 | 160.00 | | 1465.00 | 2000.00 | 2000.00 | 16.00 | 2000.00 | 80.00 |
| TOTAL | | 63500.00 | 13068.65 | 6209.60 | 7656.92 | 0.00 | 36564.83 | 61300.00 | 19500.00 | 156.00 | 19500.00 | 780.00 |

# A.4 Mortgage Manager: A Complete Driver-Based System

This example demonstrates all the major features of a driver-based macro system. It uses many of the macro concepts and techniques explained earlier. Although you may not have mortgages to manage, it is easily adapted to perform many other tasks. For instance, it can be used to manage partnerships, real estate, or investments. It works well with any set of activities that require large amounts of detail to be kept on individual items, but also need to produce reports in a consolidated form.

The individual macros can be used in many different worksheet applications to solve information problems. At first glance, it may appear that such a system would be difficult and time-consuming to develop. In fact, a system will perform only one task at a time, so that the process is actually made up of many small pieces that are built separately.

## Background

The Mortgage Manager was constructed to solve a problem in a trust operation. There were about 100 notes and mortgages that had been placed into the trusts. Some of them were given a value different from the balance remaining on the note. Each of them received periodic payments (monthly, quarterly, and so forth), and the income and principal had to be separated and entered into a bank computer. The totals of all the notes had to be reconciled to the computer balances. Annual statements were to be sent to the payors of the notes to show them their income tax deductions. The trust managers needed to know the details of the note at any time.

1-2-3 was able to solve this problem by using a separate file for each note. Each file was numbered sequentially, so that they could be retrieved by using counters in looping macros. They had "header" lines, which contained all the information of the notes that would be needed for consolidated reports. A driver worksheet contained all the macros, formulas, print screens, and consolidated lists.

Menus and input forms keep the user from making errors that could destroy the information. Data sort and extract routines manipulate the lists to provide useful information. Printouts of the notes, lists, address labels, and computer input forms are produced. New mortgages can be added and old ones dropped. All the files can be updated annually to start the new year with the year end closing balances.

You will notice that many of the macros look very similar. This is because macros were written, tested, and their cores shared with other macros performing similar functions. In the same way, you can take these macros and modify them to fit your own unique needs.

## Summary

The driver for the system is a worksheet named MORTGAGE. If your computer system uses floppy disks, the number of mortgages the system will handle is limited to 45 (35 for 320k floppies). This is because all the notes must be on one disk, and 1-2-3 uses a lot of memory for each worksheet. If you have a hard disk system, there can be up to 2000 notes, limited to the number of rows 1-2-3 provides.

Each individual note is kept on a separate worksheet. The permanent information such as the payor, payee, addresses, rate, beginning balance, and gain/loss data are placed in the top portion of one screen. Beneath this are the payment dates and amounts. Under this is the "header" line with all the information from the note needed for the consolidated reports. It is organized this way so that transaction summaries can be printed at the end of the year, and also more detailed reports can be printed for the manager of the account.

The system assigns a file number to each note so they will remain in consecutive order. In this way looping macros can manipulate each file to consolidate, print, or do the year-end closing. If a note needs to be updated with new information or payments, it is brought to the driver worksheet. After the work is done on it, it is saved by being extracted back to disk, using the file number as its name. All the repetitive information and formulas are erased by a macro before the file is extracted. This saves a great deal of disk space. This information is on a master template, which is copied into place before a note is combined with the driver worksheet.

For the consolidated lists, the macros need only to pull in the summary line that has been given the range name HEADER on the individual notes. The cursor is positioned at the top of the Accounts file and the first summary line is File Combined. The cursor is moved down one line, and the next summary line is obtained, and so on. After all the note summaries have been obtained, a portion of this list is copied to the File file, where notes can be looked up by their file number. The Accounts file is then sorted into account number order. The Data Query Extract command is used to select all the notes with the last payment date more than 65 days before today's date (which must be in the computer). All these notes are then copied to the Late file.

This system will print various reports and also produce the input forms necessary for a mainframe computer system. It is possible to extract this information into a file that could be transferred directly to another computer. As each computer system is very specific as to how it will accept input, it is necessary to work with the programmers on the system to be sure the information is correctly transferred. This step would be helpful because direct transfer eliminates data entry errors from the forms to the computer system.

## The Structure of the Mortgage Manager

The main menu will show the main functions of the system.

It performs the following tasks:

**VIEW**

To see different portions of the worksheet

| | |
|---|---|
| **ACCOUNT** | To see a listing of notes by account number |
| **FILE** | To see a listing of notes by file number |
| **LATE** | To see a listing of late notes |
| **CURRENT** | To see a current note being worked on |
| **RETURN** | To return to main menu |

**RECORD**

To record payments or changes to a note

**SAVE**

To save changes to the note

**PRINT**

To print out information from the note system

| | |
|---|---|
| **TICKET** | To print tickets for computer input and to save the file |
| **FILE** | To print the list of notes by file number |
| **ACCOUNT** | To print the list of notes by account number |
| **LATE** | To print the list of late payments |
| **DETAIL** | To print detail of individual notes |
| **TRANSACTIONS** | To print the transactions of the notes |
| **OFFICE** | To print the details of notes for the office records |
| **PAYOR** | To print Payor labels |
| **HOLDER** | To print Holder labels |
| **RETURN** | To return to print menu |
| **RETURN** | To return to the main menu |

**UPDATE**

To update the summaries of note information and save new file

**CREATE**

To create a new note on the system

**ERASE**

To remove information from the note system

| | |
|---|---|
| **RETURN** | To return to the main menu |
| **PURGE ACCOUNT** | To remove a note from the system |
| **DELETE YEAR** | To delete the year's transactions and bring the balances forward |

**QUIT**

To leave the note system

The following are specific instructions:

**VIEW** Choose this to see the files or the current note. To return to the main menu press ALT-M .

**RECORD** Choose this to record each payment made on the note, and additions or changes to the permanent information of the note. Be sure to SAVE your work. This will be done automatically if you have the system print the computer input tickets.

The system will ask for the file number. After entering it and pressing return, the note will be displayed. The cursor will move to the cells for data entry by using the arrow keys. After entering each item, press an arrow key. When you are done, press return twice. The main menu will be displayed. If there are more items to enter, choose RECORD again.

**Acc/Num** Enter the account number.

**File num** This number is assigned by the system. If a note is purged, the number may be used again for a new note by using the RECORD function and specifying this number.

**Acct Name** Enter the name and address of the account holder. The street number of the address must be preceded by an apostrophe.

**Payor** Enter the name and address of the payor. The street number of the address must be preceded by an apostrophe.

**Mgr num** Enter the manager number.

**Pymt. amt** Enter the amount paid with each installment.

**Int. rate** Enter the annual interest rate of the note.

**Pymt freq** A formula representing the number of payments per year must be entered. The normal note has payments made 12 times per year. This is represented as the formula 1/12, or .833333. The formula for quarterly payments = 1/4 or .25, semi-annual = 1/2 or .5, annual = 1.

**Orig. Note Balance** Enter the balance of the note at the time it was received.

**Sec. Num.** Enter the security number of the note if it is different.

**Due date** Enter the frequency and day of payments, for example, mo16 for a payment due on the 16th of each month.

**Description** Enter a short description of the note. Be sure it fits within the space provided.

**Orig. Bookval.** Enter the Bookvalue of the note at the time it was received.

**ID Num.** Enter the identification number if different.

**PAYMENTS** The first Date, Note Balance, and B/V Balance in the PAYMENTS section must be the balances and date of the original note or of the last payment received prior to the first payment to be recorded.

**Date** All dates in Lotus 1-2-3 must be entered in the form @date(yr,mo,da), where the year, month, and day are all numbers. Thus, April 17, 1984 would be recorded: @date(84,4,17). This allows the 1-2-3 math function to work.

**Payment** Enter the amount of the payment, less any service charges.

**SAVE** This function will save any changes made to the note. The Print Ticket function also saves the note, so do not use this function if a ticket is printed.

**PRINT** To print the files, notes, or address labels. Make sure the printer is on and the paper is in position. Some of the reports are wider than normal paper, so the macros print them in condensed print using the Epson printer codes. The macros can be modified to other codes simply by changing the print commands.

All the consolidated files will print without any further input. However, the first and last file numbers must be given for the detail reports from the individual notes. If only one note is to be printed, enter its file number as the first and last number.

**UPDATE** Choose this to update the summary listings (by file number, account number, and late payment).

**CREATE**   To create a new file number for a new note. First be sure that there are no file numbers available from notes that have been purged. If information is entered into the note, be sure to save the note by printing tickets or using Save.

**ERASE**   Choose this to remove information from the file.

   **DELETE** will remove the year's transaction information from every account and bring the balances forward.

   **PURGE** will remove a note from the system. The file number can be used again by choosing RECORD.

**QUIT**   To leave the Mortgage Manager system.

## Design

As you can see below, the first three sections are the consolidated lists of information from the individual notes. The Account # file has all the important information from the notes in account number order. The File # file is a cross reference tool to find the account number. The Late file lists all the accounts that have not received a payment for 65 days.

The master template is used to create the form for the individual notes. It contains all the formulas, headings, and layout of the notes. It was created in the location where the notes are placed by the File Combine macros. This area is Range Named ACCOUNT. The template was then copied to a location below the note and this area Range Named MASTER. Each time a note is File Combined, MASTER is first copied to ACCOUNT. This automatically erases all the old data in the ACCOUNT range, and the formulas refer to the correct cells. Before the note is saved back to disk, all the information from the template is erased to conserve disk memory.

The menu macros and system macros are next. These are organized into a tree structure so they can be easily found, and so their relationships are clear.

The computer input forms are to the right. These produce the information necessary to post the transactions to the bank computer. Again, templates are used to produce the actual forms. The information from the note is copied into the forms, and the forms printed

The next area provides user aids. Screens with instructions are displayed by the macros. The screens can be "frozen" so that the macros can send the cursor around the worksheet without changing the screen. Other messages can be displayed by shifting the screen to a new area.

The last area is the input screen for printing information from the notes. It allows the user to insert the first and last file number to be printed. The macros will copy that information into themselves to control looping.

The organization of the worksheet is presented below:

| Account# file | File# file | Late pymt file | detail of note | Menu macros | System macros | Cash BD1-BN29 | Window blanks | Input blank |
|---|---|---|---|---|---|---|---|---|
| A-J | K-O | P-V | Y1-AG34 | AJ1-AS33 | AT1-BC160 | | BP1-BQ20 | BR1-BZ20 |
| " | " | P-V | Y1-AG34 | | " | Cash | BP21-BQ40 | |
| " | " | " | | System | " | template | BP41-BQ60 | |
| " | " | " | | macros | " | BD35-BN63 | | |
| " | " | " | | AJ34-AS155 | " | | | |
| " | " | " | Master | " | " | Sell | | |
| " | " | " | template | " | " | BD66-BN101 | | |
| " | " | " | Y40-AF71 | " | " | | | |
| " | " | " | | " | " | | | |
| " | " | " | Menu | " | " | Sell | | |
| " | " | " | blanks | " | " | template | | |
| " | " | " | AD121-AI140 | " | " | BD104-BN139 | | |
| " | " | " | AD141-AI160 | | | | | |

The menu macros and system macros follow a tree structure. The main menu (menu1) is the trunk. The macros call other menu branches or are leaves (final selections). In this way each individual macro can be found quickly by following the branching structure. It is very easy to modify the structure, because each function is a complete unit.

The tree structure of the menu system is shown in Diagram 4-2.

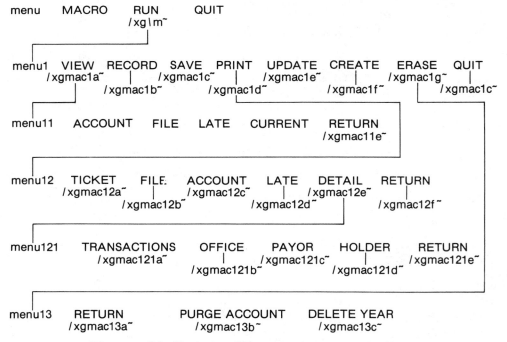

Diagram 4-2. Mortgage Manager menu organization

## Macros

These are the macros that run the system. Each macro line is documented to show what it is doing. For more detailed explanations of the macro concepts, consult the previous sections. First the menu macros and then the system macros will be shown. If you did not buy the disk with this book, the macros will work if they are typed in (beware of typos). Note that the menu entries have been arranged so that they can be read. They must be entered in the menu format for the menu to work.

## Menu Macros

**Entry menu.**   This menu is only for the needs of the disk with the book. It allows direct access to the macros, or runs the system. The system itself does not use it.

```
menu     Macro  Run  Quit
```

(macro) to view the macros
        {goto}m~/xq

(run)    to start the system
         /xg\m~

(quit)   to return to the macro directory
         /frmenu~

**Main menu.**   This menu controls all the functions of the system. Some of the choices call subsidiary menus, others call macros directly. The Quit selection should be modified to leave the worksheet if the system is used separately from the book disk.

```
menu1 VIEW  RECORD  SAVE  PRINT  UPDATE  CREATE  ERASE  QUIT
```

(view)  To see different portions of the worksheet
        {goto}blank1~
        /xgmac1a~

(record) To record payments or changes to a note
         /xcfreeze~
         /xgmac1b~

(save)  To save changes to the note
        /xcfreeze~
        /xgmac1c~

(print) To print out information from the note system
        {goto}blank1~
        /xgmac1d~

(update) To update the summaries of note information and
save new file
```
/xcfreeze~
/xgmac1e~
```

(create) To create a new note on the system
```
/xcfreeze~
/xgmac1f~
```

(erase) To remove information from the note system
```
{goto}blank1~
/xgmac1g~
```

(quit) To leave the note system
```
{goto}blank~
/xgmac1·h~
```

**Viewing menu.** This menu lets the user go to different parts of the
worksheet to see the files.

menu11    ACCOUNT    FILE    LATE    CURRENT    RETURN

(accnt) To see the listing of notes by account number
```
{home}/xq
```

(file) To see the listing of notes by file number
```
{goto}K1~/xq
```

(late) To see the listing of late notes
```
{goto}Q1~/xq
```

(curr) To see the current note being worked on
```
{goto}Y1~/xq
```

(retn) To return to the main menu
```
/xgmac11e~
```

**Print menu.** This menu will print the files on the driver worksheet. The
Detail selection calls the print submenu.

menu12    TICKET    FILE    ACCOUNT    LATE    DETAIL    RETURN

(ticket) To print tickets for computer input and to save
the file
```
/xcfreeze~
/xgmac12a~
```

(file) To print the list of notes by file number
```
/xcfreeze~
/xgmac12b~
```

(accnt) To print the list of notes by account number
```
/xcfreeze~
/xgmac12c~
```

(late)  `To print the list of late payments`
`/xcfreeze~`
`/xgmac12d~`

(detail) `To print the detail of individual notes`
`/xgmac12e~`

(return)`To return to the main menu`
`/xgmac12f~`

**Print submenu.**  This menu prints information from the individual files. The user will be asked for the range of file numbers to be printed (from one to all).

`menu121 TRANSACTIONS    OFFICE    PAYOR    HOLDER    RETURN`

(trans)  `To print the transactions of the notes`
`/xgmac121a~`

(office) `To print the details of notes for the office`
`records`
`/xgmac121b~`

(payor) `To print Payor labels`
`/xgmac121c~`

(holder)`To print Holder labels`
`/xgmac121d~`

(return)`To return to the print menu`
`/xgmac121e~`

**Erase menu.**  This menu provides for the removing of a note or the deletion of the year's transactions after the balances have been brought forward.

`menu13   RETURN    PURGE ACCOUNT    DELETE YEAR`

(return)`To return to the main menu`
`/xgmac13a~`

(purge) `To remove a note from the system`
`/xcfreeze~`
`/xgmac13b~`

(delete) `To delete the year's transactions and bring the`
`balances forward`
`/xcfreeze~`
`/xgmac13c~`

## System Macros

You will notice that each macro that calls a menu ends with a command to call the menu the macro is in (the entry macros call themselves). This command is not executed unless the escape key is pressed while viewing a menu. This allows the menus to move back and forth like the 1-2-3 command menus.

Some of the macros in the system are not named using the tree system. This is because they are only called by other macros, or they are the macros to get into the system. The first two macros are the latter type.

| Name | Macro | comments |
|------|-------|----------|
|  |  | ----------------------------------DISPLAY  ENTRY  MENU |
| \0 | {goto}BLANK~/wgpe/xmMENU~/xg\0~ |  |
|  |  | -----------------------------------DISPLAY  MAIN  MENU |
| \m | {goto}BLANK1~/wgpe/xmMENU1~/xg\M~ |  |

These two macros "freeze" the screen during macro operations. `freeze` is called as a subroutine, which returns to the macro when it is done. The screen will show a message while the cursor is busy moving around. When the macro is done, the clear macro is called, clearing the screen and bringing back the main menu.

|  |  |  |
|------|-------|----------|
|  | ---------------------------------FREEZE  SCREEN  SUBROUTINE | |
| freeze | {goto}UL~ | move to upper left corner |
|  | {goto}BR~ | move to bottom right corner |
|  | /wwv/wwu | create window |
|  | {window}/xr | move cursor out, start macro |
|  | ---------------------------------CLEAR  SCREEN  SUBROUTINE | |
| clear | /wwc/xg\M~ | clear screen, return to menu |

The mac1 series are the main menu macros. Mac1a calls the view menu.

|  |  |  |
|------|-------|----------|
|  | --------------------------------CALL  VIEW  MENU | |
| mac1a | /xmMENU11~/xg\M~ | |

This macro sets up the template for the note and then gets the specified note from disk memory. It uses two windows. The first freezes the screen while the note is retrieved. The second displays a message to show how to enter the information. After the new information is recorded, the main menu returns.

|  |  |  |
|------|-------|----------|
|  | --------------------------------RECORD  INFORMATION | |
| mac1b | {window}{pgdn}{window} | move screen |
|  | /wgpd{goto}ACCOUNT~/reACCOUNT~ | erase area |
|  | /cMASTER~ACCOUNT~ | get template |
|  | /fccnACCOUNT~{?}~ | get requested file |
|  | /wwc{goto}BLK~{down}/wwh/wwu | get message |
|  | {window}/riACCOUNT~/wwc/xg\M~ | insert info; get menu |

This macro sets up the header line and erases all the standard information included on the template. It then extracts the note to disk memory.

|  |  |  |
|------|-------|----------|
|  | -------------------------------FORMAT  AND  SAVE  NOTE | |
| mac1c | /wgpd/cY3..AC3~Y34~/mAC34~AB34~ | header: copy top line |
|  | /cY9..Z9~AC34~ | copy mgr, pymt |

```
          /dfAE34~@max(Y17..Y31)~~~              copy date
          /xi@count(AC32..AF32)=0~/xgNEXT~       skip balances if empty
          /dfAF34~AC32~~~                        copy note balances
          /dfAG34~AF32~~~                        copy bookvalue balances
next      /cY3~NAME~                             get file name
          /reY1..AC2~/reY8..AD8~                 erase standard information
          /reY12..AD12~/reY15..AF16~
          /reAA18..AF32~
          /rpY34..ag34~                          protect header cells
          /wwc/fxf                               extract file
name      1
          ~Y1..AG34~r
          /xg\m                                  return to menu
```

This macro gets the main print menu.

```
          --------------------------------GET PRINT MENU
mac1d     /xmMENU12~/xg\M~
```

This macro updates each of the consolidated files on the worksheet. It appears to be lengthy, but it is broken up into separate modules.

**mac1e** is a looping macro that increments a counter each time it loops. It uses the counter to find the note, and then pulls the header line into the Accounts list. The pointer is reset to the next line of the worksheet. The macro has copied in the last file number as the test for the end of the notes. When the counter equals the last file number, the macro named Copy is called.

Copy makes a partial copy of the Accounts list, which is now in file number order, and places it in the File list. The Accounts list can then be sorted into account number order by the Sort macro.

The list of late accounts is then produced. The input range for the list must be defined, because new accounts may have been created. The Late macro is actually using hidden titles to perform the data base operations. The row beneath the titles of the accounts and late files has spaces inserted into the cells. The Data Query command sees these spaces as the titles, and does the selection and output based on them. The criterion formula tests the dates to see if they are older than 65 days. Each note that meets the test will be copied into the late file.

```
          ---------------------------UPDATE FILES
mac1e     /wgpd{goto}COUNTER~'1~               to initialize counter
          /cFILENUM~ONE~                       to get last file number
          /reA10..W2048~                       to erase spreadsheet
          /dfDATE~@TODAY~~~                     to enter current date
          /cDATE~M2~/cDATE~S3~                  to copy date
          {goto}A10~                           to start list on correct line
          /rndPOINTER~/rncPOINTER~~            to name pointer
loop1     {goto}POINTER~                       to go to next entry
```

| | | |
|---|---|---|
| | /fccnHEADER~ | to get data from account |
| counter | 8 | Counter—file number |
| | ~/rndPOINTER~{down}/rncPOINTER~~ | to move pointer down one |
| | /cCOUNTER~TWO~/xi | copy counter; test to see if |
| one | 8 | filenumber |
| | = | equals |
| two | 8 | counter |
| | ~/xgCOPY~ | if at end go to copy macro |
| | {goto}COUNTER~{edit}{home}{del} | routine to increment counter |
| | 1+{calc}{home}'~ | |
| | /xgloop1~ | to loop1 |
| copy | {goto}A10~/c{end}{down}{right} | to make list by file number |
| | {right}{right}{right}~K10~ | |
| | /xgSORT~ | to start sort routine |
| sort | {goto}A10~/dsd{bs}.{end}{down} | to sort file by account number |
| | ..{end}{right} | |
| | pB10~a~g/xgLATE~ | to start late routine |
| C | >criterion | (seven spaces) |
| C | +G10<($DATE-65) >range | |
| | | extract late paying notes |
| late | {goto}A9~/rndI~/rncI~{end}{down} | to define input range |
| | ..{end}{right}~ | |
| | /dqiI~cC~oO~eq | to extract late payments |
| | /wwc/fs~r | close window, save file |
| | /xg\M~ | get menu |

To create a new file, the cell containing the last file number (filenum) must be increased by one and used as the name of the new account. This number is placed in the header so that the Update macro can extract it, and it is placed in the macro so the file can be saved to disk. The date on the file is set to 1/1/99 so that blank notes can be identified in the consolidated lists and so that the Late macro will not select it.

After saving the note and the worksheet, the Master template is copied and the user can enter information. A horizontal window displays a message of how to enter the information. The macro then returns to the main menu so computer tickets can be printed or the new data saved.

| | | |
|---|---|---|
| | ------------------------------NUMBER OF LAST FILE CREATED | |
| filenum | 8 | |
| | ------------------------------CREATE NEW NOTE | |
| mac1f | /wgpd/reACCOUNT~ | erase area |
| | {goto}FILENUM~ | increment filenum |
| | {edit}{home}{del}1+ | |
| | {calc}{home}'~/c~Y3~ | copy to account |
| | /cY3~Y34~/cY3~NAME2~/cY3~NAME3~ | copy to header and macro |
| | /dfAE34~36161~~~/cAE34~Y17~ | put 1/1/99 as date |
| | /fxv | extract file |
| name2 | 8 | |

```
              ~ACCOUNT~
              /wwc/fs~r                          close window, save file
              {goto}BR~/wwv/wwu{window}          freeze screen
              {goto}ACCOUNT~/cMASTER~ACCOUNT~    get template
              /fccnACCOUNT~                      get file
name3         8
              ~/wwc{goto}BLK~{down}/wwh/wwu      get message
              {window}/riACCOUNT~/wwc/xg\M~      insert info; get menu
```
These two macros display additional menus.

```
              -------------------------------GET ERASE MENU
mac1g         /xmMENU13~/xg\M~
              -------------------------------GET ENTRY MENU
mac1h         /xmMENU~/xg\M~
```
This macro is the only one for menu11. It calls the main menu.

```
              ---------------------------DISPLAY MAIN MENU
mac11e        /xmMENU1~/xgMAC1A~
```

The **mac12** series performs the print functions. The first one, **mac12a**, prints the computer tickets for input into the bank computer. The interest of the note goes on the cash ticket, the principal on the sell ticket. This macro is rather long because the information can't be placed in the forms by having cell addresses in the appropriate cells in the form. Labels cannot be moved this way, and the numeric data will be in different places on the note schedule as the payments are made. Thus, the cursor must move to the correct cell and copy its information into the form. This also means that formulas must be turned into values before they can be copied.

```
              --------------------------PRINT COMPUTER TICKETS
mac12a        /wgpd/cCASHBLANK~CASH~             prepare blank cash
              /cSELLBLANK~SELL~                  prepare blank sell
              {goto}Y31~{end}{up}/c~BI16~/c~BK91~    last date
              {right}{right}{edit}{calc}~/c~BK8~     income cash
              {right}{edit}{calc}~/c~BK74~/c~BK90~   Principal cash
              {right}{edit}{calc}~/c~BK95~           new balance
              {up}{edit}{calc}~/c~BK15~{down}        old balance
              {right}{right}{edit}{calc}~/c~BN74~    bookvalue
              /cY9~BK2~/cY9~BI98~                manager
              /cZ3~BE8~/cZ3~BE74~                account number
              /cAA3~BD12~/cAA3~BI69~             account name
              /cAD9~BG8~/cAD9~BG74~              security number
              /cAD13~BK12~/cAD13~BG78~           I D number
              /cZ13~BH17~/cZ13~BJ92~             loan desc. 1
              /cZ14~BH18~/cZ14~BJ93~             loan desc. 2
              /pprCASH~agpq                      print cash ticket
              /pprSELL~agpq/xgMAC1C~             print sell ticket
```

Macros **mac12b**, **c**, and **d** print the consolidated lists. As the number of accounts may change, the range of the print area must be defined each time.

```
                --------------------------PRINT FILE NUMBER LIST
mac12b    {goto}K1~/ppr{bs}.{end}{down}        set range
          {end}{down}{end}{down}{right}{right}
          {right}{right}~os\018~qagpq           set for normal print
          /xgCLEAR~                             clear screen, return to menu
                --------------------------PRINT ACCOUNT NUMBER LIST
mac12c    {goto}A1~/ppr{bs}.{end}{down}            set range
          {end}{down}{right}{right}
          {right}{right}{right}{right}
          {right}{right}~os\015~qagp           set for condensed print
          os\018~qq                            reset to normal print
          /xgCLEAR~                            clear screen, return to menu
                --------------------------PRINT LATE PAYMENTS
mac12d    {goto}Q1~/ppr{bs}.{end}{down}{end}       set range
          {down}{end}{end}{down}{right}{right}
          {right}{right}{right}{right}~
          os{esc}\018~qagpq                       set printer
          /xgCLEAR~                            clear screen, return to menu
These two macros display menus
                --------------------------GET PRINT DETAIL MENU
mac12e    /xmMENU121~/xgMAC1D~                 To display detail menu
                --------------------------RETURN TO MAIN MENU
mac12f    /xmMENU1~/xgMAC1D~
```

This series of macros prints the detail from the individual accounts. An input screen is displayed so that the first and last file number may be given. The default value is always the first account, so the printer will not be tied up long if Return is accidentally pressed. The transaction statements do not show the book value data, which is only needed by the office. Address labels may be produced for either the holder of the note or the person paying it.

```
                --------------------------PRINT TRANSACTION STATEMENTS
mac121a   /wgpd/dfFIRST~1~~~/dfLAST~1~~~       set default file numbers
          /cFILENUM~NUMBER~                    set ending file number
          {goto}ENTER~/riENTER~                enter range to be printed
          /xcFREEZE~                           freeze screen
          /cFIRST~COUNTER1~                    set counter
          {goto}COUNTER1~{edit}{home}'~        turn number to label
          /cLAST~FIVE~                         set last file number to print
          {goto}FIVE~{edit}{home}'~            turn number to label
loop3     {goto}Y1~                            loop3 and Restart start here
          /reY1..AI34~/cMASTER~~               erase area; get template
          /fccnACCOUNT~                        to get file
counter11
          ~/pprY1..AC32~agpq                   number of file to get
          /cCOUNTER1~SIX~                      to print file
          /xi                                  copy current value to test
five      1                                    test to see if
          <=                                   last number
                                               is less than or equals
```

```
six       1                                      counter
          ~/xgCLEAR~                             then: clear screen; menu
          {goto}COUNTER1~{edit}{home}            to increase counter
          {del}1+{calc}{home}'~
          /xgLOOP3~                              to loop
          -------------------------------PRINT OFFICE STATEMENTS
mac121b   /wgpd/dfFIRST~1~~~/dfLAST~1~~~         set default file numbers
          /cFILENUM~NUMBER~                      set ending file number
          {goto}ENTER~/riENTER~                  enter range to be printed
          /xcFREEZE~                             freeze screen
          /cFIRST~COUNTER2~                      set counter
          {goto}COUNTER2~{edit}{home}'~          turn number to label
          /cLAST~THREE~                          set last file number to print
          {goto}THREE~{edit}{home}'~             turn number to label
          /ppos{esc}\015~qq                      set printer:condensed print
loop4     {goto}Y1~/wgpd                         loop4 and Continue start here
          /reY1..AI34~/cMASTER~~                 erase area; get template
          /fccnACCOUNT~                          to get file
counter21                                        counter2
          ~/pprY1..AF32~agpq                     to print file
          /cCOUNTER2~FOUR~/xi                    check to see if
three     1                                      last number
          <=                                     is less than or equals
four      1                                      counter
          ~/ppos{esc}\018~qq/xgCLEAR~            then:reset printer; clear screen
          {goto}COUNTER2~                        to increase counter
          {edit}{home}{del}1+{calc}{home}'~
          ~/xgLOOP4~                             to loop
          -------------------------------PRINT PAYOR LABELS
mac121c   /wgpd/dfFIRST~1~~~/dfLAST~1~~~         set default file numbers
          /cFILENUM~NUMBER~                      set ending file number
          {goto}ENTER~/riENTER~                  enter range to be printed
          /xcFREEZE~                             freeze screen
          /cFIRST~COUNTER6~                      set counter
          {goto}COUNTER6~{edit}{home}'~          turn number to label
          /cLAST~ELEVEN~                         set last file number to print
          {goto}ELEVEN~{edit}{home}'~            turn number to label
loop7     {goto}LABEL~                           move cursor to label area
          /reLABEL~                              erase former data
          /fccnPAYOR~                            get holder address
counter61                                        counter6
          ~/pprLABEL~oouqagq                     print label
          /cCOUNTER6~TWELVE~/xi                  test to see if
eleven    1                                      last number
          <=                                     is less than or equals
twelve    1                                      counter
          ~/xgCLEAR~                             then:clear screen;return to menu
          {goto}COUNTER6~{edit}{home}{del}increase counter
          {calc}{home}'~
```

```
              /xgLOOP7~                          loop
              --------------------------------PRINT HOLDER LABELS
    mac121d   /wgpd/dfFIRST~1~~~/dfLAST~1~~~    set default file numbers
              /cFILENUM~NUMBER~                 set ending file number
              {goto}ENTER~/riENTER~             enter range to be printed
              /xcFREEZE~                        freeze screen
              /cFIRST~COUNTER5~                 set counter
              {goto}COUNTER5~{edit}{home}'~     turn number to label
              /cLAST~NINE~                      set last file number to print
              {goto}NINE~{edit}{home}'~         turn number to label
    loop6     {goto}LABEL~                      move cursor to label area
              /reLABEL~                         erase former data
              /fccnHOLDER~                      get holder address
    counter51                                   counter5
              ~/pprLABEL~oouqagq                print label
              /cCOUNTER5~TEN~/xi                test to see if
    nine      1                                 last number
              =                                 equals
    ten       1                                 counter
              ~/xgCLEAR~                        then:clear screen;return to menu
              {goto}COUNTER5~{edit}{home}{del}increase counter
              {calc}{home}'~
              /xgLOOP6~                         loop
              --------------------------------RETURN TO PRINT MENU
    mac121e   /xmMENU12~/xgMAC12E~
```

These macros will eliminate information from the individual notes. To help prevent accidental erasures, the Return function is placed first in the Erase menu. The purge macro removes all the information from a note but the file number. This must be retained or the looping macros will fail when they get to the purged note. The date 1/1/99 is put into the note so that it may be identified in the consolidated files, and so that it will not be selected by the Late macro.

```
              --------------------------------RETURN TO MAIN MENU
    mac13a    /xmMENU1~/xgMAC1G~
              --------------------------------PURGE CONTENTS FROM NOTE
    mac13b    {window}{pgdn}{pgdn}{window}      place message on screen
              /wgpd/reY1..AI34~{goto}Y1~        erase area
              /fcce{?}~                         get file
              {window}{pgup}{pgup}{window}      place message on screen
              /reY1..AG33~                      erase data
              /cY34~Y3~/reZ34..AG34~            reenter file number/erase header
              /dfY17~36161~~~/cY17~AE34~        enter 1/1/99 as date
              /cY3~NAME1~/fxv                   copy empty account to file
    name1     1
              ~ACCOUNT~r/xgCLEAR~              return to menu
```

This macro is used at year's end. After all the notes have been printed and a backup floppy disk copy made, the macro may be run. It will take each note and move the ending balances to the start of the file. The year's transactions are then erased, leaving the note ready for the new year.

```
                 -----------------------------DELETE YEAR'S WORK FROM FILE
mac13c   /wgpd{goto}COUNTER3~'1~              to set counter3
         {goto}COUNTER4~'1~                   to set counter4
         /cFILENUM~SEVEN~                     to set ending file number
loop5    {goto}Y1~/reY1..AI34~/fcce           erase area and get file
counter31                                     number of file to get - counter3
         ~/cAE34~Y17~/cAF34~AC17~             move ending balances to beginning
         /cAG34~AF17~/reY18..Z30~             erase old transactions
         /ruY17~/ruAC17~/wwc                  unprotect cells, clear window
         /fxv                                 extract file
counter41                                     number of file to send - counter4
         ~ACCOUNT~r
         /xcFREEZE~                           freeze screen
         /cCOUNTER3~EIGHT~/xi                 test to see if
seven    1                                    filenumber
         =                                    equals
eight    1                                    counter
         ~/xgCLEAR~                           then: return to menu
         {goto}COUNTER3~{edit}{home}          to increase counter3
         {del}1+{calc}{home}'~
         /c~COUNTER4~                         copy to counter4
         /xgLOOP5~                            to loop
```

The formulas to run the mortgage manager are only in the macros and the Master template. Listed here are the contents and the cell status of the cells of the Master Template:

```
Cell Format Contents
---- -- --------
AA40: (D1) @TODAY
Y41:  'File num
Z41:  'Acc/Num
AA41: 'Acct Name
AC41: 'Mortgagor
Y47:  'Mgr num
Z47:  'Pymt. amt.
AA47: ^Int.rate
AB47: ^Pymt freq
AC47: 'Orig. Note Bal.
AD47: ' Sec. Num.
AB48: (F5) U 0.0833333333
AD48: U 'N00010
Y51:  'Due date
Z51:  'Description
AC51: 'Orig. Bookval.
AD51: ' ID Num.
```

```
AB52:  'XXXXXXX
AD52:  U '000000001
AB53:  'XXXXXXX
AD54:  ^G/L
Y55:   'Date
Z55:   "Payment
AA55:  "Interest
AB55:  "Principal
AC55:  "Note Balance
AD55:  (F5) @IF(AC48=0,0,(AC48-AC52)/AC48)
AE55:  "B/V adj.
AF55:  "B/V Balance
```

This group of formulas is copied from AA58 to AF69:

```
AA57:  (C2) @IF(Z57=0,0,AC56*$AA$9*$AB$9)
AB57:  (C2) +Z57-AA57
AC57:  (C2) +AC56-AB57
AD57:  (C2) +$AD$16*AB57
AE57:  (C2) +AB57-AD57
AF57:  (C2) +AF56-AE57


Z70:   (C2) "----------
AA70:  (C2) "----------
AB70:  (C2) "----------
AD70:  (C2) "----------
AE70:  (C2) "----------
Z71:   (C2) @SUM(Z57..Z69)
AA71:  (C2) @SUM(AA57..AA69)
AB71:  (C2) @SUM(AB57..AB69)
AC71:  (C2) @MIN(AC56..AC69)
AD71:  (C2) @SUM(AD57..AD69)
AE71:  (C2) @SUM(AE57..AE69)
AF71:  (C2) @MIN(AF56..AF69)
```

The following cells are unprotected so the user may enter data into them when the template is copied to the note area:

```
Z42
AA42..46
AC42..46
Y48..AD48
Y52
Z52..53
AC52..AD52
Y56
AC56
AF56
Y57..Z69
```

Listed here are the Range Names of cells or areas that are not in macros or created by macros (those are listed with the macros):

```
ACCOUNT      Y1..AG34
ACCT         Y1..AC33
BLANK        AD121..AI139
BLANK1       AC138
BLK          BP1..BQ20
BR           BQ40
CASH         BD1..BN29
CASHBLANK    BD35..BN63
DATE         D1
ENTER        BR1..BZ20
FIRST        BV12
HEADER       Y34..AG34
HOLDER       AA3..AA7
LABEL        Y76..Y84
LAST         BV14
MASTER       Y40..AF71
NUMBER       BX7
O            P9..V9
PAYOR        AC3..AC7
SELL         BD66..BN101
SELLBLANK    BD104..BN139
UL           BP21
```

While the macros are running, they bring up different screens to give user instructions. Shown below are the screens with their locations.

```
Screen for entry menu    (AD121..AI140)


                Note Control System



                      Please make a selection



        If you wish to return to this menu from the files,
        press ALT M.
```

This screen is for the submenus (AD141..AI160)

```
Please make a selection
```

These three screens are seen when the screen is "frozen". They are only 2 columns wide, the first 71 spaces, the second 1 space. The row of bars will form the bottom of a box during the macro.

```
Main freeze screen              (BP21..BQ40)


                             Please be patient
                        The macro will be done soon


     ------------·!!!!!!!!!!!!!!!!!!!!!!!!!!!!!!!!!!!!!!!!!!!!!!
```

This screen prompts for a file number. (BP41..BQ60)

```
Please enter the file number of the file to be retrieved

                    and press return


!!!!!!!!!!!!!!!!!!!!!!!!!!!!!!!!!!!!!!!!!!!!!!!!! !!!!!!!!!!!!!!!!!!
```

This screen prompts for the file to be purged. (BP61..BQ80)

```
Please enter the file number of the file to be purged

                    and press return


!!!!!!!!!!!!!!!!!!!!!!!!!!!!!!!!!!!!!!!!!!!!!!!!!!!!!!!!!!!!!!!
```

This message is displayed on the top line of the screen during data entry. (BP1..BQ20)

```
  - Use arrow keys to enter data. Press <ENTER> to return to
menu. -
```

This screen is the input form for determining which notes should printed. After the first and last file numbers are given, the numbers are copied into the macros to control looping. (BR1..BZ20)

```
          Please prepare your printer and

    enter the first and last file numbers to be printed

          (the current ending file number is 3    )



            First File Number     1

            Last file number      1
```

## System Printouts

The three consolidated files, different forms of the individual notes, and other information can be printed out from the system. Because some of the files are wider than a normal page, the print setup is designed for an Epson-type printer, which can print in reduced print. The print macros can be modified to accommodate any printer. Looping macros produce copies of note transactions and address labels for envelopes. Shown below are the different files and information that can be printed by the system.

### Summary listing of notes in account number order:

```
                              09-Sep-84
        Totals File
                         Tot. notes      Tot. B/V
                      $252,907.88    $250,924.87
        Account listing by account number
```

| File | Acct | Account name | Payee name | Mgr | Payment | Pymt date | Note Balance | B/V balance |
|---|---|---|---|---|---|---|---|---|
| 2 | AC3400 | Tim Franklin | Eddy Black | W3 | $500.00 | 14-Jul-83 | $57,000.00 | $47,000.00 |
| 1 | AC6420 | Stone, George L #2 | Gary T. Reynolds | W2 | $850.00 | 10-Aug-83 | $98,885.96 | $98,885.96 |
| 3 | AC6666 | Susan Lowe | Pat Sanders | W5 | $100.00 | 14-Jun-83 | $8,418.19 | $14,662.29 |

### Listing of notes by file number order:

```
                              04-Feb-84
            Account listing by file number
```

| File | Acct | Account name | Payee name | Mgr |
|---|---|---|---|---|
| 1 | AC6420 | Stone, George L #2 | Gary T. Reynolds | W2 |
| 2 | AC3400 | Tim Franklin | Eddy Black | W3 |
| 3 | AC6666 | Susan Lowe | Pat Sanders | W5 |

### Listing of notes with 65 days since last payment:

```
                              24-Jan-84
                Payments in arrears
```

| File | Acct | Account Name | Payee name | Mgr | Pymt | Date |
|---|---|---|---|---|---|---|
| 2 | AC3400 | Tim Franklin | Eddy Black | W3 | $500.00 | 14-Jul-83 |
| 1 | AC6420 | Stone, George L #2 | Gary T. Reynolds | W2 | $850.00 | 10-Aug-83 |
| 3 | AC6666 | Susan Lowe | Pat Sanders | W5 | $100.00 | 14-Jun-83 |

### Transaction statement:

```
                              04-Feb-84
```

| File num | Acc/Num | Acct Name | Mortgagor |
|---|---|---|---|
| 3 | AC6666 | Susan Lowe | Pat Sanders |
| | | 25 Main | 93c Center |
| | | Chicago, IL 54333 | Hillsdale, Il 56332 |

| Mgr num | Pymt. amt. | Int.rate | Pymt freq | Orig. Note Bal. |
|---|---|---|---|---|
| W5 | $100.00 | 0.04500 | 0.08333 | $15,000.00 |

```
Due date  Description                        Orig. Bookval.
mo 14     mortgage note payable XXXXXXX $12,500.00
          for 20 years XXXXXXX
```

| Date | Payment | Interest | Principal | Note Balance |
|------|---------|----------|-----------|--------------|
| 14-Dec-82 | | | | $8,823.45 |
| 14-Jan-83 | $100.00 | $33.09 | $66.91 | $8,756.54 |
| 14-Feb-83 | $100.00 | $32.84 | $67.16 | $8,689.37 |
| 14-Mar-83 | $100.00 | $32.59 | $67.41 | $8,621.96 |
| 14-Apr-83 | $100.00 | $32.33 | $67.67 | $8,554.29 |
| 14-May-83 | $100.00 | $32.08 | $67.92 | $8,486.37 |
| 14-Jun-83 | $100.00 | $31.82 | $68.18 | $8,418.19 |
| | | $0.00 | $0.00 | $8,418.19 |
| | | $0.00 | $0.00 | $8,418.19 |
| | | $0.00 | $0.00 | $8,418.19 |
| | | $0.00 | $0.00 | $8,418.19 |
| | | $0.00 | $0.00 | $8,418.19 |
| | | $0.00 | $0.00 | $8,418.19 |
| | | $0.00 | $0.00 | $8,418.19 |
| | ---------- | ---------- | ---------- | |
| | $600.00 | $194.74 | $405.26 | $8,418.19 |

## Office statement:

```
                      10-Oct-84
File num  Acc/Num    Acct Name          Mortgagor
1         AC6420     Stone, George L #2  Gary T. Reynolds
                     73 Berry Ave        999 Brook Lane
                     Newton, MA 02664    Stevens, AR 55774
```

```
Mgr num  Pymt. amt.  Int.rate  Pymt freq Orig. Note Bal. Sec. Num.
W2        $850.00    0.08000    0.08333    $110,000.00 N00010
```

```
Due date  Description                     Orig. Bookval.  ID Num.
mo 10     Gary T.Reynolds cont.XXXXXXX    $110,000.00 000000001
          for deed dtd 12/30/77 XXXXXXX
```

| | | | | | G/L | | B/V |
|------|---------|----------|-----------|--------------|---------|----------|---------|
| Date | Payment | Interest | Principal | Note Balance | 0.00000 | B/V adj. | Balance |
| 10-Dec-82 | | | | $100,367.26 | | | $100,367.26 |
| 10-Jan-83 | $850.00 | $669.12 | $180.88 | $100,186.38 | $0.00 | $180.88 | $100,186.38 |
| 10-Feb-83 | $850.00 | $667.91 | $182.09 | $100,004.28 | $0.00 | $182.09 | $100,004.28 |
| 10-Mar-83 | $850.00 | $666.70 | $183.30 | $99,820.98 | $0.00 | $183.30 | $99,820.98 |
| 10-Apr-83 | $850.00 | $665.47 | $184.53 | $99,636.45 | $0.00 | $184.53 | $99,636.45 |
| 10-May-83 | $850.00 | $664.24 | $185.76 | $99,450.70 | $0.00 | $185.76 | $99,450.70 |
| 10-Jun-83 | $850.00 | $663.00 | $187.00 | $99,263.70 | $0.00 | $187.00 | $99,263.70 |

| | | | | | | |
|---|---|---|---|---|---|---|
| 10-Jul-83 | $850.00 | $661.76 | $188.24 | $99,075.46 | $0.00 | $188.24 | $99,075.46 |
| 10-Aug-83 | $850.00 | $660.50 | $189.50 | $98,885.96 | $0.00 | $189.50 | $98,885.96 |
| | | $0.00 | $0.00 | $98,885.96 | $0.00 | $0.00 | $98,885.96 |
| | | $0.00 | $0.00 | $98,885.96 | $0.00 | $0.00 | $98,885.96 |
| | | $0.00 | $0.00 | $98,885.96 | $0.00 | $0.00 | $98,885.96 |
| | | $0.00 | $0.00 | $98,885.96 | $0.00 | $0.00 | $98,885.96 |
| | | $0.00 | $0.00 | $98,885.96 | $0.00 | $0.00 | $98,885.96 |

```
          -------   ---------   ---------               -------   -------
          $500.00  $5,318.70   $1,481.30   $98,885.96     $0.00  $1,481.30   $98,885.96
```

## Address labels:

Susan Lowe
25 Main
Chicago, IL 54333

## Income form:

```
CASH                                    ----------------------
  PRINCIPAL  !--!   INCOME  !--!        W5        !         30-Jun-83
  PRINCIPAL  !--!   INCOME  !-X!    ----------    !
  cd  acct  sec. num. tran    date   u/c   cash    link est book val
  -2----6-------6---- --4-- -----6-----1----10--------4-- -2------10-----
    !01!AC6666!N00010  !        !30-Jun-83 ! !     $31.82 !     ! !
                              trade   i. d. number  c tax b item reg i
  ACCOUNT NAME                  -----6---------.--9--.----1--3-2---5---3--1--
  Susan Lowe                    !         !   000000001  !Y!120! !     ! ! !
  --2-1-------------------------------------------------------------------
  !cd!L!units-10-3-!----42-----Description-of-entry--------!
  K!02!-!--------!--! Rec'd Interest on      $8,486.37 due   !
  L!03!-!           !        14-Jun-83 on                    !
  M!04!-!           ! mortgage note payable                  !
  N!05!-!           ! for 20 years                           !
  O!06!-!           !                                        !
  P!07!-!           !                                        !  ----------
  Q!08!-!           !                                        ! $amount
  R!09!-!           !                                        !
  S!10!-!           !                                        !
  J!11!-!           !                                        !  ----------
  K!12!-!           !                                        ! checked by
  L!13!-!           !                                        !
  M!14!-!           !                                        !
  N!15!-!           !                                        !
  O!16!-!           !                                        !
```

**Principal form:**

```
SELL                 -------------------------------------------------------
                     :        30-Jun-83
                     :
                     :        Susan Lowe
   cd  acct  sec. num. tran      date     u/c    cash       link est book val
   -2----6-------6---- --4-- -----6-----1-----10--------4-- -2------10-----
   :01:AC6666:N00010   :      :30-Jun-83 : :    $68.18 :      :05:    $56.81
                                                                  :
   trade date   i. d. number   c tax b item reg i               :
   -----6---- --.--9--.--------1--3--2---5---3--1-----------:------a------
           :000000001      :Y:120: :      :   : :              :
                                                                  :
   cd  acct  sec. num. tran      date     u/c    cash       link:
   -2----6-------6---- --4-- -----6-----1-----10--------4--:------a------
   :01:       :         : 4755:          : :            :     :
   ------------------------------------------------------------:------a------
   broker no : commission  : certificate numbers            :
   ----------:------------:------------------------------:
   lot                                                     :
   ------------------------------------------------------------:-----$-------
   quantity : security description :    special delivery instructions
            :                      :
   ----------:                     : rec'd    $68.18  principal pymt
                                   : due    14-Jun-83 on
       promissory note ------>     :   mortgage note payable
   --------------------------------:   for 20 years
       cusip : broker              : leaving a principal balance of
   ---------------------------------------- $8,418.19 --------------------
   DTC:-:-NYSE:-:-ASE:-:-REGL:-:-OTC:-:-Out:-:-Cust:-:-Off:-:-free:-:   :
   -:sell-:X:other:---------:- acct-off-:-inv-off-:-units-w-:-balance-----:
   -:wdr--:-:all---:-part--: W5     :         :         :              :
   ---------------------------:-----------:---------:---------:-------------:
   Holding ver : vault  :sec cage : del date : pay date:              :
   ------------:--------:----------:----------:---------:--------------:
```

# Backup

The files of the note system should be copied onto separate disks for protection of the records at a minimum of a weekly basis (that way you will lose at most a week's work if the files are damaged).

At December 31 of each year the consolidated files, and the office and transaction records for each note should be printed. A backup copy of the files should be made on a diskette to be stored separately.

## Changing the Macros

The system can have slight modifications, changes to the type of reporting, or major modifications. Each level of change requires a different amount of work.

The easiest changes are those that change titles, contents of an area already used for another purpose, or print formats. To change the titles, the templates used to produce the forms are changed. When they are copied into the working area, the new titles will appear. The categories used in the current forms can be changed to fit many different purposes, or just blanked out. It will be easier if similar sized information is used to replace the current information. The titles on the consolidated reports can be changed by typing over them. The size of the address labels is changed by changing the area of the Range Name LABEL. Print codes for condensed print are indicated in the Print macros. If different ones are needed, merely replace the current ones.

It is fairly easy to change the nature of the reports being generated. Completely new templates can be designed to solve different problems. Various macros will need to be adapted. The ones to produce the headers and save the files, to pass the information to computer input forms, and to record new information will need to include the new cell addresses. The consolidated file headings will change to reflect the new headers, and the update macro will be changed if the structure of the files changed.

Completely new systems can use these macros for a major portion of their work. The macros for extraction and retrieving files, looping to move through different files, inputting information, or printing out a series of reports, can all be easily lifted out of this system and used for different tasks. As the macros use Range Names for most of their activities, just set up the same names on the new worksheet, or modify the names in the macros to reflect the ones to be used on the new worksheet.

# A.5　List of Macros

| Page | Macro | |
|---|---|---|
| | Number | Name |
| 12 | 2-1 | First Macro |
| 16 | 2-2 | Label Macro |
| 17 | 2-3 | Number Macro |
| 18 | 2-4 | Command Macro |
| 23 | 2-5 | Entry Beneath Macro |
| 24 | 2-6 | Macro with Blank Cell |
| 26 | 2-7 | Print Macro, Example 1 |

# Index

# Index

# RELATED RESOURCES SHELF

## Financial Analysis With Lotus 1-2-3
*Lois Graff and Neil Cohen*

Beginning with fundamental business statements, balance sheet and income statements, and ratio analysis, the reader will move into 1-2-3's more advanced uses. Includes use of command language capabilities to develop integrated decision packages.

☐ 1984/304pp/paper/D4517-1/$16.95

## Lotus 1-2-3 Self-Taught On The IBM PC *Ira Krakow*

This practical guide is a comprehensive tutorial providing users with the information needed to use 1-2-3 on the IBM PC. Discusses graphics, data base management, macros, and writing 1-2-3 programs.

☐ 1985/320pp/paper/D6285-3/$19.95

## Understanding and Using dBASE II *Robert Krumm*

Here's an easy-to-use guide that succinctly explains the fundamental concepts behind computerized information systems. Emphasizes techniques for organizing and adding records, using command files, creating loops, formatting input/output, and more.

☐ 1984/350pp/spiral/D9160-5/$19.95

TO ORDER, simply clip this entire page, check off your selection, and complete the coupon below. Enclose a check or money order for the stated amount. (Please add $2.00 postage and handling per book plus local sales tax.)

Mail to: **Brady Communications Co., Inc., Dept. TS, Bowie, MD 20715**

Name _____

Address _____

City/State/Zip _____

Charge my credit card instead: ☐ MasterCard ☐ Visa

Account# _____ Expiration Date _____

Signature _____
Dept. Y                                                    Y0510-BB(5)

*Prices subject to change without notice.*